Horace Walpole, Leonard Benton Seeley

Horace Walpole and his World

Horace Walpole, Leonard Benton Seeley

Horace Walpole and his World

ISBN/EAN: 9783743344839

Manufactured in Europe, USA, Canada, Australia, Japa

Cover: Foto ©ninafisch / pixelio.de

Manufactured and distributed by brebook publishing software (www.brebook.com)

Horace Walpole, Leonard Benton Seeley

Horace Walpole and his World

HORACE WALPOLE
AND HIS WORLD

SELECT PASSAGES FROM HIS LETTERS

EDITED BY

L. B. SEELEY, M.A.

Sometime Fellow of Trinity College, Cambridge

AUTHOR OF
"FANNY BURNEY AND HER FRIENDS"

NEW EDITION

NEW YORK
CHARLES SCRIBNER'S SONS
1895

CONTENTS.

CHAPTER I.

PAGE

Introduction — Birth and Parentage — Education — Appointments — Travels — Parliamentary Career — Retirement — Fortune — Strawberry Hill—Collections—Writings—Printing Press—Accession to Title—Death—Character—Political Conduct and Opinions—The Slave Trade—Strikes—Views of Literature—Friendships—Charities—Chatterton—Letters 1

CHAPTER II.

Country Life—Ranelagh Gardens—The Rebel Lords—The Earthquake—A Frolic at Vauxhall—Capture of a Housebreaker—Strawberry Hill—The Beautiful Gunnings—Sterne 33

CHAPTER III.

A new Reign—Funeral of the late King—Houghton revisited—Election at Lynn—Marriage of George III.—His Coronation 62

CHAPTER IV.

General Taste for Pleasure— Entertainments at Twickenham and Esher—Miss Chudleigh's Ball—Masquerade at Richmond House—The Gallery at Strawberry Hill—Balls—The Duchess of Queensberry—Petition of the Periwig-makers—Ladies' Head-gear—Almack's—"The Castle of Otranto"—Plans for a Bower—A late Dinner—Walpole's Idle Life—Social Usages 78

vi *Contents.*

CHAPTER V.

PAGE

The Gout — Visits to Paris — Bath — John Wesley — Bad Weather — English Summers — Quitting Parliament— Madame du Deffand—Human Vanity—The Banks of the Thames—A Subscription Masquerade—Extravagance of the Age—The Pantheon—Visiting Stowe with Princess Amelia —George Montagu—The Countess of Ossory—Powder-Mills Blown up at Hounslow—Distractions of Business and Pleasure . . . . - 99

CHAPTER VI.

Lord Nuneham—Madame de Sévigné—Charles Fox—Mrs. Clive and Cliveden—Goldsmith and Garrick—Dearth of News—Madame de Trop—A Bunch of Grapes—General Election—Perils by Land and Water—Sir Horace Mann— Lord Clive—The History of Manners—A Traveller from Lima—The Sçavoir Vivre Club—Reflections on Life—The Pretender's Happiness—Paris Fashions—Madame du Deffand ill — Growth of London — Sir Joshua Reynolds— Change in Manners—Our Climate 124

CHAPTER VII.

The American War—Irish Discontent—Want of Money—The Houghton Pictures sold—Removal to Berkeley Square—Ill-health—A Painting by Zoffani—The Rage for News— The Duke of Gloucester—Wilkes—Fashions, Old and New— Mackerel News—Pretty Stories—Madame de Sévigné's Cabinet—Picture of his Waldegrave Nieces—The Gordon Riots—Death of Madame du Deffand—The Blue Stockings 151

CHAPTER VIII.

Walpole in his Sixty-fourth Year—The Royal Academy— Tonton—Charles Fox—William Pitt—Mrs. Hobart's *Sans Souci*—Improvements at Florence—Walpole's Dancing Feats—No Feathers at Court—Highwaymen—Loss of the *Royal George*—Mrs. Siddons—Peace—Its Social Consequences—The Coalition—The Rivals—Political Excitement —The Westminster Election—Political Caricatures—Conway's Retirement—Lady Harrington—Balloons—Illness— Recovery 183

Contents.

CHAPTER IX.

Lady Correspondents—Madame de Genlis—Miss Burney and Hannah More—Deaths of Mrs. Clive and Sir Horace Mann—Story of Madame de Choiseul—Richmond—Queensberry House—Warren Hastings—Genteel Comedy—St. Swithin—Riverside Conceits—Lord North—The Theatre again—Gibbon's History — Sheridan — Conway's comedy — A Turkish War—Society Newspapers—The Misses Berry—Bonner's Ghost—The Arabian Nights—King's College Chapel—Richmond Society—New Arrivals—The Berrys' visit Italy—A Farewell Letter 221

CHAPTER X.

Walpole's Love of English Scenery—Richmond Hill—Burke on the French Revolution—The Berrys at Florence—Death of George Selwyn—London Solitude—Repairs at Cliveden—Burke and Fox—The Countess of Albany—Journal of a Day—Mrs. Hobart's Party—Ancient Trade with India—Lady Hamilton—A Boat Race—Return of the Berrys—Horace succeeds to the Peerage—Epitaphium Vivi Auctoris—His Wives—Mary Berry—Closing Years—Love of Moving Objects—Visit from Queen Charlotte—Death of Conway—Final Illness of Horace—His last Letter 262

HORACE WALPOLE AND HIS WORLD.

CHAPTER I.

Introduction.—Birth and Parentage.—Education.—Appointments.—Travels.—Parliamentary Career.—Retirement.—Fortune.—Strawberry Hill.—Collections.—Writings.—Printing Press.—Accession to Title.—Death.—Character.—Political Conduct and Opinions.—The Slave-Trade.—Strikes.—Views of Literature.—Friendships.—Charities.—Chatterton.—Letters.

WE offer to the general reader some specimens of Horace Walpole's correspondence. Students of history and students of literature are familiar with this great mine of facts and fancies, but it is too extensive to be fully explored by those who have not both ample leisure and strong inclination for such employment. Yet most persons, we imagine, would be glad to have some acquaintance with the prince of English letter-writers. Many years have passed since Walter Scott pronounced Walpole's letters to be the best in our language, and since Lord Byron declared them to be incomparable. The fashion in style and composition has changed during the interval almost as often as the fashion in dress: other candidates, too, for fame in the same department have come forward; but no one, we think, has succeeded in setting aside the verdict given, in the early part of our century, by the two most famous writers of their time. Meanwhile, to the collections of letters by Walpole that were known to Scott and Byron have been added several others, no way inferior to the first, which have been published at different periods; besides numerous detached letters, which have come to light from various quarters. In the years 1857-9, appeared a complete edition of Walpole's letters in nine large octavo volumes.* The editor of this expressed his confidence that no additions of moment would afterwards be made to the mass of correspondence which his industry had brought together. Yet he proved to be mistaken. In 1865 came out Miss Berry's Journals and Correspondence,† containing a large quantity of letters and parts of letters addressed to her and her sister by Walpole, which had not previously been given to the world, as well as several interesting letters to other persons, the manuscripts of which had passed into and remained in Miss Berry's possession. Other letters, too, have made their appearance, singly and incidentally, in more recent publications.‡ The total number of Walpole's published letters cannot now fall much short of three thousand;

* "The Letters of Horace Walpole, Earl of Orford, edited by Peter Cunningham."
† A second edition was published in 1866.
‡ E.g., in Jesse's " Memoirs of George III.'

the earliest of these is dated in November, 1735,* the latest in January, 1797. Throughout the intervening sixty years, the writer, to use his own phrase, lived always in the big busy world; and whatever there passed before him, his restless fingers, restless even when stiffened by the gout, recorded and commented on for the amusement of his correspondents and the benefit of posterity. The extant results of his diligence display a full picture of the period, distorted indeed in many places by the prejudices of the artist, but truthful on the whole, and enlivened everywhere by touches of genius. From this mass of narratives and descriptions, anecdotes and good-sayings, criticisms, reflections and raillery, we shall endeavour to make as representative a selection as our limits will permit.

It is hardly necessary to say that Horace Walpole entered life as the son of the foremost Englishman of his time. He was born on the 24th of September, 1717, O.S., and was the youngest of the six children whom Sir Robert Walpole's first wife, Catherine Shorter, brought to her illustrious husband. This family included two other sons, Robert and Edward, and two daughters, besides a fourth son, William, who died in infancy. Horace, whose birth took place

---

* Or in 1732, if the dates of some letters published in *Notes and Queries*, 4th Series, vol. iii., p. 2, can be trusted. But as the second of these letters, the date of which is given as Sep. 18, 1732, refers to the death of Walpole's mother, and as we know, from his own statement, that Lady Walpole died Aug. 20, 1737, there seems to be an error.

eleven years after that of the fifth child, bore no resemblance, either in body or mind, to the robust and hearty Sir Robert. He was of slight figure and feeble constitution; his features lacked the comeliness of the Walpole race; and his temperament was of that fastidious, self-conscious, impressionable cast which generally causes a man or boy to be called affected. The scandalous, noting these things, and comparing the person and character of Horace Walpole with those of the Herveys, remembered that Sir Robert and his first wife had been estranged from one another in the later years of their union, and that the lady had been supposed to be intimate with Carr Lord Hervey, elder brother of Pope's Sporus. Horace himself has mentioned that this Carr was reckoned of superior parts to the more known John Lord Hervey, but nowhere in our author's writings does it appear that the least suspicion of spurious parentage* had entered his thoughts. Everywhere he exults in being sprung from the great Prime Minister; everywhere he is devoted to the memory of his mother, to whom he raised a monument in Westminster Abbey, with an inscription

---

* The story that Horace was of Hervey blood was first published in some Introductory Anecdotes prefixed to the later editions of the works of Lady Mary Wortley Montagu. These anecdotes were contributed by Lady Louisa Stuart, daughter of Lord Bute, the Prime Minister, and grand-daughter of Lady Mary. Her statement about Walpole, though generally accepted, has perhaps received more credit than it deserves, but *se non è vero, è ben trovato*. The similarity, both in matter and composition, between the memoirs of Lord Hervey and those of Horace Walpole is certainly remarkable.

from his own pen celebrating her virtue. And in the concluding words of this epigraph, he repeated a saying, which he has elsewhere recorded, of the poet Pope, that Lady Walpole was " untainted by a Court."

Walpole tells us that, in the first years of his life, being an extremely delicate child, he was much indulged both by his mother and Sir Robert; and as an instance of this, he relates the well-known story, how his longing to see the King was gratified by his mother carrying him to St. James's to kiss the hand of George I. just before his Majesty began his last journey to Hanover. Shortly after this, the boy was sent to Eton, from which period we hear no more of Lady Walpole, though she survived till August, 1737. In 1735, young Horace proceeded from Eton to King's College, Cambridge, where he resided, though with long intervals of absence, until after he came of age. On quitting the University, he was in possession of a handsome income arising from the patent place of Usher of the Exchequer, to which he had recently been appointed, and which was then reckoned worth £900 a year, and from two other small patent places in the Exchequer, those of Clerk of the Escheats and Controller of the Pipe, producing together about £300 a year, which had been held for him during his minority. All these offices had been procured for him by Sir Robert Walpole, and were sinecures, or capable of being executed by deputy.

Finding himself thus provided for and at leisure, the fortunate youth set out on the continental tour which was considered indispensable for a man of fashion.

He travelled, as he tells us, at his own expense; and being well able to afford the luxury of a companion, he took with him Thomas Gray the poet, who had been his associate at Eton and Cambridge. The pair visited together various parts of France and Italy, making a stay of some duration at several places. After a few weeks spent in Paris, they settled at Rheims for three months to study French. They lived here with their former school-mate, Henry Seymour Conway,* Walpole's maternal cousin; and here appears to have been cemented the lifelong friendship between Conway and Walpole which forms perhaps the most honourable feature in the history of the latter. At Florence, Walpole resided for more than twelve months in the house of Horace Mann, British Envoy to the Court of Tuscany, with whom he formed an intimacy, which was maintained, from the time of his leaving Italy until the death of Mann forty-five years after, by correspondence only, without the parties ever meeting again. Gray remained with Walpole at Florence, and accompanied him in visits which he made thence to Rome, Naples, and other places; but

* Born in July, 1719. He was second son of the first Lord Conway by his third wife, Charlotte Shorter, sister of Lady Walpole. He was Secretary in Ireland during the vice-royalty of William, fourth Duke of Devonshire; then Groom of the Bedchamber to George II. and to George III.; became Secretary of State in 1765; Lieutenant-General of the Ordnance in 1770; Commander-in-Chief in 1782; and was created a Field-Marshal in 1793. He married the Dowager Countess of Aylesbury, by whom he had an only child, Mrs. Damer, the sculptor, to whom Walpole left Strawberry Hill.

at Reggio a dissension arose between them, and they parted to return home by different routes. Walpole subsequently took the blame of this dispute upon himself. "It arose," he says, "from Gray being too serious a companion. Gray was for antiquities, I was for perpetual balls and plays; the fault was mine." According to another account, Walpole had opened a letter addressed to Gray. Whatever was the cause of the breach, it was repaired three years later, and during the rest of the poet's life he continued on friendly terms with his early companion.

Walpole reached England in September, 1741, just before the meeting of a new Parliament, and at the commencement of the Session took his seat as member for Callington, in Cornwall, for which place he had been elected during his absence. Sir Robert's Government was at that time in the midst of the difficulties which soon afterwards caused its downfall. In February, 1742, the defeated Minister resigned, and was created Earl of Orford. Horace, as was to be expected, took no prominent part in the struggle. His maiden speech was delivered in March, 1742, on a motion for an inquiry into the conduct of Sir Robert Walpole during the last ten years of his administration. The young orator was received with favour by the House, and obtained a compliment from the great William Pitt; but the success of his effort, which is preserved in one of his letters to Mann, must be attributed entirely to the circumstances under which it was uttered. It does not appear that he afterwards acquired any reputation in debate. Indeed, he was generally content to be a listener. That he was a constant attendant at the House, his correspondence sufficiently proves, but he rarely took an active part in its proceedings. He has recorded a dispute he had with Speaker Onslow in his second Parliament. In 1751 he moved the address to the King at the opening of the Session, and five years later we find him speaking on a question of employing Swiss troops in the Colonies. In 1757 he exerted himself with much zeal in favour of the unfortunate Admiral Byng. This, however, was by argument and solicitation outside the House. In like manner, some years afterwards, he made strenuous, though vain, endeavours, at the conferences of his party, to persuade them not to support the exclusion of the King's mother from the Regency which was provided for on the first serious illness of George III.

These are the chief incidents of Walpole's public career, although he remained in the House of Commons for twenty-seven years. At the General Election of 1754 he was chosen for the family borough of Castle Rising in Norfolk, but vacated this seat soon afterwards in order to be a candidate for the town of King's Lynn, which had for many years returned his father to Parliament. Horace continued to represent Lynn until the Dissolution of 1768, when he took leave of his constituents, and was no longer seen in Westminster Hall. Perhaps the final reason for his retirement was the failure of his friend Conway to retain a foremost position in politics. After serving as Secretary of State and Leader of the House of Commons under three successive Premiers, Conway, through feebleness of purpose, lost his hold upon office, and fell for some years into the background. But with disappointment for his friend, there must have mingled in Walpole's mind a feeling of dissatisfaction with himself. Few men acquire much weight in Parliament who do not at least occasionally take a share in its discussions; and Horace had more than once found that his influence in the House was by no means proportioned to his general reputation for ability. He was therefore quite ready to withdraw when Conway could no longer profit by his vote. Though at all times a keen politician, and extremely social in his habits, he was unfitted by nature for the conflicts of the Parliamentary arena. Desultory skirmishing with the pen was more to his taste than the close fighting of debate. During more than half his life, the war of parties was largely carried on by anonymous pamphlets, and Walpole gave powerful help in this way to his side; afterwards, when letters and articles in newspapers took the place of pamphlets, he became an occasional contributor to the public journals.

But Walpole found in art and literature the chief employment of his serious hours. His reading was extensive, the most solid portion of it being in the regions of history and archæology. More engrossing than his love of books was his passion for collecting and imitating antiquities and curiosities of all kinds. His ample fortune furnished him with the means of indulging these expensive pursuits. The emoluments of the Usher of the Exchequer greatly increased during his tenure of that post: in time of war—and England was often at war in those days—they were sometimes very large. Walpole admits that in one year he received as much as £4,200 from this source; and the Commissioners of Accounts in 1782 thought that the annual value of the place might fairly be stated at that sum. There was an antique flavour about these gains which gave Walpole almost as much pleasure as the money itself. The duties of the Usher were to shut the gates of the Exchequer, and to provide the Exchequer and Treasury with the paper, parchment, pens, ink, sand, wax, tape, and other articles of a similar nature used in those departments. The latter of these duties, which was said to be as old as the reign of Edward III. at least, formed the lucrative part of the Usher's employment, as he was allowed large profits on the goods he thus purveyed to the Crown. Obviously the income of such an office, while varying with the financial business of each year, must have steadily advanced on the whole with the progress of the nation. Besides this place, and the two other patent places before mentioned, in all of which he continued until his death, Walpole enjoyed for many years a principal share in the income of the Collectorship of the Customs. Sir Robert Walpole held the last appointment under a patent which entitled him to dispose as he pleased of the reversion during the lives of his two eldest sons, Robert and Edward. Accordingly, he appointed that, after his death, £1,000 a year of the income should be paid to his youngest son Horace during the subsistence of the patent, and that the remainder should be divided equally between Horace and Edward. By this arrangement, Horace at the age of twenty-seven—for his father died in March, 1745—stepped into another income of about £1,400 a year, which lasted until the death of his brother Sir Edward Walpole in 1784. In his writings he speaks, with becoming gratitude, of the places and emoluments bestowed on him by his father as being a noble provision for a third son. Having thus nobly provided at the public expense for a child who had not yet shown any merit or capacity, Sir Robert did not find it needful to do much for him out of his private property. By his will, he bequeathed Horace only a sum of £5,000 charged on his Norfolk estate, and a leasehold house in Arlington Street. The greater part of the legacy remained unpaid for forty years; the house Horace occupied until the term expired in 1781, when he bought a residence in Berkeley Square. As Walpole was never married, it is not surprising that he died worth ninety-one thousand pounds in the funds, besides other property, including his town house just mentioned, and his villa at Twickenham with its collection of pictures and other works of art.

The fantastic little pile of buildings which he raised on the margin of the Thames engaged his chief attention for many years. He purchased the site of this in 1748, there being nothing then on the land but a cottage, and called it Strawberry Hill, a name which he found in one of the title-deeds. He had taken a lease the year before of the cottage, with part of the land, from Mrs. Chenevix, a fashionable toy-dealer, and thus describes his acquisition in a letter to Conway: "It is a little plaything-house that I got out of Mrs. Chenevix's shop, and is the prettiest bauble you ever saw. It is set in enamelled meadows, with filigree hedges:

> '"A small Euphrates through the piece is rolled,
> And little finches wave their wings in gold."

Two delightful roads, that you would call dusty, supply me continually with coaches and chaises: barges as solemn as Barons of the Exchequer move under my window; Richmond Hill and Ham walks bound my prospect; but thank God! the Thames is between me and the Duchess of Queensberry. Dowagers as plenty as flounders inhabit all around, and Pope's ghost is just now skimming under my window by a most poetical moonlight. I have about land enough to keep such a farm as Noah's, when he set up in the Ark with a pair of each kind; but my cottage is rather cleaner than I believe his was after they had been cooped up together forty days. The Chenevixes had tricked it out for themselves: up two pair of stairs is what they call Mr. Chenevix's library, furnished with three maps, one shelf, a bust of Sir Isaac Newton, and a lame telescope without any glasses. Lord John Sackville *predeceased* me here, and instituted certain games called *cricketalia*, which have been celebrated this very evening in honour of him in a neighbouring meadow."

Having completed his purchase, Walpole proceeded to make improvements. His antiquarian studies had inspired him with a fondness for Gothic architecture. But his zeal was not according to much knowledge, nor guided by a very pure taste. Gradually the little cottage became merged in a strange nondescript edifice, half castle, half cloister, with all kinds of grotesque decorations. "The Castle," so Walpole called it, "was," he tells us, "not entirely built from the ground, but formed at different times, by alterations of, and additions to, the old small house. The Library and Refectory, or Great Parlour, was entirely new-built in 1753; the Gallery, Round Tower, Great Cloister, and Cabinet, in 1760 and 1761; the Great North Bed-chamber in 1770; and the Beauclerk Tower with the Hexagon Closet in 1776." In a small cloister, outside the house, stood the blue and white china bowl, commemorated by Gray, in which Walpole's cat was drowned. On the staircase was the famous armour of Francis I. In the Gallery, among many other treasures, were placed the Roman eagle and the bust of Vespasian, so often mentioned in their owner's correspondence. The buildings were no more substantial in structure than they were correct in style. Much cheap ridicule has been poured upon "the Castle," as "a most trumpery piece of ginger-bread Gothic," with "pie-crust battlements," and "pinnacles of lath and plaster." Many of its faults and absurdities must in justice be referred to the novelty of the attempt to apply a disused style to the requirements of a modern domestic residence. Walpole himself was by no means blind to the flimsiness and incongruities of his creation. He was rather indignant, indeed, when a French visitor censured it as "non digne de la solidité Anglaise;" but in his own description of it he calls it "a paper fabric," and speaks of the house and its decorations as "a mixture which may be denominated, in some words of Pope:

'A Gothic Vatican of Greece and Rome.'"

With the help of Mr. Essex, who assisted him in designing the later portions, he gradually learned the depth of the architectural ignorance in which he and the "Committee," who were his first advisers, had been involved at the commencement of his work. In short, Strawberry Hill, child's baby-house as it was, proved the first step in the renascence of Gothic art.

As chamber after chamber was added to the Castle, it became Walpole's next care to fill them with fresh antiques in furniture, pictures, bronzes, armour, painted glass, and other like articles. "In his villa," says Lord Macaulay, "every apartment is a museum, every piece of furniture is a curiosity; there is something strange in the form of the shovel; there is a long story belonging to the bell-rope. We wander among a profusion of rarities, of trifling intrinsic value, but so quaint in fashion, or connected with such remarkable names and events, that they may well detain our attention for a moment. A moment is enough. Some new relic, some new unique, some new carved work, some new enamel, is forthcoming in an instant. One cabinet of trinkets is no sooner closed than another is opened."

Of Walpole's writings other than his letters, we do

not propose to offer any detailed account or criticism. His earliest work, "Ædes Walpolianæ," was published as early as 1747; it was merely a description of his father's pictures at Houghton Hall, the family seat in Norfolk. Among his next efforts were some papers contributed in 1753 and following years to a periodical work of the day, called *The World.** Most persons have read the "Castle of Otranto," so warmly applauded by the author of "Ivanhoe." Most students of art, we suppose, are acquainted with Walpole's "Anecdotes of Painting," and his "Catalogue of Engravers." His "Catalogue of Noble and Royal Authors," though abounding in agreeable anecdotes, is probably now consulted by few; and his "Historic Doubts on the Life and Reign of Richard III.," acute and ingenious as it was, cannot detain anyone who is aware of the recent researches on the same subject. His "Reminiscences of the Courts of George I. and George II.," and his "Memoirs" and "Journals" relating to the reigns of George II. and George III., are, and must ever remain, among the most valuable historical documents of the eighteenth century. The Reminiscences were written for the amusement of the Misses Berry, and have been extolled with justice as being, both in manner and matter, the very perfection

---

* One of his papers in *The World* contains an account of an escape which he had, in 1749, of being shot by highwaymen in Hyde Park. His face was grazed by a ball from the pistol of one of his assailants, which went off accidentally before aim had been taken. An allusion to this adventure will be found in one of our extracts.

of anecdote writing. The rest of Walpole's works, including his tragedy of "The Mysterious Mother"—the merits of which, whatever they may be, are cancelled by the atrocity of the fable—are as nearly as possible forgotten.

Not content with writing and collecting books, Horace in 1757 established a printing press in the grounds of Strawberry Hill. The first printer employed by him was William Robinson; the last, Thomas Kirgate, whose name will often be found in the following extracts. The first work printed at this press was Gray's "Odes," with Bentley's Illustrations. Its other productions include Walpole's own Royal and Noble Authors, Anecdotes of Painting, Engravers, and Tragedy; his "Description of Strawberry Hill," and "Fugitive Pieces;" besides several works by other authors, such as Bentley's "Lucan," Lord Herbert's Life, a translation of Hentzner's "Travels," and Lord Whitworth's "Account of Russia;" as well as small collections of verses by sundry friends. These "Strawberry Hill" editions are now scarce, and command high prices.

The rest of our author's career may be summed up in a few words. His eldest brother had died early, and had been succeeded by an only son, whose profligacy and occasional fits of insanity caused much trouble. In December, 1791, when seventy-four years of age, Horace became, by the death of this nephew, Earl of Orford, which made little addition to his income, the family estate being heavily incumbered. The inheritance was far from welcome. In a letter to a friend, he says he does not understand the management of such an estate, and is too old to learn. "A source of lawsuits among my near relations, endless conversations with lawyers, and packets of letters to read every day and answer—all this weight of new business is too much for the rag of life that yet hangs about me.* He never took his seat in the House of Lords. He lived for upwards of five years longer, in the full possession of all his faculties, though suffering great bodily infirmity from the effects of gout, to which he was long a martyr. He died at his house, No. 11, Berkeley Square, on the 2nd of March, 1797, in his eightieth year, and was buried at the family seat of Houghton. With him the male line of Sir Robert Walpole and the title of Orford became extinct. The estate of Houghton descended to the fourth Earl of Cholmondeley, grandson of Horace Walpole's younger sister Mary, who married the third earl of that ilk. Strawberry Hill was at its founder's absolute disposal, and he left it, as already mentioned, to Mrs. Damer, Conway's daughter, but for life only, with limitations over in strict settlement.

"It is somewhat curious," says his biographer, "as a proof of the inconsistency of the human mind, that, having built his Castle with so little view to durability, Walpole entailed the perishable possession with a degree of strictness which would have been more fitting for a baronial estate. And that, too, after having written a fable entitled 'The Entail,' in consequence of some one having asked him whether he did not intend

* Letter to John Pinkerton, Dec. 26, 1791.

to entail Strawberry Hill, and in ridicule of such a proceeding."

Inconsistency, caprice, eccentricity, affectation, are faults which have been freely charged against the character of Horace Walpole. His strong prejudices and antipathies, his pride of rank, his propensity to satire, even his sensitive temperament, made him many enemies, who not only exaggerated his failings, but succeeded, in some instances at least, in transmitting their personal resentments to men of the present century.

As a politician, especially, Walpole has received rather hard measure from the partisan critics on both sides. A generation back, Whig Reviewers and Tory Reviewers vied with each other in defaming his memory. Macaulay and Croker, who seldom agreed in anything, were of one accord in this. To Croker, of course, Horace was just a place-holder who furnished a telling example of Whig jobbery. To rake up all the details of his places in the Exchequer, and his "rider," or charge, on the place in the Customs, to compute and exaggerate his gains from each of these sources, to track him in dark intrigues for extending his tenure of one appointment and bettering his position in another; all this was congenial employment for the Rigby of the nineteenth century, as it would have been for his prototype in the eighteenth. The motive of Macaulay's deadly attack is not quite so obvious. Walpole's politics were those of his father and of the old Whigs generally. While in theory inclined to Republicanism—though he was never, as he tells us, quite a Republican*—it was his habit, on practical questions, to consider what course the great Sir Robert would have taken under similar circumstances. There seems nothing in all this to excite the wrath of the most atrabilious Liberal. The truth appears to be that, in the Whig circles of Macaulay's time, there existed a traditional grudge against Horace Walpole. In the "Memorials of Charles James Fox," which were arranged by Lord Vassall-Holland, and edited by Lord John Russell, both the noble commentators speak of Horace in terms of undisguised bitterness. Nor is the cause very far to seek. In politics, Conway was under the dominion of Walpole; and Conway, on more than one critical occasion, disobliged the Rockingham faction, from which the modern Whigs deduce their origin. "Conway," says Lord John Russell, writing of the events of 1766, "had been made Secretary of State by Lord Rockingham, and ought to have resigned when Lord Rockingham left office; but Mr. Walpole did not choose that this should be so." Sixteen years later, Conway sat again in a Cabinet presided over by Lord Rockingham, and when that nobleman died, he again refused to resign. It will be remembered that, on this occasion, the Cavendishes and Fox quitted their places when the Treasury was given to Lord Shelburne, instead of their own nominee, the Duke of Portland, whose only recommendations were that he was Lord of Welbeck, and had married a daughter of the House of Devonshire.

* "I have been called a Republican; I never was quite that."—Walpole to Lady Ossory, July 7, 1782.

In 1782, the Duke of Richmond, Conway's son-in-law, concurred with Conway in declining to desert the new Premier; and we know that Walpole stoutly supported, if he did not dictate, the joint resolution of his two friends. Lord Holland tells us that Fox did not like Walpole at all, and accounts for this dislike by suggesting that his uncle may have imbibed some prejudice against Walpole for unkindness shown to the first Lord Holland. But this seems going needlessly far back for an explanation. There can be no doubt that Fox looked on Walpole as having assisted to thwart his design of governing England in the name of the insignificant Duke of Portland, and detested him accordingly. Nor did subsequent events tend to soften Fox's recollection of this passage in his life, or of the persons concerned in it. Had he overcome his jealousy of Lord Shelburne, or had he succeeded in compelling his rival to bow before the "wooden idol"—so Lord John Russell himself calls Portland—which he had set up, he would probably, in either case, have avoided the ill-famed coalition with Lord North, which was the main cause of his long-continued exclusion from power. Walpole had spoken his mind very plainly on the subject. "It is very entertaining," he wrote, "that two or three great families should persuade themselves that they have an hereditary and exclusive right of giving us a head without a tongue."* And he told Fox himself: "My Whiggism is not confined to the Peak of Derbyshire."† We can imagine with what

* Letter to Mann, July 10, 1782.
† Letter to Lady Ossory, July 7, 1782.

horror such utterances as these were received by the believers in the Whig doctrine of divine right. No wonder that Mr. Fox did not like Walpole. And what Mr. Fox disliked was, of course, anathema to every true Whig, and especially to an Edinburgh Reviewer of 1833.

What do the complaints of Walpole's political tergiversation amount to? It was certainly not a wise act of Horace to hang up in his bedroom an engraving of the death warrant of Charles I. with the inscription "Major Charta." But the Whig essayist, while reproving Walpole's strange fancy that, without the instrument in question, the Great Charter would have become of little importance, might have recollected that he had himself professed his inability to see any essential distinction between the execution of the Royal Martyr and the deposition of his son. Again, there was inconsistency, no doubt, between Walpole's admiration of the Long Parliament, and his detestation of the National Assembly; yet it should be borne in mind that, in the midst of his disgust at the excesses of the French Revolution, he protested that he was very far from subscribing to the whole of Burke's "Reflections." Why then should we be told that "he was frightened into a fanatical royalist, and became one of the most extravagant alarmists of those wretched times?" We may surely ask on his behalf the question which Macaulay put when the consistency of his own master, Sir James Mackintosh, was impugned: "Why is one person to be singled out from among millions, and arraigned before posterity as a traitor to his opinions, only because events produced on him the effect which they produced on a whole generation?"

When the critic tells us that Walpole was a mischief-maker who "sometimes contrived, without showing himself, to disturb the course of Ministerial negotiations, and to spread confusion through the political circles," we cannot avoid seeing in these words a resentful reference to the part taken by Conway on the occasions above referred to.

It was not Walpole's fault that the party conflicts of his time were mainly about persons. We have seen the importance which Fox attached to these personal questions. We may safely say that this great man's disapproval of Walpole's conduct did not spring from any difference on matters of principle. If Horace was an opponent of Parliamentary Reform, this was an open question among Fox's most intimate associates. If he objected to the enfranchisement of the Roman Catholics, most Whigs of his time did the same. In the dispute with America, as we shall see, he maintained, from the first, the right of the Colonies to liberty and independence. Nor did he retract his expressions of sympathy with the American Republic when the horrors of the French Revolution made him a supporter of Tory policy in England and on the Continent. He always lamented as one of the worst effects of the French excesses that they must necessarily retard the progress and establishment of civil liberty.*

* Miss Berry.

There were questions of social politics on which he was far in advance of his times. "We have been sitting," he wrote, on the 25th of February, 1750, "this fortnight on the African Company. We, the British Senate, that temple of liberty, and bulwark of Protestant Christianity, have, this fortnight, been considering methods to make more effectual that horrid traffic of selling negroes. It has appeared to us that six-and-forty thousand of these wretches are sold every year to our plantations alone! It chills one's blood—I would not have to say I voted for it for the Continent of America! The destruction of the miserable inhabitants by the Spaniards was but a momentary misfortune that followed from the discovery of the New World, compared with the lasting havoc which it brought upon Africa. We reproach Spain, and yet do not even pretend the nonsense of butchering these poor creatures for the good of their souls."* The sentiments thus declared by Walpole nine years before Wilberforce was born, he steadily adhered to through life. On this point, at least, no one has ever charged him with any wavering or inconsistency.

We will mention, before passing on to different topics, one other matter on which Walpole shows a liberality of feeling quite unusual at any period of his life. In the summer of 1762, he writes: 'I am in distress about my Gallery and Cabinet: the latter was on the point of being completed, and is really striking beyond description. Last Saturday night my work-

* Letter to Sir Horace Mann.

men took their leave, made their bow, and left me up to the knees in shavings. In short, the journeymen carpenters, like the cabinet-makers, have entered into an association not to work unless their wages are raised; and how can one complain? The poor fellows, whose all the labour is, see their masters advance their prices every day, and think it reasonable to touch their share."*

In the domain of literature, Walpole's opinions were largely influenced by his social position and personal connexions. He rated the class of professional writers as much below as they have ever been rated above their real deserts; and this may perhaps help to explain the rancour with which he has been pursued by some critics. He could see nothing wonderful in the art of stringing sentences together. He met famous authors daily in society, and did not find that they were wiser or more accomplished than their neighbours. Most of them showed to little advantage in the drawing-rooms in which he felt his own life completest. Gray seldom opened his lips; Goldsmith "talked like poor poll"; Johnson was Ursa Major—a brute with whom Horace declined to be acquainted; Hume's powers of mind did not appear in his broad unmeaning face, nor animate his awkward conversation; even Gibbon made a bad figure as often as any doubt was hinted as to the transcendent importance of his luminous or voluminous history. As for the novelists, neither Fielding nor Richardson ever ascended to the sublime heights in

* Letter to Sir Horace Mann, July 1, 1762.

which Horace dwelt at ease. Stories circulated there of vulgar orgies amidst which the biographer of Tom Jones performed his police functions, and of requests made by the author of "Clarissa" to his female admirers for information as to the manners of polite life. Walpole shrank from the coarseness of the one, and smiled at the attempts of the other to describe a sphere which he had never entered. We are not to suppose, however, that Horace was as blind to the gradations of literary rank as some would have us believe. When he told Mann that *The World* was the work of "our first writers," instancing Lord Chesterfield, Sir Charles Hanbury Williams, and other well-born dilettanti whose names have now sunk into oblivion or neglect, it is clear that he was speaking with reference to the matter in hand. It did not occur to him that great historians and poets would be likely or suitable contributors to a series of light papers intended for the macaronis of the hour. What he regarded as the chief qualification of himself and his friends who wrote for this fashionable journal was their familiarity with the tone of the best society. For himself, Walpole constantly disclaimed all pretence to learning or exact knowledge of any kind, and, due allowance made for the vanity of which undoubtedly he owned an ample share, there seems no reason to question his sincerity. We conceive, indeed, that his estimate of his own talents and acquirements was much more accurate than it has usually been considered. In all that related to literary fame, his vanity showed itself rather in depreciating the advantages which he had not, than in exalting those which he possessed. If he did not worship style, still less was he disposed to bow down before study and research. Hence the low esteem in which he held authors of all kinds. Some excuses may be made for his disparaging criticisms. The literati of his day were certainly eclipsed by the contemporary orators. What writer was left in prose or verse, on the death of Swift, who could compare with Mansfield or the first William Pitt? Which of the poets or historians of the next generation won the applause which was called forth by the speeches of Fox or Sheridan or the younger Pitt? If Fox and Sheridan could obtain their greatest triumphs in the midst of gambling and dissipation, and apparently without pains or application, there was some apology for slighting the labours of Robertson and the carefully polished verses of Goldsmith. With the exception of Lord Chatham, whom he strongly disliked, Walpole generally does justice to the great speakers of his time, on whichever side in politics they were ranged; if he gives no credit for genius to the writers of the age, this was partly at least because their genius was of no striking or signal order. Judgment, sense, and spirit were Pope's three marks for distinguishing a great writer from an inferior one, and these continued to be the criteria applicable, even in the department of so-called works of imagination, down to the end of the century.

Walpole, as in duty bound, was a professed worshipper of Shakespeare and Milton, but we suspect that his worship was not very hearty. It is clear that Pope was the poet of his choice; and he seems to have known every line of his favourite by heart. He admired also the exquisite poetry of Gray, and this admiration was no doubt sincere; but we are disposed to think that it arose entirely from the early connexion between Horace and the author, and from the feeling that Gray, in some sort, belonged to him. Gray was Walpole's poet, as Conway was his statesman; and the sense of ownership, which converted his cousinly regard for Conway into a species of idolatry. turned to enthusiasm for Gray's "Odes" the critical estimate which would otherwise, we feel sure, have ended in a pretty strong aversion.

What Walpole said, rather uncharitably, of Sir Joshua Reynolds, may, we fear, be applied with more justice to Walpole himself. All his geese were swans, as the swans of others were geese in his eyes. Conway was a man of integrity and honour, an excellent soldier, a fluent speaker, but he was a timid and vacillating politician. That phase of their weakness which makes the vainglorious pique themselves on having remarkable friends, is certainly not unamiable, though it is sometimes fatiguing. We all know the man who congratulates himself on his good fortune in being the associate of the versatile Dr. A., the high-souled Mr. B., the original Mr. C., and so on. Had Horace possessed a wife, he would have wearied all his acquaintance with encomiums on her beauty, wit, wisdom, and other matchless perfections. Having no wife to celebrate, he chose to sing the praises of General Conway, and sang them lustily, and with good courage. This was the more disinterested, as Conway appears to have been distinctly one of those persons who allow themselves to be loved. There is no questioning the genuineness of a devotion which undoubtedly entailed on Walpole great sacrifices. The time and labour which Horace bestowed in the service of his friend's ambition entitle him to full credit for honesty in the offer which he made to share his fortune with the latter, when, at an early stage of his career, he was dismissed from his employments for opposing the Ministry of the day.

This was not the only occasion on which Walpole showed himself capable of uncommon generosity. He made a similar offer to Madame du Deffand, when she was threatened with the loss of her pension. That clever leader of French society was not, like Conway, a connexion of long standing, but a mere recent acquaintance of Horace, who had no claim on him beyond the pleasure she had shown in his company, and the pity which her blind and helpless old age demanded. In the event, the lady did not require his assistance, but her letters prove that she had full confidence in his intentions, notwithstanding the harshness with which he sometimes repressed her expressions of affection. The same temperament which made him fond of displaying his intimacy with Conway, caused him to dread the ridicule of being supposed to have an attachment for the poor old Marquise. Hence arose the occasional semblance of unkindness, which was contradicted by substantial proofs of regard, and which must be set down to undue sensitiveness on the gentleman's side rather than to want of consideration.

The coldness of heart with which Walpole is reproached has, we think, been exaggerated. "His affections were bestowed on few; for in early life they had never been cultivated." So much is admitted by Miss Berry, a most favourable witness. But in society generally, Horace appears to have shown himself friendly and obliging. His aristocratic pride did not prevent him from mixing freely with persons much his inferiors in station. Miss Hawkins, daughter of the historian of music, who for many years lived near him at Twickenham, testifies to his sociable and liberal temper; and Walpole's own letters show that he was at some trouble to assist Sir John Hawkins in collecting materials for his work. The correspondence between Horace and his deputies in the Exchequer proves the kindly feeling that subsisted between him and them; and also reveals the fact that he employed them from time to time in dispensing charities which he did not wish to have disclosed. And Miss Berry records that, during his later life, although no ostentatious contributor to public charities and schemes of improvement, the friends in whose opinion he could confide had always more difficulty to repress than to excite his liberality.

His temper, says Sir Walter Scott, was precarious. Walpole, we believe, would readily have pleaded guilty to this charge. That he felt his infirmity in this respect his Letters sufficiently show; he assigns it as the chief reason why he preferred to live alone. Gray was not the only one of his early friends with whom he quarrelled. He became estranged at different times from Ashton, another college companion; from Bentley, whose taste and talent he had employed in decorating his Castle; from George Montagu,* who, next to Conway, was long his most intimate friend; and from Mason the poet; not to mention other names. Whatever blame may attach to Walpole for these ruptures, it seems to be now pretty well agreed that in the matter of Chatterton he was guiltless. On this subject, we need only quote a few sentences from Scott. "His memory," says Sir Walter, "has suffered most on account of his conduct towards Chatterton, in which we have always thought he was perfectly defensible. That unhappy son of genius endeavoured to impose upon Walpole a few stanzas of very inferior merit, as ancient; and sent him an equally gross and palpable imposture under the shape of a pretended 'List of Painters.' Walpole's sole crime lies in not patronizing at once a young man who only appeared before him in the character of a very inartificial impostor, though he afterwards proved himself a gigantic one. The fate of Chatterton lies, not at the door of Walpole, but

---

* Son of Brigadier-General Edward Montagu, and nephew to the second Earl of Halifax. He was member of Parliament for Northampton, usher of the Black Rod in Ireland during the lieutenancy of the Earl of Halifax, ranger of Salsey Forest, and private secretary to Lord North when Chancellor of the Exchequer.

of the public at large, who two years, we believe, afterwards were possessed of the splendid proofs of his natural powers, and any one of whom was as much called upon as Walpole to prevent the most unhappy catastrophe."*

We turn from Walpole's life and character to his Letters. We have already mentioned the friends to whom the earlier portion of these were chiefly addressed. Other friends to whom he occasionally wrote were Lord Hertford, Conway's elder brother, Lord Strafford, Cole, the antiquary of Cambridge, and John Chute, with whom he had been intimate at Florence. The names of some later correspondents will appear as we proceed, of whom such an account as may seem necessary will be given as they come before us. Of the pains and skill with which the matter of each letter is adapted to the person for whom it was intended, our readers will be able to judge for themselves. That the author had studied letter-writing as an art, is a remark almost too trivial to be repeated. It is hardly too much to say that he made it his chief literary business. "Mine," he said, "is a life of letter-writing." That he counted on being remembered by his letters far more than by any other of his writings, we hold to be as certain as any statement of the kind

* Had Chatterton appealed simply to Walpole's charity, he would not have been rejected. This was the opinion of those who knew Horace best. But, apart from the imposture sought to be palmed on him, Walpole did not profess to be a patron of literature or the arts. An artist has pencils, he would say, and an author has pens, and the public must reward them as it sees fit.

can be. He had, we believe, gauged his powers far more correctly than is commonly supposed, and was satisfied that in this kind of composition, more than in any other, he had produced something of permanent value. He had studied closely the letters of Gray and Madame de Sévigné, and formed his own style from them. The letters of the latter were his especial delight. He read them over until they became part of his own mind. Nothing interested him so much as a rumour that some fresh letters of "Notre Dame des Rochers" had been discovered. It may be too much to say, as Miss Berry has said, that Walpole has shown our language to be capable of all the graces and all the charms of the French of the great writer whom he imitated. But, due allowance made for the superiority of French idiom and French finesse in a department where they appear to most advantage, it may safely be affirmed that, if variety and interest of topics be regarded as well as style, Walpole's letters are unrivalled. It was only by degrees that Horace attained to the perfection of easy engaging writing. His earlier letters betray signs of considerable labour. It is said that a summary prepared beforehand of one of his letters to Montagu was found in looking over some of his correspondence. In later days he wrote with the greatest facility, even carrying on a conversation the while. But he continued to the last the habit of putting down on the backs of letters or slips of paper, a note of facts, of news, of witticisms, or of anything he wished not to forget for the amusement of his correspondents.

CHAPTER II.

Country Life.—Ranelagh Gardens.—The Rebel Lords.—The Earthquake.—A Frolic at Vauxhall.—Capture of a Housebreaker.—Strawberry Hill.—The Beautiful Gunnings.—Sterne.

WE pass over such of Walpole's letters as were written before his return from his travels. They are interesting chiefly as parts of a correspondence carried on by four young men of talent—Gray, West, Ashton, and Horace himself—who, having been schoolfellows, had formed what they called a quadruple alliance; and it must be owned that Walpole in this correspondence shines less than Gray, who appears to have been the mentor of the group, and less, too, perhaps than West, whose early death disappointed great hopes. We omit, besides, all reference to the letters in which Horace described the great Walpolean battle, and traced the fortunes of the Broad Bottom Administration. And, with few exceptions, his accounts of later political events have also been excluded. The additions which his gossiping chronicles have made to our knowledge of these matters have been incorporated in most recent histories of the period; the extracts given in the present volume are designed, as a rule, to illustrate the history of manners rather than of politics.

From the moment of his return from the Continent until he lost his father, Horace lived in the old statesman's house, dividing his time, for the most part, between the House of Commons and the amusements of fashionable society. In the latter sphere, the Honourable Mr. Walpole soon achieved success. Several years afterwards, he defined himself as a dancing senator. His first season witnessed the opening of Ranelagh Gardens, which at once became the resort of the great world. Grave ministers and privy councillors were to be seen there in the crowd of beauties and macaronis. Horace relates that he carried Sir Robert thither just before attending him on his retreat to Houghton. Constrained by filial duty, the young man revisited the family seat in each of the two following years, but he went sorely against his will. With his father's coarse habits and boisterous manners he had nothing in common; his feeble constitution was unequal to the sports of the field, and the drinking that then accompanied them; nor could the scenery of Norfolk, which he disliked, make him forget the excitements of Westminster and Chelsea. Yet to these visits to Houghton his readers owe some entertaining sketches of English country life in the middle of the eighteenth century. Take, for instance, the following lively letter addressed to John Chute, whose acquaintance he had made at Florence:

"Houghton, August 20, 1743.

"Indeed, my dear Sir, you certainly did not use to be stupid, and till you give me more substantial proof that you are so, I shall not believe it. As for your temperate diet and milk bringing about such a metamorphosis, I hold it impossible. I have such lamentable proofs every day before my eyes of the stupifying qualities of beef, ale, and wine, that I have contracted a most religious veneration for your spiritual nouriture. Only imagine that I here every day see men, who are mountains of roast beef, and only seem just roughly hewn out into the outlines of human form, like the giant-rock at Pratolino! I shudder when I see them brandish their knives in act to carve, and look on them as savages that devour one another. I should not stare at all more than I do, if yonder Alderman at the lower end of the table was to stick his fork into his neighbour's jolly cheek, and cut a brave slice of brown and fat. Why, I'll swear I see no difference between a country gentleman and a sirloin; whenever the first laughs, or the latter is cut, there run out just the same streams of gravy! Indeed, the sirloin does not ask quite so many questions. I have an Aunt here, a family piece of goods, an old remnant of inquisitive hospitality and economy, who, to all intents and purposes, is as beefy as her neighbours. She wore me so down yesterday with interrogatories, that I dreamt all night she was at my ear with 'who's' and 'why's,' and 'when's' and 'where's,' till at last in my very sleep I cried out, 'For heaven's sake, Madam, ask me no more questions!'

"Oh! my dear Sir, don't you find that nine parts in ten of the world are of no use but to make you wish yourself with that tenth part? I am so far from growing used to mankind by living amongst them, that my natural ferocity and wildness does but every day grow worse. They tire me, they fatigue me; I don't know what to do with them; I don't know what to say to them; I fling open the windows, and fancy I want air; and when I get by myself, I undress myself, and seem to have had people in my pockets, in my plaits, and on my shoulders! I indeed find this fatigue worse in the country than in town, because one can avoid it there and has more resources; but it is there too. I fear 'tis growing old; but I literally seem to have murdered a man whose name was Ennui, for his ghost is ever before me. They say there is no English word for *ennui*; I think you may translate it most literally by what is called 'entertaining people,' and 'doing the honours:' that is, you sit an hour with somebody you don't know and don't care for, talk about the wind and the weather, and ask a thousand foolish questions, which all begin with, 'I think you live a good deal in the country,' or, 'I think you don't love this thing or that.' Oh! 'tis dreadful!

"I'll tell you what is delightful—the Dominichin!* My dear Sir, if ever there was a Dominichin, if there was ever an original picture, this is one. I am quite

---

* Thus described by Walpole in his account of the pictures at Houghton: "The Virgin and Child, a most beautiful, bright, and capital picture, by Dominichino: bought out of the Zambeccari Palace at Bologna by Horace Walpole, junior."

happy; for my father is as much transported with it as I am. It is hung in the gallery, where are all his most capital pictures, and he himself thinks it beats all but the two Guidos. That of the Doctors and the Octagon —I don't know if you ever saw them? What a chain of thought this leads me into! but why should I not indulge it? I will flatter myself with your some time or other passing a few days here with me. Why must I never expect to see anything but Beefs in a gallery which would not yield even to the Colonna?"

Again the following to Sir Horace Mann:

"Newmarket, Oct. 3, 1743.

"I am writing to you in an inn on the road to London. What a paradise should I have thought this when I was in the Italian inns! in a wide barn with four ample windows, which had nothing more like glass than shutters and iron bars! no tester to the bed, and the saddles and portmanteaus heaped on me to keep off the cold. What a paradise did I think the inn at Dover when I came back! and what magnificence were two-penny prints, salt cellars, and boxes to hold the knives; but the *summum bonum* was small-beer and the newspaper.

"'I bless'd my stars, and call'd it luxury!'

"Who was the Neapolitan ambassadress* that could not live at Paris, because there was no macaroni? Now am I relapsed into all the dissatisfied repinement of a true English grumbling voluptuary. I could find

* The Princess of Campoflorido.

in my heart to write a Craftsman against the Government, because I am not quite so much at my ease as on my own sofa. I could persuade myself that it is my Lord Carteret's fault that I am only sitting in a common arm-chair, when I would be lolling in a *péché-mortel*. How dismal, how solitary, how scrub does this town look; and yet it has actually a street of houses better than Parma or Modena. Nay, the houses of the people of fashion, who come hither for the races, are palaces to what houses in London itself were fifteen years ago. People do begin to live again now, and I suppose in a term we shall revert to York Houses, Clarendon Houses, etc. But from that grandeur all the nobility had contracted themselves to live in coops of a dining-room, a dark back-room, with one eye in a corner, and a closet. Think what London would be, if the chief houses were in it, as in the cities in other countries, and not dispersed like great rarity-plums in a vast pudding of country. Well, it is a tolerable place as it is! Were I a physician, I would prescribe nothing but recipe, CCCLXV drachm. Londin. Would you know why I like London so much? Why, if the world must consist of so many fools as it does, I choose to take them in the gross, and not made into separate pills, as they are prepared in the country. Besides, there is no being alone but in a metropolis: the worst place in the world to find solitude is the country: questions grow there, and that unpleasant Christian commodity, neighbours. Oh! they are all good Samaritans, and do so pour balms and nostrums upon one, if one has but the toothache, or a journey to take, that they break one's head. A journey to take—ay! they talk over the miles to you, and tell you, you will be late in. My Lord Lovel says, *John* always goes two hours in the dark in the morning, to avoid being one hour in the dark in the evening. I was pressed to set out to-day before seven: I did before nine; and here am I arrived at a quarter past five, for the rest of the night.

"I am more convinced every day, that there is not only no knowledge of the world out of a great city, but no decency, no practicable society—I had almost said not a virtue. I will only instance in modesty, which all *old Englishmen* are persuaded cannot exist within the atmosphere of Middlesex. Lady Mary has a remarkable taste and knowledge of music, and can sing—I don't say, like your sister; but I am sure she would be ready to die if obliged to sing before three people, or before one with whom she is not intimate. The other day there came to see her a Norfolk heiress; the young gentlewoman had not been three hours in the house, and that for the first time of her life, before she notified her talent for singing, and invited herself upstairs, to Lady Mary's harpsichord; where, with a voice like thunder, and with as little harmony, she sang to nine or ten people for an hour. 'Was ever nymph like Rossymonde?'—no, *d'honneur*. We told her she had a very strong voice. 'Why, Sir! my master says it is nothing to what it was.' My dear child, she brags abominably; if it had been a thousandth degree louder, you must have heard it at Florence."

Arrived in London, he is again in his element. "You must be informed," he writes to Conway, "that every night constantly I go to Ranelagh, which has totally beat Vauxhall. Nobody goes anywhere else—everybody goes there. My Lord Chesterfield is so fond of it, that he says he has ordered all his letters to be directed thither. If you had never seen it, I would make you a most pompous description of it, and tell you how the floor is all of beaten princes—that you can't set your foot without treading on a Prince of Wales or Duke of Cumberland. The company is universal: there is from his Grace of Grafton down to children out of the Foundling Hospital—from my Lady Townshend to the kitten—from my Lord Sandys* to your humble cousin and sincere friend."

From scenes like this Conway's humble cousin was removed, though not for long, by the last illness and death of Lord Orford. The Rebellion of 1745, which quickly followed, produced only a momentary stir in London. But the trials and executions of the rebel Lords, occurring in the Capital itself, excited longer interest. We give Walpole's narrative of the execution of Lords Kilmarnock and Balmerino:

"Just before they came out of the Tower, Lord Balmerino drank a bumper to King James's health. As the clock struck ten, they came forth on foot, Lord Kilmarnock all in black, his hair unpowdered in a bag, supported by Forster, the great Presbyterian, and by

* Lord Orford's successor as Chancellor of the Exchequer.

Mr. Home, a young clergyman, his friend. Lord Balmerino followed, alone, in a blue coat, turned up with red, (his rebellious regimentals,) a flannel waistcoat, and his shroud beneath; their hearses following. They were conducted to a house near the scaffold: the room forwards had benches for spectators, in the second Lord Kilmarnock was put, and in the third backwards Lord Balmerino: all three chambers hung with black. Here they parted! Balmerino embraced the other, and said, 'My lord, I wish I could suffer for both!' He had scarce left him, before he desired again to see him, and then asked him, 'My Lord Kilmarnock, do you know anything of the resolution taken in our army, the day before the battle of Culloden, to put the English prisoners to death?' He replied, 'My lord, I was not present; but since I came hither, I have had all the reason in the world to believe that there was such order taken; and I hear the Duke has the pocket-book with the order.' Balmerino answered, 'It was a lie raised to excuse their barbarity to us.'—Take notice, that the Duke's charging this on Lord Kilmarnock (certainly on misinformation) decided this unhappy man's fate! The most now pretended is, that it would have come to Lord Kilmarnock's turn to have given the word for the slaughter, as lieutenant-general, with the patent for which he was immediately drawn into the rebellion, after having been staggered by his wife, her mother, his own poverty, and the defeat of Cope. He remained an hour and a half in the house, and shed tears. At last he came to the scaffold, certainly much terrified, but with a resolution that prevented his behaving in the least meanly or unlike a gentleman.* He took no notice of the crowd, only to desire that the baize might be lifted up from the rails, that the mob might see the spectacle. He stood and prayed some time with Forster, who wept over him, exhorted and encouraged him. He delivered a long speech to the Sheriff, and with a noble manliness stuck to the recantation he had made at his trial; declaring he wished that all who embarked in the same cause might meet the same fate. He then took off his bag, coat and waistcoat, with great composure, and after some trouble put on a napkin-cap, and then several times tried the block; the executioner, who was in white, with a white apron, out of tenderness concealing the axe behind himself. At last the Earl knelt down, with a visible unwillingness to depart, and after five minutes dropped his handkerchief, the signal, and his head was cut off at once, only hanging by a bit of skin, and was received in a scarlet cloth by four of the undertaker's men kneeling, who wrapped it up and put it into the coffin with the body; orders having been given not to expose the heads, as used to be the custom.

* When he [Kilmarnock] beheld the fatal scaffold covered with black cloth; the executioner, with his axe and his assistants; the saw-dust, which was soon to be drenched with his blood; the coffin, prepared to receive the limbs which were yet warm with life; above all, the immense display of human countenances which surrounded the scaffold like a sea, all eyes being bent on the sad object of the preparation,—his natural feelings broke forth in a whisper to the friend on whose arm he leaned, "Home, this is terrible!" No sign of indecent timidity, however, affected his behaviour.—*Sir Walter Scott's Tales of my Grandfather.*

"The scaffold was immediately new-strewed with saw-dust, the block new-covered, the executioner new-dressed, and a new axe brought. Then came old Balmerino, treading with the air of a general. As soon as he mounted the scaffold, he read the inscription on his coffin, as he did again afterwards: he then surveyed the spectators, who were in amazing numbers, even upon masts of ships in the river; and pulling out his spectacles, read a reasonable speech, which he delivered to the Sheriff, and said, the young Pretender was so sweet a Prince, that flesh and blood could not resist following him; and lying down to try the block, he said, 'If I had a thousand lives, I would lay them all down here in the same cause.' He said, if he had not taken the sacrament the day before, he would have knocked down Williamson, the lieutenant of the Tower, for his ill-usage of him. He took the axe and felt it, and asked the headsman how many blows he had given Lord Kilmarnock; and gave him three guineas. Two clergymen, who attended him, coming up, he said, 'No, gentlemen, I believe you have already done me all the service you can.' Then he went to the corner of the scaffold, and called very loud for the warder, to give him his periwig, which he took off, and put on a night-cap of Scotch plaid, and then pulled off his coat and waistcoat and lay down; but being told he was on the wrong side, vaulted round, and immediately gave the sign by tossing up his arm, as if he were giving the signal for battle. He received three blows, but the first certainly took away all sensation. He was not a quarter of an hour on the scaffold; Lord Kilmarnock above half a one. Balmerino certainly died with the intrepidity of a hero, but with the insensibility of one too. As he walked from his prison to execution, seeing every window and top of house filled with spectators, he cried out, 'Look, look, how they are all piled up like rotten oranges!'"

Horace was now in the full tide of fashion, not to say dissipation. For a good many years the opera, plays, balls, routs, and other diversions public and private occupy as much space in his letters as the war or the peace, the debates in Parliament, and the intrigues of party leaders. Mingled with topics of both kinds, we have journeys to visit great houses in the country, schemes for their improvement, designs for the Gothic villa at Strawberry Hill, abundance of scandal, and playful satire on the follies of the day. Here is an amusing account of the sensation produced by the earthquake which alarmed London in 1750. It will be seen that the more serious feelings which the event awakened were as ridiculous in Walpole's eyes as any part of the panic:

"'Portents and prodigies are grown so frequent,
That they have lost their name.'

"My text is not literally true; but as far as earthquakes go towards lowering the price of wonderful commodities, to be sure we are overstocked. We have had a second, much more violent than the first; and you must not be surprised if by next post you hear of a burning mountain sprung up in Smithfield. In the night between Wednesday and Thursday last, (exactly a month since the first shock,) the earth had a shivering fit between one and two; but so slight that, if no more had followed, I don't believe it would have been noticed. I had been awake, and had scarce dozed again—on a sudden I felt my bolster lift up my head; I thought somebody was getting from under my bed, but soon found it was a strong earthquake, that lasted near half a minute, with a violent vibration and great roaring. I rang my bell; my servant came in, frightened out of his senses: in an instant we heard all the windows in the neighbourhood flung up. I got up and found people running into the streets, but saw no mischief done: there has been some; two old houses flung down, several chimneys, and much china-ware. The bells rang in several houses. Admiral Knowles, who has lived long in Jamaica, and felt seven there, says this was more violent than any of them: Francesco prefers it to the dreadful one at Leghorn. The wise say, that if we have not rain soon, we shall certainly have more. Several people are going out of town, for it has nowhere reached above ten miles from London: they say, they are not frightened, but that it is such fine weather, 'Why, one can't help going into the country!' The only visible effect it has had, was on the ridotto, at which, being the following night, there were but four hundred people. A parson, who came into White's the morning of earthquake the first, and heard bets laid on whether it was an earthquake or the blowing up of powder-mills, went away exceedingly scandalised, and said, 'I protest, they are such an impious set of people, that I believe if the last trumpet was to sound, they would bet puppet-show against Judgment.' If we get any nearer still to the torrid zone, I shall pique myself on sending you a present of cedrati and orange-flower water: I am already planning a *terreno* for Strawberry Hill. . . .

"You will not wonder so much at our earthquakes as at the effects they have had. All the women in town have taken them up upon the foot of *Judgments;* and the clergy, who have had no windfalls of a long season, have driven horse and foot into this opinion. There has been a shower of sermons and exhortations: Secker,* the jesuitical Bishop of Oxford, began the mode. He heard the women were all going out of town to avoid the next shock; and so, for fear of losing his Easter offerings, he set himself to advise them to await God's good pleasure in fear and trembling. But what is more astonishing, Sherlock,† who has much better sense, and much less of the Popish confessor, has been running a race with him for the old ladies, and has written a pastoral letter, of which ten thousand were sold in two days; and fifty thousand have been subscribed for, since the two first editions.

"I told you the women talked of going out of town: several families are literally gone, and many more

---

* Afterwards Archbishop of Canterbury. Walpole had a strong and unreasonable prejudice against him.

† Thomas Sherlock, Master of the Temple; first, Bishop of Salisbury, and afterwards of London.—WALPOLE.

going to-day and to-morrow; for what adds to the absurdity is, that the second shock having happened exactly a month after the former, it prevails that there will be a third on Thursday next, another month, which is to swallow up London. I am almost ready to burn my letter now I have begun it, lest you should think I am laughing at you: but it is so true, that Arthur of White's told me last night, that he should put off the last ridotto, which was to be on Thursday, because he hears nobody would come to it. I have advised several who are going to keep their next earthquake in the country, to take the bark for it, as it is so periodic. Dick Leveson and Mr. Rigby, who had supped and stayed late at Bedford House the other night, knocked at several doors, and in a watchman's voice cried, 'Past four o'clock, and a dreadful earthquake!' But I have done with this ridiculous panic: two pages were too much to talk of it. . . .

"I had not time to finish my letter on Monday. I return to the earthquake, which I had mistaken; it is to be to-day. This frantic terror prevails so much, that within these three days seven hundred and thirty coaches have been counted passing Hyde Park Corner, with whole parties removing into the country. Here is a good advertisement which I cut out of the papers to-day:

"'On Monday next will be published (price 6*d*.) A true and exact List of all the Nobility and Gentry who have left, or shall leave, this place through fear of another Earthquake.'

"Several women have made earthquake gowns; that

is, warm gowns to sit out of doors all to-night. These are of the more courageous. One woman, still more heroic, is come to town on purpose; she says, all her friends are in London, and she will not survive them. But what will you think of Lady Catherine Pelham, Lady Frances Arundel, and Lord and Lady Galway, who go this evening to an inn ten miles out of town, where they are to play at brag till five in the morning, and then come back—I suppose, to look for the bones of their husbands and families under the rubbish? The prophet of all this (next to the Bishop of London) is a trooper of Lord Delawar's, who was yesterday sent to Bedlam. His *colonel* sent to the man's wife, and asked her if her husband had ever been disordered before. She cried, ' Oh dear! my lord, he is not mad now; if your *lordship* would but get any *sensible* man to examine him, you would find he is quite in his right mind.' . . .

"I did not doubt but you would be diverted with the detail of absurdities that were committed after the earthquake: I could have filled more paper with such relations, if I had not feared tiring you. We have swarmed with sermons, essays, relations, poems, and exhortations on that subject. One Stukely, a parson, has accounted for it, and I think prettily, by electricity —but that is the fashionable cause, and everything is resolved into electrical appearances, as formerly everything was accounted for by Descartes's vortices, and Sir Isaac's gravitation. But they all take care, after accounting for the earthquake systematically, to assure you that still it was nothing less than a judgment. Dr. Barton, the Rector of St. Andrew's, was the only sensible, or at least honest divine, upon the occasion. When some women would have had him pray to them in his parish church against the intended shock, he excused himself on having a great cold. 'And besides,' said he, 'you may go to St. James's Church; the Bishop of Oxford is to preach there all night about earthquakes.' Turner, a great china-man, at the corner of next street, had a jar cracked by the shock: he originally asked ten guineas for the pair: he now asks twenty, 'because it is the only jar in Europe that has been cracked by an earthquake.'"

Not long after the earthquake, we find Walpole engaged in a frolic at Vauxhall, though in the best company, Lady Caroline Petersham, his hostess on the occasion, being the dashing wife* of Lord Petersham, eldest son of the Earl of Harrington, who had been Secretary of State. We insert Walpole's history of the affair for the reason which he gives for telling it. It is part of a letter to George Montagu. After a jest about the habits of Buxton, where his friend's sister was then drinking the waters, the writer proceeds:

"As jolly and as abominable a life as she may have been leading, I defy all her enormities to equal a party of pleasure that I had t'other night. I shall relate it to you to show you the manners of the age, which are always as entertaining to a person fifty miles off as to

* She was daughter of the Duke of Grafton.

one born an hundred and fifty years after the time. I
had a card from Lady Caroline Petersham to go with
her to Vauxhall. I went accordingly to her house, and
found her and the little Ashe, or the Pollard Ashe, as
they call her; they had just finished their last layer of
red, and looked as handsome as crimson could make
them. . . . We issued into the Mall to assemble our
company, which was all the town, if we could get it;
for just so many had been summoned, except Harry
Vane, whom we met by chance. We mustered the
Duke of Kingston, whom Lady Caroline says she has
been trying for these seven years; but alas! his beauty
is at the fall of the leaf; Lord March, Mr. Whitehed, a
pretty Miss Beauclerc, and a very foolish Miss Sparre.
These two damsels were trusted by their mothers for
the first time of their lives to the matronly care of Lady
Caroline. As we sailed up the Mall with all our colours
flying, Lord Petersham,* with his hose and legs twisted
to every point of crossness, strode by us on the outside,
and repassed again on the return. At the end of the
Mall she called to him; he would not answer: she gave
a familiar spring, and, between laugh and confusion,
ran up to him, ' My lord, my lord! why, you don't see
us!' We advanced at a little distance, not a little
awkward in expectation how all this would end, for my
ord never stirred his hat, or took the least notice of
anybody: she said, ' Do you go with us, or are *you
going anywhere else?*'—' I don't go with you, I am going
somewhere else;' and away he stalked, as sulky as a

* His gait was so singular, that he was called Peter Shamble.

ghost that nobody will speak to first. We got into the best order we could, and marched to our barge, with a boat of French horns attending, and little Ashe singing. We paraded some time up the river, and at last debarked at Vauxhall: there, if we had so pleased, we might have had the vivacity of our party increased by a quarrel; for a Mrs. Lloyd,* who is supposed to be married to Lord Haddington, seeing the two girls following Lady Petersham and Miss Ashe, said aloud, 'Poor girls, I am sorry to see them in such bad company!' Miss Sparre, who desired nothing so much as the fun of seeing a duel—a thing which, though she is fifteen, she has never been so lucky as to see,—took due pains to make Lord March resent this; but he, who is very lively and agreeable, laughed her out of this charming frolic with a great deal of humour. Here we picked up Lord Granby.... If all the adventures don't conclude as you expect in the beginning of a paragraph, you must not wonder, for I am not making a history, but relating one strictly as it happened, and I think with full entertainment enough to content you. At last, we assembled in our booth, Lady Caroline in the front, with the vizor of her hat erect, and looking gloriously jolly and handsome. She had fetched my brother Orford from the next box, where he was enjoying himself with his *petite partie*, to help us to mince chickens. We minced seven chickens into a china dish, which Lady Caroline stewed over a lamp with

---

* Mrs. Lloyd of Spring Gardens, to whom the Earl of Haddington was married this year.

three pats of butter and a flagon of water, stirring, and rattling, and laughing, and we every minute expecting to have the dish fly about our ears. She had brought Betty, the fruit-girl, with hampers of strawberries and cherries from Rogers's, and made her wait upon us, and then made her sup by us at a little table. The conversation was no less lively than the whole transaction. There was a Mr. O'Brien arrived from Ireland, who would get the Duchess of Manchester from Mr. Hussey,* if she were still at liberty. I took up the biggest hautboy in the dish, and said to Lady Caroline, 'Madam, Miss Ashe desires you would eat this O'Brien strawberry;' she replied immediately, 'I won't, you hussey.' You may imagine the laugh this reply occasioned. After the tempest was a little calmed, the Pollard said, 'Now, how anybody would spoil this story that was to repeat it, and say, I won't, you jade!' In short, the whole air of our party was sufficient, as you will easily imagine, to take up the whole attention of the garden; so much so, that from eleven o'clock till half an hour after one we had the whole concourse round our booth: at last, they came into the little gardens of each booth on the sides of ours, till Harry Vane took up a bumper, and drank their healths, and was proceeding to treat them with still greater freedom. It was three o'clock before we got home."

Our next extract displays even better than the last

* An Irish adventurer, whose fine person had induced the Dowager Duchess of Manchester to marry him. He was afterwards created Earl of Beaulieu. O'Brien, it seems, was even taller than Hussey.

our author's skill in telling a story. It also contains some pleasant references to his life at Strawberry Hill:

"I have just been in London for two or three days, to fetch an adventure, and am returned to my hill and my castle. I can't say I lost my labour, as you shall hear. Last Sunday night, being as wet a night as you shall see in a summer's day, about half an hour after twelve, I was just come home from White's, and undressing to step into bed, when I heard Harry, who you know lies forwards, roar out, 'Stop thief!' and run down stairs. I ran after him. Don't be frightened; I have not lost one enamel, nor bronze, nor have been shot through the head again. A gentlewoman, who lives at Governor Pitt's, next door but one to me, and where Mr. Bentley used to live, was going to bed too, and heard people breaking into Mr. Freeman's house, who, like some acquaintance of mine in Albemarle Street, goes out of town, locks up his doors, and leaves the community to watch his furniture. N.B. It was broken open but two years ago, and I and all the chairmen vow they shall steal his house away another time, before we will trouble our heads about it. Well, madam called out 'Watch!' two men, who were sentinels, ran away, and Harry's voice after them. Down came I, and with a posse of chairmen and watchmen found the third fellow in the area of Mr. Freeman's house. Mayhap you have seen all this in the papers, little thinking who commanded the detachment. Harry fetched a blunderbuss to invite the thief up. One of the chairmen, who was drunk, cried,

'Give me the blunderbuss, I'll shoot him!' But as the general's head was a little cooler, he prevented military execution, and took the prisoner, without bloodshed, intending to make his triumphal entry into the metropolis of Twickenham with his captive tied to the wheels of his post-chaise. I find my style rises so much with the recollection of my victory, that I don't know how to descend to tell you that the enemy was a carpenter, and had a leather apron on. The next step was to share my glory with my friends. I despatched a courier to White's for George Selwyn, who, you know, loves nothing upon earth so well as a criminal, except the execution of him. It happened very luckily that the drawer, who received my message, has very lately been robbed himself, and had the wound fresh in his memory. He stalked up into the club-room, stopped short, and with a hollow trembling voice said, 'Mr. Selwyn! Mr. Walpole's compliments to you, and he has got a housebreaker for you!' A squadron immediately came to reinforce me, and having summoned Moreland with the keys of the fortress, we marched into the house to search for more of the gang. Col. Seabright with his sword drawn went first, and then I, exactly the figure of Robinson Crusoe, with a candle and lanthorn in my hand, a carbine upon my shoulder, my hair wet and about my ears, and in a linen night-gown and slippers. We found the kitchen shutters forced, but not finished; and in the area a tremendous bag of tools, a hammer large enough for the hand of a Jael, and six chisels! All which *opima spolia*, as there was no temple of

Jupiter Capitolinus in the neighbourhood, I was reduced to offer on the altar of Sir Thomas Clarges.

"I am now, as I told you, returned to my plough with as much humility and pride as any of my great predecessors. We lead quite a rural life, have had a sheep-shearing, a hay-making, a syllabub under the cow, and a fishing of three gold-fish out of Poyang,* for a present to Madam Clive. They breed with me excessively, and are grown to the size of small perch. Everything grows, if tempests would let it; but I have had two of my largest trees broke to-day with the wind, and another last week. I am much obliged to you for the flower you offer me, but by the description it is an Austrian rose, and I have several now in bloom. Mr. Bentley is with me, finishing the drawings for Gray's Odes; there are some mandarin-cats fishing for gold-fish, which will delight you. . . .

"You will be pleased with a story of Lord Bury, that is come from Scotland: he is quartered at Inverness; the magistrates invited him to an entertainment with fire-works, which they intended to give on the morrow for the Duke's birth-day. He thanked them, assured them he would represent their zeal to his Royal Highness; but he did not doubt it would be more agreeable to him, if they postponed it to the day following, the anniversary of the battle of Culloden. They stared, said they could not promise on their own authority, but would go and consult their body. They returned, told

* Walpole had given this Chinese name to a pond of gold-fish at Strawberry Hill.

him it was unprecedented, and could not be complied with. Lord Bury replied, he was sorry they had not given a negative at once, for he had mentioned it to his soldiers, who would not bear a disappointment, and was afraid it would provoke them to some outrage upon the town. This did;—they celebrated Culloden. . . ."

A few years later Strawberry Hill had attained its greatest celebrity. In June, 1759, Walpole writes:

" Strawberry Hill is grown a perfect Paphos; it is the land of beauties. On Wednesday the Duchesses of Hamilton and Richmond, and Lady Ailesbury dined there; the two latter stayed all night. There never was so pretty a sight as to see them all three sitting in the shell; a thousand years hence, when I begin to grow old, if that can ever be, I shall talk of that event, and tell young people how much handsomer the women of my time were than they will be then: I shall say, ' Women alter now; I remember Lady Ailesbury looking handsomer than her daughter, the pretty Duchess of Richmond, as they were sitting in the shell on my terrace with the Duchess of Hamilton, one of the famous Gunnings.' Yesterday t'other more famous Gunning [Lady Coventry] dined there. She has made a friendship with my charming niece, to disguise her jealousy of the new Countess's beauty: there were they two, their lords, Lord Buckingham, and Charlotte. You will think that I did not choose men for my parties so well as women. I don't include Lord Waldegrave in this bad election."

The famous Gunnings referred to in the last passage figure often in Walpole's letters. These two ladies were the daughters of Irish parents, and though of noble blood on the mother's side, are said to have been originally so poor that they had thought of being actresses; and when they were first presented at Dublin Castle, they were supplied with clothes for the occasion by Mrs. Woffington, the actress. On their arrival in England, their beauty created such an impression, that they were followed by crowds in the Park and at Vauxhall. We even read that Maria, the elder, some years after her marriage, having been mobbed in the Park, was attended by a guard of soldiers. Maria married the Earl of Coventry, and died many years before her husband. Her younger sister, Elizabeth, who was reckoned the less beautiful of the two, married, first, the Duke of Hamilton, and, secondly, Colonel John Campbell, afterwards Duke of Argyll, for whom she had refused the Duke of Bridgewater. The penniless Irish girl, Elizabeth Gunning, was the mother of two Dukes of Hamilton and two Dukes of Argyll. Walpole's niece, of whom he suggests Lady Coventry was jealous, was a natural daughter of his brother, Sir Edward Walpole, and was then the bride of the Earl of Waldegrave, after whose death she became Duchess of Gloucester, by a clandestine marriage with George III.'s younger brother. By her first husband she had three daughters, the Ladies Waldegrave, whose portraits, by Reynolds, are included in this volume.

Before we leave that portion of Horace Walpole's correspondence which belongs to the reign of George II., we will give one letter of a character different from those we have previously selected. It is addressed to Sir David Dalrymple, afterwards Lord Hailes, and deals entirely with literary subjects. The "Irish poems" referred to in it are, of course, the first fragments of "Ossian," then recently published by Macpherson:

"Strawberry Hill, April 4, 1760.

"As I have very little at present to trouble you with myself, I should have deferred writing till a better opportunity, if it were not to satisfy the curiosity of a friend; a friend whom you, Sir, will be glad to have made curious, as you originally pointed him out as a likely person to be charmed with the old Irish poetry you sent me. It is Mr. Gray, who is an enthusiast about those poems, and begs me to put the following queries to you; which I will do in his own words, and I may say truly, *Poeta loquitur*.

"'I am so charmed with the two specimens of Erse poetry, that I cannot help giving you the trouble to inquire a little farther about them, and should wish to see a few lines of the original, that I may form some slight idea of the language, the measures, and the rhythm.

"'Is there anything known of the author or authors, and of what antiquity are they supposed to be?

"'Is there any more to be had of equal beauty, or at all approaching to it?

"'I have been often told, that the poem called Hardykanute* (which I always admired and still admire) was the work of somebody that lived a few years ago. This I do not at all believe, though it has evidently been retouched in places by some modern hand; but, however, I am authorised by this report to ask, whether the two poems in question are certainly antique and genuine. I make this inquiry in quality of an antiquary, and am not otherwise concerned about it; for if I were sure that anyone now living in Scotland had written them, to divert himself and laugh at the credulity of the world, I would undertake a journey into the Highlands only for the pleasure of seeing him.'

"You see, Sir, how easily you may make our greatest southern bard travel northward to visit a brother. The young translator has nothing to do but to own a forgery, and Mr. Gray is ready to pack up his lyre, saddle Pegasus, and set out directly. But seriously, he, Mr. Mason, my Lord Lyttelton, and one or two more, whose taste the world allows, are in love with your Erse elegies: I cannot say in general they are so much admired—but Mr. Gray alone is worth satisfying.

"The 'Siege of Aquileia,' of which you ask, pleased less than Mr. Home's other plays.† In my own opinion,

---

* It was written by Mrs. Halket of Wardlaw. Mr. Lockhart states, that on the blank leaf of his copy of Allan Ramsay's "Evergreen," Sir Walter Scott has written, "Hardyknute was the first poem that I ever learnt, the last that I shall forget."

† The "Siege of Aquileia," a tragedy, by John Home, produced at Drury Lane, 21st February, 1760.

'Douglas' far exceeds both the others. Mr. Home seems to have a beautiful talent for painting genuine nature and the manners of his country. There was so little of nature in the manners of both Greeks and Romans, that I do not wonder at his success being less brilliant when he tried those subjects; and, to say the truth, one is a little weary of them. At present, nothing is talked of, nothing admired, but what I cannot help calling a very insipid and tedious performance: it is a kind of novel, called 'The Life and Opinions of Tristram Shandy;' the great humour of which consists in the whole narration always going backwards. I can conceive a man saying that it would be droll to write a book in that manner, but have no notion of his persevering in executing it. It makes one smile two or three times at the beginning, but in recompense makes one yawn for two hours. The characters are tolerably kept up, but the humour is for ever attempted and missed. The best thing in it is a Sermon, oddly coupled with a good deal of indecency, and both the composition of a clergyman. The man's head, indeed, was a little turned before, now topsy-turvy with his success and fame. Dodsley has given him six hundred and fifty pounds for the second edition and two more volumes (which I suppose will reach backwards to his great-great-grandfather); Lord Fauconberg, a donative* of one hundred and sixty pounds a year; and Bishop Warburton gave him a purse of gold and this compliment (which happened to be a contradiction), 'that it was

* The living of Coxwold, in Yorkshire.

quite an original composition, and in the true Cervantic vein :' the only copy that ever was an original, except in painting, where they all pretend to be so. Warburton, however, not content with this, recommended the book to the bench of bishops, and told them Mr. Sterne, the author, was the English Rabelais. They had never heard of such a writer. Adieu!"

CHAPTER III.

A new reign.—Funeral of the late King.—Houghton revisited.—Election at Lynn.—Marriage of George the Third.—His Coronation.

THE accession of George III. was the beginning of a new era in English society. The character of George II. could inspire no respect. His successor, with all his faults, did as much perhaps towards reforming the manners of the higher classes as a more enlightened prince could have effected. His regular life and the strictness of his Court applied a pressure answering to that which grew daily stronger from below. The chief want of the aristocracy at this time was not so much culture as something more vitally important. Culture they did, indeed, sorely lack, but many influences among themselves were tending to promote this. What they mainly needed to have enforced upon them from without was some regard to the first principles of social order, some recognition of moral and religious obligations. Those who despise the formalism of George III.'s reign, may reflect that to impose external decorum on the society represented in Hogarth's pictures was of itself no trifling improvement. Even this was some time in coming. It was retarded by the mistaken system of government which for a long while rendered the Crown unpopular. Still the signs of a change for the better gradually became apparent; and when the close of the American War had removed the last subject of national discontent, the great majority of the upper, as well as of the middle ranks, rallied round the throne as the mainstay of public morality, supporting the King and the sedate minister of his choice against a rival whose irregularities recalled the disorders of a former time.

We give the letter in which Walpole describes the funeral of George II. It should be stated that the writer did not long retain the favourable opinion he here expresses of the new Sovereign :

"Arlington Street, Nov. 13, 1760.

" Even the honeymoon of a new reign don't produce events every day. There is nothing but the common saying of addresses and kissing hands. The chief difficulty is settled; Lord Gower yields the Mastership of the Horse to Lord Huntingdon, and removes to the Great Wardrobe, from whence Sir Thomas Robinson was to have gone into Ellis's place, but he is saved. The City, however, have a mind to be out of humour; a paper has been fixed on the Royal Exchange, with these words, ' No petticoat Government, no Scotch Minister, no Lord George Sackville ;' two hints totally unfounded, and the other scarce true. No petticoat ever governed less, it is left at Leicester-house; Lord George's breeches are as little concerned ; and, except

Lady Susan Stuart and Sir Harry Erskine, nothing has yet been done for any Scots. For the King himself, he seems all good-nature, and wishing to satisfy everybody; all his speeches are obliging. I saw him again yesterday, and was surprised to find the levee-room had lost so entirely the air of the lion's den. This Sovereign don't stand in one spot, with his eyes fixed royally on the ground, and dropping bits of German news; he walks about, and speaks to everybody. I saw him afterwards on the throne, where he is graceful and genteel, sits with dignity, and reads his answers to addresses well; it was the Cambridge address, carried by the Duke of Newcastle in his Doctor's gown, and looking like the *Médecin malgré lui*. He had been vehemently solicitous for attendance, for fear my Lord Westmoreland, who vouchsafes himself to bring the address from Oxford, should outnumber him. Lord Lichfield and several other Jacobites have kissed hands; George Selwyn says, 'They go to St James's, because now there are so many *Stuarts* there.'

"Do you know, I had the curiosity to go to the burying t'other night; I had never seen a royal funeral; nay, I walked as a rag of quality, which I found would be, and so it was, the easiest way of seeing it. It is absolutely a noble sight. The Prince's chamber, hung with purple, and a quantity of silver lamps, the coffin under a canopy of purple velvet, and six vast chandeliers of silver on high stands, had a very good effect. The Ambassador from Tripoli and his son were carried to see that chamber. The procession, through a line of foot-guards, every seventh man bearing a torch, the horse-guards lining the outside, their officers with drawn sabres and crape sashes on horseback, the drums muffled, the fifes, bells tolling, and minute-guns,—all this was very solemn. But the charm was the entrance of the Abbey, where we were received by the Dean and Chapter in rich robes, the choir and almsmen bearing torches; the whole Abbey so illuminated, that one saw it to greater advantage than by day; the tombs, long aisles, and fretted roof, all appearing distinctly, and with the happiest *chiaroscuro*. There wanted nothing but incense, and little chapels here and there, with priests saying mass for the repose of the defunct; yet one could not complain of its not being catholic enough. I had been in dread of being coupled with some boy of ten years old; but the heralds were not very accurate, and I walked with George Grenville, taller and older, to keep me in countenance. When we came to the chapel of Henry the Seventh, all solemnity and decorum ceased; no order was observed, people sat or stood where they could or would; the yeomen of the guard were crying out for help, oppressed by the immense weight of the coffin; the Bishop read sadly, and blundered in the prayers; the fine chapter, *Man that is born of a woman*, was chanted, not read; and the anthem, besides being immeasurably tedious, would have served as well for a nuptial. The real serious part was the figure of the Duke of Cumberland, heightened by a thousand melancholy circumstances. He had a dark brown adonis, and a cloak of black cloth, with a train of five yards.

Attending the funeral of a father could not be pleasant: his leg extremely bad, yet forced to stand upon it near two hours; his face bloated and distorted with his late paralytic stroke, which has affected, too, one of his eyes, and placed over the mouth of the vault, into which, in all probability, he must himself so soon descend; think how unpleasant a situation! He bore it all with a firm and unaffected countenance. This grave scene was fully contrasted by the burlesque Duke of Newcastle. He fell into a fit of crying the moment he came into the chapel, and flung himself back in a stall, the Archbishop hovering over him with a smelling-bottle; but in two minutes his curiosity got the better of his hypocrisy, and he ran about the chapel with his glass to spy who was or was not there, spying with one hand, and mopping his eyes with the other. Then returned the fear of catching cold; and the Duke of Cumberland, who was sinking with heat, felt himself weighed down, and turning round, found it was the Duke of Newcastle standing upon his train, to avoid the chill of the marble. It was very theatric to look down into the vault where the coffin lay, attended by mourners with lights. Clavering, the groom of the bedchamber, refused to sit up with the body, and was dismissed by the King's order."

The demise of the Crown, of course, dissolved Parliament. Horace Walpole went down to Houghton to be re-elected for Lynn:

"Houghton, March 25, 1761.

" Here I am at Houghton! and alone! in this spot, where (except two hours last month) I have not been in sixteen years! Think, what a crowd of reflections! No; Gray, and forty churchyards, could not furnish so many; nay, I know one must feel them with greater indifference than I possess, to have patience to put them into verse. Here I am, probably for the last time of my life, though not for the last time: every clock that strikes tells me I am an hour nearer to yonder church—that church, into which I have not yet had courage to enter, where lies that mother on whom I doated, and who doated on me! There are the two rival mistresses of Houghton, neither of whom ever wished to enjoy it! There too lies he who founded its greatness, to contribute to whose fall Europe was embroiled; there he sleeps in quiet and dignity, while his friend and his foe, rather his false ally and real enemy, Newcastle and Bath, are exhausting the dregs of their pitiful lives in squabbles and pamphlets.*

"The surprise the pictures gave me is again renewed; accustomed for many years to see nothing but wretched daubs and varnished copies at auctions, I look at these as enchantment. My own description of them seems poor; but shall I tell you truly, the majesty of Italian ideas almost sinks before the warm nature of Flemish colouring. Alas! don't I grow old? My young imagination was fired with Guido's ideas: must they be plump as Abishag to warm me now? Does great

* " My flatterers here are all mutes. The oaks, the beeches, the chestnuts, seem to contend which best shall please the Lord of the Manor. They cannot deceive, they will not lie."—*Sir Robert Walpole to General Churchill*, Houghton, June 24th, 1743.

youth feel with poetic limbs, as well as see with poetic eyes? In one respect I am very young, I cannot satiate myself with looking: an incident contributed to make me feel this more strongly. A party arrived, just as I did, to see the house, a man and three women in riding-dresses, and they rode post through the apartments. I could not hurry before them fast enough; they were not so long in seeing for the first time, as I could have been in one room, to examine what I knew by heart. I remember formerly being often diverted with this kind of *seers;* they come, ask what such a room is called, in which Sir Robert lay, write it down, admire a lobster or a cabbage in a market-piece, dispute whether the last room was green or purple, and then hurry to the inn for fear the fish should be overdressed. How different my sensations! not a picture here but recalls a history; not one, but I remember in Downing-street or Chelsea, where queens and crowds admired them, though seeing them as little as these travellers!

"When I had drunk tea, I strolled into the garden; they told me it was now called the *pleasure-ground.* What a dissonant idea of pleasure! those groves, those *allées,* where I have passed so many charming moments, are now stripped up or overgrown—many fond paths I could not unravel, though with a very exact clew in my memory: I met two gamekeepers, and a thousand hares! In the days when all my soul was tuned to pleasure and vivacity (and you will think, perhaps, it is far from being out of tune yet), I hated Houghton and its solitude; yet I loved this garden, as now, with many regrets, I love Houghton; Houghton, I know not what to call it, a monument of grandeur or ruin! How I have wished this evening for Lord Bute! how I could preach to him! For myself, I do not want to be preached to; I have long considered, how every Balbec must wait for the chance of a Mr. Wood. The servants wanted to lay me in the great apartment—what, to make me pass my night as I have done my evening! It were like proposing to Margaret Roper to be a duchess in the court that cut off her father's head, and imagining it would please her. I have chosen to sit in my father's little dressing-room, and am now by his scrutoire, where, in the height of his fortune, he used to receive the accounts of his farmers, and deceive himself, or us, with the thoughts of his economy. How wise a man at once, and how weak! For what has he built Houghton? for his grandson to annihilate, or for his son to mourn over. If Lord Burleigh could rise and view his representative driving the Hatfield stage, he would feel as I feel now. Poor little Strawberry! at least, it will not be stripped to pieces by a descendant! You will find all these fine meditations dictated by pride, not by philosophy. Pray consider through how many mediums philosophy must pass, before it is purified—

"'——how often must it weep, how often burn!'

"My mind was extremely prepared for all this gloom by parting with Mr. Conway yesterday morning; moral reflections or commonplaces are the livery one likes to wear, when one has just had a real misfortune. He is going to Germany: I was glad to dress myself up in transitory Houghton, in lieu of very sensible concern. To-morrow I shall be distracted with thoughts, at least images of very different complexion. I go to Lynn, and am to be elected on Friday. I shall return hither on Saturday, again alone, to expect Burleighides on Sunday, whom I left at Newmarket. I must once in my life see him on his grandfather's throne.

"*Epping, Monday night, thirty-first.*—No, I have not seen him; he loitered on the road, and I was kept at Lynn till yesterday morning. It is plain I never knew for how many trades I was formed, when at this time of day I can begin electioneering, and succeed in my new vocation. Think of me, the subject of a mob, who was scarce ever before in a mob, addressing them in the town-hall, riding at the head of two thousand people through such a town as Lynn, dining with above two hundred of them, amid bumpers, huzzas, songs, and tobacco, and finishing with country dancing at a ball and sixpenny whist! I have borne it all cheerfully; nay, have sat hours in *conversation,* the thing upon earth that I hate; have been to hear misses play on the harpsichord, and to see an alderman's copies of Rubens and Carlo Marat. Yet to do the folks justice, they are sensible, and reasonable, and civilised; their very language is polished since I lived among them. I attribute this to their more frequent intercourse with the world and the capital, by the help of good roads and postchaises, which, if they have abridged the King's dominions, have at least tamed his subjects. Well, how comfortable it will be to-morrow, to see my parroquet, to play at loo, and not be obliged to talk seriously! The Ieraclitus of the beginning of this letter will be overjoyed on finishing it to sign himself your old friend,

"DEMOCRITUS.

"P.S. I forgot to tell you that my ancient aunt Hammond came over to Lynn to see me; not from any affection, but curiosity. The first thing she said to me, though we have not met these sixteen years, was, 'Child, you have done a thing to-day, that your father never did in all his life; you sat as they carried you,—he always stood the whole time.' 'Madam,' said I, 'when I am placed in a chair, I conclude I am to sit in it; besides, as I cannot imitate my father in great things, I am not at all ambitious of mimicking him in little ones.' I am sure she proposes to tell her remarks to my uncle Horace's ghost, the instant they meet."

The King's marriage followed a few months later:

"Arlington Street, Sept. 10, 1761.

"When we least expected the Queen, she came, after being ten days at sea, but without sickness for above half-an-hour. She was gay the whole voyage, sung to her harpsichord, and left the door of her cabin open. They made the coast of Suffolk last Saturday, and on Monday morning she landed at Harwich; so prosperously has Lord Anson executed his commission. She lay that night at your old friend Lord Abercorn's, at Witham in Essex; and, if she judged by her host, must have thought she was coming to reign in the realm of taciturnity. She arrived at St. James's a quarter after three on Tuesday the 8th. When she first saw the Palace she turned pale: the Duchess of Hamilton smiled. 'My dear Duchess,' said the Princess, '*you* may laugh: you have been married twice; but it is no joke to me.' Is this a bad proof of her sense? On the journey they wanted her to curl her toupet. 'No, indeed,' said she, 'I think it looks as well as those of the ladies who have been sent for me: if the King would have me wear a periwig, I will; otherwise I shall let myself alone.' The Duke of York gave her his hand at the garden-gate: her lips trembled, but she jumped out with spirit. In the garden the King met her; she would have fallen at his feet; he prevented and embraced her, and led her into the apartments, where she was received by the Princess of Wales and Lady Augusta: these three princesses only dined with the King. At ten the procession went to chapel, preceded by unmarried daughters of peers, and peeresses in plenty. The new Princess was led by the Duke of York and Prince William; the Archbishop married them; the King talked to her the whole time with great good humour, and the Duke of Cumberland have her away. She is not tall, nor a beauty; pale, and very thin; but looks sensible, and is genteel. Her hair is darkish and fine; her forehead low, her nose very well, except the nostrils spreading too wide; her mouth has the same fault, but her teeth are good.* She talks a good deal, and French tolerably; possesses herself, is frank, but with great respect to the King. After the ceremony, the whole company came into the drawing-room for about ten minutes, but nobody was presented that night. The Queen was in white and silver; an endless mantle of violet-coloured velvet, lined with ermine, and attempted to be fastened on her shoulder by a bunch of large pearls, dragged itself and almost the rest of her clothes halfway down her waist. On her head was a beautiful little tiara of diamonds; a diamond necklace, and a stomacher of diamonds, worth three score thousand pounds, which she is to wear at the Coronation too. Her train was borne by the ten bridesmaids, Lady Sarah Lenox, Lady Caroline Russell, Lady Caroline Montagu, Lady Harriot Bentinck, Lady Anne Hamilton, Lady Essex Kerr (daughters of Dukes of Richmond, Bedford, Manchester, Portland, Hamilton, and Roxburgh); and four daughters of the Earls of Albemarle, Brook, Harcourt, and Ilchester,—Lady Elizabeth Keppel, Louisa Greville, Elizabeth Harcourt, and Susan Fox Strangways: their heads crowned with diamonds, and in robes of white and silver. Lady Caroline Russell is extremely

* "Queen Charlotte had always been if not ugly, at least ordinary, but in her later years her want of personal charms became of course less observable, and it used to be said that she was grown better looking. I one day said something to this effect to Colonel Disbrowe, her Chamberlain. 'Yes,' replied he, 'I do think that the *bloom* of her ugliness is going off.'"—CROKER.

handsome; Lady Elizabeth Keppel very pretty; but with neither features nor air, nothing ever looked so charming as Lady Sarah Lenox; she has all the glow of beauty peculiar to her family. As supper was not ready, the Queen sat down, sung, and played on the harpsichord to the Royal Family, who all supped with her in private. They talked of the different German dialects; the King asked if the Hanoverian was not pure—'Oh, no, sir,' said the Queen; 'it is the worst of all.'—She will not be unpopular.

"The Duke of Cumberland told the King that himself and Lady Augusta were sleepy. The Queen was very averse to leave the company, and at last articled that nobody should accompany her but the Princess of Wales and her own two German women, and that nobody should be admitted afterwards but the King—they did not retire till between two and three.

"The next morning the King had a Levee. After the Levee there was a Drawing-Room; the Queen stood under the throne: the women were presented to her by the Duchess of Hamilton, and then the men by the Duke of Manchester; but as she knew nobody, she was not to speak. At night there was a ball, drawing-rooms yesterday and to-day, and then a cessation of ceremony till the Coronation, except next Monday, when she is to receive the address of the Lord Mayor and Aldermen, sitting on the throne attended by the bridesmaids. A ridiculous circumstance happened yesterday; Lord Westmoreland, not very young nor clear-sighted, mistook Lady Sarah

Lenox for the Queen, kneeled to her, and would have kissed her hand if she had not prevented him. People think that a Chancellor of Oxford was naturally attracted by the blood of Stuart. It is as comical to see Kitty Dashwood, the famous old beauty of the Oxfordshire Jacobites, living in the palace as Duenna to the Queen. She and Mrs. Broughton, Lord Lyttelton's ancient Delia, are revived again in a young court that never heard of them. There, I think you could not have had a more circumstantial account of a royal wedding from the Heralds' Office. Adieu!

"Yours to serve you,
"HORACE SANDFORD,
"Mecklenburgh King-at-Arms."

The Coronation of the King and Queen took place on the 22nd of September, 1761, a fortnight after their marriage. Walpole writes to Mann:

"Strawberry Hill, Sept. 28, 1761.

"What is the finest sight in the world? A Coronation. What do people talk most about? A Coronation. Indeed, one had need be a handsome young peeress not to be fatigued to death with it. After being exhausted with hearing of nothing else for six weeks, and having every cranny of my ideas stuffed with velvet and ermine, and tresses, and jewels, I thought I was very cunning in going to lie in Palace-yard, that I might not sit up all night in order to seize a place. The consequence of this wise scheme was, that I did not get a wink of sleep all night; hammering of scaffolds, shouting of people, relieving guards, and jangling of bells, was the concert I heard from twelve to six, when I rose; and it was noon before the procession was ready to set forth, and night before it returned from the Abbey. I then saw the Hall, the dinner, and the champion, a gloriously illuminated chamber, a wretched banquet, and a foolish puppet-show. A Trial of a peer, though by no means so sumptuous, is a preferable sight, for the latter is interesting. At a Coronation one sees the peerage as exalted as they like to be, and at a Trial as much humbled as a plebeian wishes them. I tell you nothing of who looked well; you know them no more than if I told you of the next Coronation. Yes, two ancient dames whom you remember, were still ornaments of the show,—the Duchess of Queensberry and Lady Westmoreland. Some of the peeresses were so fond of their robes, that they graciously exhibited themselves for a whole day before to all the company their servants could invite to see them. A maid from Richmond begged leave to stay in town because the Duchess of Montrose was only to be seen from two to four. The Heralds were so ignorant of their business, that, though pensioned for nothing but to register lords and ladies, and what belongs to them, they advertised in the newspaper for the Christian names and places of abode of the peeresses. The King complained of such omissions and of the want of precedent; Lord Effingham, the Earl Marshal, told him, it was true there had been great neglect in that office, but he had now taken such care of registering directions, that *next coronation* would be conducted with the greatest order imaginable. The King was so diverted with this *flattering* speech that he made the earl repeat it several times.

"On this occasion one saw to how high-water-mark extravagance is risen in England. At the Coronation of George II. my mother gave forty guineas for a dining-room, scaffold, and bedchamber. An exactly parallel apartment, only with rather a worse view, was this time set at three hundred and fifty guineas—a tolerable rise in thirty-three years! The platform from St. Margaret's Round-house to the church-door, which formerly let for forty pounds, went this time for two thousand four hundred pounds. Still more was given for the inside of the Abbey. The prebends would like a Coronation every year. The King paid nine thousand pounds for the hire of jewels; indeed, last time, it cost my father fourteen hundred to bejewel my Lady Orford. A single shop now sold six hundred pounds' sterling worth of nails—but nails are risen—so is everything, and everything adulterated. If we conquer Spain, as we have done France, I expect to be poisoned."

An observation as awkward as that of Lord Effingham had been made by the beautiful Lady Coventry to George II. "She was tired of sights," she said; "there was only one left that she wanted to see, and that was a coronation." The old man, says Walpole, told the story himself at supper to his family with great good humour. As it happened, he outlived Lady Coventry by a few days.

CHAPTER IV.

General Taste for Pleasure.—Entertainments at Twickenham and Esher.—Miss Chudleigh's Ball.—Masquerade at Richmond House.—The Gallery at Strawberry Hill.—Balls.—The Duchess of Queensberry.—Petition of the Periwig-makers.—Ladies' Headgear.—Almack's.—The Castle of Otranto.—Plans for a Bower.—A Late Dinner.—Walpole's Idle Life.—Social usages.

For some years after the arrival of the Queen, the enlivening influence of a new reign is clearly traceable in Walpole's letters. The Court, indeed, did not willingly contribute much to the national gaiety. Its plainness and economy soon incurred reproach ;* while there were intervals in which the first uncertain signs of mental derangement caused the young King to be withdrawn from public observation. Still there were christenings and birthdays, with now and then a wedding, to be celebrated in the royal family ; and the State festivities, unavoidable on these occasions, were eagerly emulated by the nobility. The Peace of Paris, too, was not only welcomed with popular rejoicings,

* "The recluse life led here at Richmond, which is carried to such an excess of privacy and economy, that the Queen's friseur waits on them at dinner, and that four pounds only of beef are allowed for their soup, disgusts all sorts of people."—*Walpole to Lord Hertford, Sep.* 9, 1764.

but produced a general stir in society by the renewed intercourse which it brought about between France and England. "The two nations," writes Horace, "are crossing over and figuring-in." A trifle restrained by the example of the Court and the presence of foreign visitors, the appetite for pleasure became universal among the English higher classes. Lord Bute and the Princess of Wales, Wilkes and the *North Briton*, the debates on privilege and on general warrants, divided the attention of Walpole's world with the last entertainment at the Duke of Richmond's or Northumberland House, with Miss Chudleigh's last ball, with the riots at Drury Lane Theatre, with the *fêtes* in honour of the marriage of the Princess Augusta and the Prince of Brunswick, or, somewhat later, of the ill-starred union between the Princess Caroline and the King of Denmark. We hear no more of frolics at Vauxhall, but we find galas, masquerades, ridottos, festinos, displays of fireworks following each other in rapid succession through our author's pages; sometimes several such scenes are described in the same letter. There is, of course, much sameness in these descriptions, but some passages serve to illustrate the tastes of the age. We will make three or four brief extracts. Our first choice is an account of two entertainments given to French guests of rank, one by Horace himself at Strawberry Hill, the other by Miss Pelham at the country seat celebrated by Pope and Thomson. The whole story is contained in a letter to George Montagu, written in May, 1763:

"'On vient de nous donner une très jolie fête au

château de Straberri: tout étoit tapissé de narcisses, de tulipes, et de lilacs; des cors de chasse, des clarionettes; des petits vers galants faits par des fées, et qui se trouvoient sous la presse; des fruits à la glace, du thé, du caffé, des biscuits, et force hot-rolls.'*—This is not the beginning of a letter to you, but of one that I might suppose sets out to-night for Paris, or rather, which I do not suppose will set out thither; for though the narrative is circumstantially true, I don't believe the actors were pleased enough with the scene, to give so favourable an account of it.

"The French do not come hither to see. *A l'Anglaise* happened to be the word in fashion; and half a dozen of the most fashionable people have been the dupes of it. I take for granted that their next mode will be *à l'Iroquaise*, that they may be under no obligation of realising their pretensions. Madame de Boufflers I think will die a martyr to a taste, which she fancied she had, and finds she has not. Never having stirred ten miles from Paris, and having only rolled in an easy coach from one hotel to another on a gliding pavement, she is already worn out with being hurried from morning till night from one sight to another. She rises every morning so fatigued with the toils of the preceding day, that she has not strength, if she had inclination, to

---

* Walpole was thinking of an anecdote he had told in a previous letter. "The old Maréchale de Villars gave a vast dinner [at Paris] to the Duchess of Bedford. In the middle of the dessert, Madame de Villars called out, 'Oh dear! they have forgot! yet I bespoke them, and I am sure they are ready; you English love hot rolls—bring the rolls.' There arrived a huge dish of hot rolls, and a sauce-boat of melted butter."

observe the least, or the finest thing she sees! She came hither to-day to a great breakfast I made for her, with her eyes a foot deep in her head, her hands dangling, and scarce able to support her knitting-bag. She had been yesterday to see a ship launched, and went from Greenwich by water to Ranelagh. Madame Dusson, who is Dutch-built, and whose muscles are pleasure-proof, came with her; there were besides, Lady Mary Coke, Lord and Lady Holdernesse, the Duke and Duchess of Grafton, Lord Hertford, Lord Villiers, Offley, Messieurs de Fleury, D'Eon, et Duclos. The latter is author of the Life of Louis Onze; dresses like a dissenting minister, which I suppose is the livery of a *bel esprit*, and is much more impetuous than agreeable. We breakfasted in the great parlour, and I had filled the hall and large cloister by turns with French horns and clarionettes. As the French ladies had never seen a printing-house, I carried them into mine; they found something ready set, and desiring to see what it was, it proved as follows:

"The Press speaks—

"For Madame De Boufflers.

"'The graceful fair, who loves to know,
Nor dreads the north's inclement snow;
Who bids her polish'd accent wear
The British diction's harsher air;
Shall read her praise in every clime
Where types can speak or poets rhyme.

"FOR MADAME DUSSON.

"Feign not an ignorance of what I speak ;
You could not miss my meaning were it Greek :
'Tis the same language Belgium utter'd first,
The same which from admiring Gallia burst.
True sentiment a like expression pours ;
Each country says the same to eyes like yours.

"You will comprehend that the first speaks English, and that the second does not ; that the second is handsome, and the first not ; and that the second was born in Holland. This little gentilesse pleased, and atoned for the popery* of my house, which was not serious enough for Madame de Boufflers, who is Montmorency, *et du sang du premier Chrétien ;* and too serious for Madame Dusson, who is a Dutch Calvinist. . . . The Gallery is not advanced enough to give them any idea at all, as they are not apt to go out of their way for one; but the Cabinet, and the glory of yellow glass at top, which had a charming sun for a foil, did surmount their indifference, especially as they were animated by the Duchess of Grafton, who had never happened to be here before, and who perfectly entered into the air of

* "The Duc de Nivernois [the French ambassador] called here the other day in his way from Hampton Court ; but, as the most sensible French never have eyes to see anything, unless they see it every day and see it in fashion, I cannot say he flattered me much, or was much struck with Strawberry. When I carried him into the Cabinet, which I have told you is formed upon the idea of a Catholic chapel, he pulled off his hat, but perceiving his error, he said, ' *Ce n'est pas une chapelle pourtant*,' and seemed a little displeased."
—*Walpole to Mann, April* 30, 1763.

enchantment and fairyism, which is the tone of the place, and was peculiarly so to-day.

"Thursday.

"I am ashamed of myself to have nothing but a journal of pleasures to send you; I never passed a more agreeable day than yesterday. Miss Pelham gave the French an entertainment at Esher; but they have been so feasted and amused, that none of them were well enough, or reposed enough, to come, but Nivernois and Madame Dusson. The rest of the company were, the Graftons, Lady Rockingham, Lord and Lady Pembroke. . . . The day was delightful, the scene transporting; the trees, lawns, concaves, all in the perfection in which the ghost of Kent* would joy to see them. At twelve we made the tour of the farm in eight chaises and calashes, horsemen, and footmen, setting out like a picture of Wouverman's. My lot fell in the lap of Mrs. Anne Pitt,† which I could have excused, as she was not at all in the style of the day, romantic, but political. We had a magnificent dinner, cloaked in the modesty of earthenware; French horns and hautboys on the lawn. We walked to the Belvidere on the summit of the hill, where a theatrical

---

* "Esher's peaceful grove
Where Kent and Nature vie for Pelham's love."—*Pope.*

"Esher's groves,
Where, in the sweetest solitude, embraced
By the soft windings of the silent Mole,
From courts and senates Pelham finds repose."—*Thomson.*

† Mrs. Anne Pitt, sister of Lord Chatham.

storm only served to heighten the beauty of the landscape, a rainbow on a dark cloud falling precisely behind the tower of a neighbouring church, between another tower and the building at Claremont. Monsieur de Nivernois, who had been absorbed all day, and lagging behind, translating my verses, was delivered of his version, and of some more lines which he wrote on Miss Pelham in the Belvidere, while we drank tea and coffee. From thence we passed into the wood, and the ladies formed a circle on chairs before the mouth of the cave, which was overhung to a vast height with woodbines, lilacs, and laburnums, and dignified by the tall shapely cypresses. On the descent of the hill were placed the French horns; the abigails, servants, and neighbours wandering below by the river; in short, it was Parnassus, as Watteau would have painted it. Here we had a rural syllabub, and part of the company returned to town; but were replaced by Giardini and Onofrio, who with Nivernois on the violin, and Lord Pembroke on the base, accompanied Miss Pelham, Lady Rockingham, and the Duchess of Grafton, who sang. This little concert lasted till past ten; then there were minuets, and as we had several couples left, it concluded with a country dance. I blush again, for I danced, but was kept in countenance by Nivernois, who has one wrinkle more than I have. A quarter after twelve they sat down to supper, and I came home by a charming moonlight. I am going to dine in town, and to a great ball with fireworks at Miss Chudleigh's, but I return hither on Sunday, to bid adieu to this abominable Arcadian life; for really when one is not young, one ought to do nothing but *s'ennuyer;* I will try, but I always go about it awkwardly."

Two days later this indefatigable chronicler of trifles describes to Conway the *fête* given by Miss Chudleigh, afterwards known as the Duchess of Kingston, but at that time a maid of honour to the Princess-Dowager of Wales:

"Oh, that you had been at her ball t'other night! History could never describe it and keep its countenance. The Queen's real birthday, you know, is not kept: this Maid of Honour kept it—nay, while the Court is in mourning, expected people to be out of mourning; the Queen's family really was so, Lady Northumberland having desired leave for them. A scaffold was erected in Hyde-park for fireworks. To show the illuminations without to more advantage, the company were received in an apartment totally dark, where they remained for two hours. . . . The fireworks were fine, and succeeded well. On each side of the court were two large scaffolds for the Virgin's* tradespeople. When the fireworks ceased, a large scene was lighted in the court, representing their Majesties; on each side of which were six obelisks, painted with emblems, and illuminated; mottoes beneath in Latin and English. . . . The lady of the house made many apologies for the poorness of the performance, which

* Miss Chudleigh.

she said was only oil-paper, painted by one of her servants; but it really was fine and pretty. Behind the house was a cenotaph for the Princess Elizabeth, a kind of illuminated cradle; the motto, *All the honours the dead can receive.* This burying-ground was a strange codicil to a festival; and, what was more strange, about one in the morning, this sarcophagus burst out into crackers and guns. The Margrave of Anspach began the ball with the Virgin. The supper was most sumptuous."

A fortnight afterwards he writes:

" June 7th.

"Last night we had a magnificent entertainment at Richmond House, a masquerade and fireworks. A masquerade was a new sight to the young people, who had dressed themselves charmingly, without having the fear of an earthquake before their eyes, though Prince William and Prince Henry* were not suffered to be there. The Duchesses of Richmond and Grafton, the first as a Persian Sultana, the latter as Cleopatra,—and such a Cleopatra! were glorious figures, in very different styles. Mrs. Fitzroy in a Turkish dress, Lady George Lenox and Lady Bolingbroke as Grecian girls, Lady Mary Coke as Imoinda, and Lady Pembroke as a pilgrim, were the principal beauties of the night. The whole garden was illuminated, and the apartments. An encampment of barges decked with streamers in the middle of the Thames, kept the people from danger,

* Afterwards Dukes of Gloucester and Cumberland.

and formed a stage for the fireworks, which were placed, too, along the rails of the garden. The ground rooms lighted, with suppers spread, the houses covered and filled with people, the bridge, the garden full of masks, Whitehall crowded with spectators to see the dresses pass, and the multitude of heads on the river who came to light by the splendour of the fire-wheels, composed the gayest and richest scene imaginable, not to mention the diamonds and sumptuousness of the habits. The Dukes of York and Cumberland, and the Margrave of Anspach, were there, and about six hundred masks."

In the intervals of these engagements, he is busy at Strawberry Hill. Thus, in arranging a short visit to George Montagu, he says (July 1):

"The journey you must accept as a great sacrifice either to you or to my promise, for I quit the Gallery almost in the critical minute of consummation. Gilders, carvers, upholsterers, and picture-cleaners are labouring at their several forges, and I do not love to trust a hammer or a brush without my own supervisal. This will make my stay very short, but it is a greater compliment than a month would be at another season; and yet I am not profuse of months. Well, but I begin to be ashamed of my magnificence; Strawberry is growing sumptuous in its latter day; it will scarce be any longer like the fruit of its name, or the modesty of its ancient demeanour, both which seem to have been in Spenser's prophetic eye, when he sung of

> "'—— the blushing strawberries
> Which lurk, close-shrouded from high-looking eyes,
> Showing that sweetness low and hidden lies.'

"In truth, my collection was too great already to be lodged humbly; it has extended my walls, and pomp followed. It was a neat, small house; it now will be a comfortable one, and, except one fine apartment, does not deviate from its simplicity. Adieu! I know nothing about the world, and am only Strawberry's and yours sincerely."

Our next extract shows that, however fond of frequenting large parties, the writer had little inclination to give them, at any rate, in his toy-house:

"We had, last Monday, the prettiest ball that ever was seen, at Mrs. Anne Pitt's, in the compass of a silver penny. There were one hundred and four persons, of which number fifty-five supped. The supper-room was disposed with tables and benches back to back, in the manner of an ale-house. The idea sounds ill; but the fairies had so improved upon it, had so *be-garlanded*, so *sweetmeated*, and so *desserted* it, that it looked like a vision. I told her she could only have fed and stowed so much company by a miracle, and that, when we were gone, she would take up twelve baskets-full of people. The Duchess of Bedford asked me before Madame de Guerchy, if I would not give them a ball at Strawberry? Not for the universe! What, turn a ball, and dust, and dirt, and a million of candles, into my charming new gallery! I said, I could not flatter myself that people would give themselves the trouble of going eleven miles for a *ball*—(though I believe they would go fifty).—' Well, then,' says she, ' it shall be a *dinner*.'—' With all my heart, I have no objection ; but no *ball* shall set its foot within my doors.' "—*Walpole to Lord Hertford, Feb.* 24, 1764.

The promised dinner was duly given. " Strawberry," we read soon afterwards, "has been more sumptuous to-day than ordinary, and banquetted their representative Majesties of France and Spain. . . . They really seemed quite pleased with the place and the day ; but I must tell you, the treasury of the abbey will feel it, for, without magnificence, all was handsomely done." Mrs. Anne Pitt, the giver of the ball, was present at the banquet. In describing to a foreigner this lady's strong likeness to her famous brother, Walpole once said happily, " Qu'ils se ressemblaient comme deux gouttes de *feu*." Another eccentric entertainer of the day was the Duchess of Queensberry, " very clever, very whimsical, and just not mad." Of her we are told :

" Last Thursday, the Duchess of Queensberry gave a ball, opened it herself with a minuet, and danced two country dances : as she had enjoined everybody to be with her by six, to sup at twelve, and go away directly. . . . The only extraordinary thing the Duchess did, was to do nothing extraordinary, for I do not call it very mad that some pique happening between her and the Duchess of Bedford, the latter had this distich sent to her,

"'Come with a whistle, and come with a call,
Come with a good will, or come not at all.'

"I do not know whether what I am going to tell you did not border a little upon Moorfields.* The gallery where they danced was very cold. Lord Lorn, George Selwyn, and I, retired into a little room, and sat comfortably by the fire. The Duchess looked in, said nothing, and sent a smith to take the hinges of the door off. We understood the hint, and left the room, and so did the smith the door. This was pretty legible."— *Walpole to Lord Hertford, March* 11, 1764.

A little later on we have more gossip about the humours of the day and of Lady Queensberry. Writing to the same correspondent, under date of Febuary 12, 1765, Horace says :

"If it was not too long to transcribe, I would send you an entertaining petition† of the periwig-makers to the King, in which they complain that men will wear their own hair. Should one almost wonder if carpenters were to remonstrate, that since the peace their trade

---

* The old Bedlam stood in Moorfields.

† The substance of this petition, and the grave answer which the King was advised to give to such a ludicrous appeal, are preserved in the *Gentleman's Magazine* for 1765, p. 95 ; where also we learn that Mr. Walpole's idea of the Carpenters' petition was put in practice, and his Majesty was humbly entreated to wear a wooden leg himself, and to enjoin all his servants to do the same. It may, therefore, be presumed that this *jeu d'esprit* was from the pen of Mr. Walpole.

decays, and that there is no demand for wooden legs? Apropos, my Lady Hertford's friend, Lady Harriot Vernon, has quarrelled with me for smiling at the enormous head-gear of her daughter, Lady Grosvenor. She came one night to Northumberland-house with such display of friz, that it literally spread beyond her shoulders. I happened to say it looked as if her parents had stinted her in hair before marriage, and that she was determined to indulge her fancy now. This, among ten thousand things said by all the world, was reported to Lady Harriot, and has occasioned my disgrace. As she never found fault with anybody herself, I excuse her! You will be less surprised to hear that the Duchess of Queensberry has not yet done dressing herself marvellously: she was at Court on Sunday in a gown and petticoat of red flannel. The same day the Guerchys made a dinner for her, and invited Lord and Lady Hyde, the Forbes's, and her other particular friends: in the morning she sent word she was to go out of town, but as soon as dinner was over, arrived at Madame de Guerchy's, and said she had been at Court."

On February 14th, he adds in the same letter:

" The new Assembly Room at Almack's was opened the night before last, and they say is very magnificent, but it was empty; half the town is ill with colds, and many were afraid to go, as the house is scarcely built yet. Almack advertised that it was built with hot bricks and boiling water—think what a rage there must be for public places, if this notice, instead of terrifying, could draw anybody thither. They tell me the ceilings were dropping with wet—but can you believe me, when I assure you the Duke of Cumberland was there?—Nay, had had a levee in the morning, and went to the Opera before the assembly! There is a vast flight of steps, and he was forced to rest two or three times. If he dies of it,—and how should he not?—it will sound very silly when Hercules or Theseus ask him what he died of, to reply, 'I caught my death on a damp staircase at a new club-room.'"

The reader will be inclined to wonder how, with so many distractions, Walpole found time for all this letter-writing, and still more how he managed to come before the public as an author. His, however, was the pen of an extremely ready writer, and, when not otherwise engaged, he plied it with unwearied diligence. This appears in the following letter to Cole, the Cambridge antiquary, in which Horace gives an account of the origin and composition of his well-known romance. The letter shows also the writer's love of collecting and designing curiosities:

"Strawberry Hill, March 9, 1765.

"I had time to write but a short note with the 'Castle of Otranto,' as your messenger called on me at four o'clock, as I was going to dine abroad. Your partiality to me and Strawberry have, I hope, inclined you to excuse the wildness of the story. You will even have found some traits to put you in mind of this place. When you read of the picture quitting its panel, did not you recollect the portrait of Lord Falkland, all in white, in my Gallery? Shall I even confess to you, what was the origin of this romance! I waked one morning, in the beginning of last June, from a dream, of which, all I could recover was, that I had thought myself in an ancient castle (a very natural dream for a head filled like mine with Gothic story), and that on the uppermost bannister of a great staircase I saw a gigantic hand in armour. In the evening I sat down, and began to write, without knowing in the least what I intended to say or relate. The work grew on my hands, and I grew fond of it—add, that I was very glad to think of anything, rather than politics. In short, I was so engrossed with my tale, which I completed in less than two months, that one evening, I wrote from the time I had drunk my tea, about six o'clock, till half an hour after one in the morning, when my hand and fingers were so weary, that I could not hold the pen to finish the sentence, but left Matilda and Isabella talking, in the middle of a paragraph. You will laugh at my earnestness; but if I have amused you, by retracing with any fidelity the manners of ancient days, I am content, and give you leave to think me as idle as you please. . . .

"When you go into Cheshire, and upon your ramble, may I trouble you with a commission? but about which you must promise me not to go a step out of your way. Mr. Bateman has got a cloister at Old Windsor, furnished with ancient wooden chairs, most of them triangular, but all of various patterns, and carved and turned in the most uncouth and whimsical forms. He picked them up one by one, for two, three, five, or six shillings a-piece from different farm-houses in Herefordshire. I have long envied and coveted them. There may be such in poor cottages, in so neighbouring a county as Cheshire. I should not grudge any expense for purchase or carriage; and should be glad even of a couple such for my cloister here. When you are copying inscriptions in a churchyard in any village, think of me, and step into the first cottage you see—but don't take further trouble than that. . . .

" My bower is determined, but not at all what it is to be. Though I write romances, I cannot tell how to build all that belongs to them. Madame Danois, in the Fairy Tales, used to *tapestry* them with *jonquils;* but as that furniture will not last above a fortnight in the year, I shall prefer something more huckaback. I have decided that the outside shall be of *treillage,* which, however, I shall not commence, till I have again seen some of old Louis's old-fashioned *Galanteries* at Versailles. Rosamond's bower, you, and I, and Tom Hearne know, was a labyrinth: but as my territory will admit of a very short clew, I lay aside all thoughts of a mazy habitation: though a bower is very different from an arbour, and must have more chambers than one. In short, I both know, and don't know, what it should be. I am almost afraid I must go and read Spenser, and wade through his allegories, and drawling stanzas, to get at a picture. But, good night! you see how one gossips, when one is alone, and at quiet on one's own dunghill! —Well! it may be trifling; yet it is such trifling as Ambition never is happy enough to know! Ambition orders palaces, but it is Content that chats for a page or two over a bower."

A large part of Walpole's correspondence was despatched at night after his return from the theatre or a reception. His habits were late. He was a late riser, and he often played cards till two or three o'clock in the morning. Whist he disliked, but gave himself to faro, while that game was in vogue, and afterwards to loo, with all the fervour of a devotee. But when not thus occupied, the hours observed by the fashionable world allowed him to retire early to his desk. How different those hours were then from what they now are, may be gathered from Walpole's amusing sketch of a retarded dinner, at which he was a sufferer, in 1765:

"Now for my disaster; you will laugh at it, though it was woful to me. I was to dine at Northumberland-house, and went a little after hour: there I found the Countess, Lady Betty Mackenzie, Lady Strafford; my Lady Finlater, who was never out of Scotland before; a tall lad of fifteen, her son; Lord Drogheda, and Mr. Worseley. At five, arrived Mr. Mitchell, who said the Lords had begun to read the Poor-bill, which would take at least two hours, and perhaps would debate it afterwards. We concluded dinner would be called for, it not being very precedented for ladies to wait for gentlemen:—no such thing. Six o'clock came,—seven o'clock came,—our coaches came,—well! we sent them away, and excuses were we were engaged. Still the Countess's heart did not relent, nor uttered a syllable of apology. We wore out the wind and the weather, the Opera and the Play, Mrs. Cornelys's and Almack's, and every topic that would do in a formal circle. We hinted, represented—in vain. The clock struck eight: my Lady, at last, said, she would go and order dinner; but it was a good half-hour before it appeared. We then sat down to a table for fourteen covers: but instead of substantials, there was nothing but a profusion of plates striped red, green, and yellow, gilt plate, blacks and uniforms! My Lady Finlater, who had never seen these embroidered dinners, nor dined after three, was famished. The first course stayed as long as possible, in hopes of the Lords: so did the second. The dessert at last arrived, and the middle dish was actually set on when Lord Finlater and Mr. Mackay arrived!— would you believe it?—the dessert was remanded, and the whole first course brought back again!—Stay, I have not done:—just as this second first course had done its duty, Lord Northumberland, Lord Strafford, and Mackenzie came in, and the whole began a third time! Then the second course and the dessert! I thought we should have dropped from our chairs with fatigue and fumes! When the clock struck eleven, we were asked to return to the drawing-room, and drink tea and coffee, but I said I was engaged to supper, and came home to bed."

A few weeks later he laments his idle life in a letter to Lady Hervey:

"It is scandalous, at my age, to have been carried backwards and forwards to balls and suppers and parties by very young people, as I was all last week. My resolutions of growing old and staid are admirable: I wake with a sober plan, and intend to pass the day with my friends—then comes the Duke of Richmond, and hurries me down to Whitehall to dinner—then the Duchess of Grafton sends for me to loo in Upper Grosvenor Street —before I can get thither, I am begged to step to Kensington, to give Mrs. Anne Pitt my opinion about a bow-window—after the loo, I am to march back to Whitehall to supper—and after that, am to walk with Miss Pelham on the terrace till two in the morning, because it is moonlight and her chair is not come. All this does not help my morning laziness; and, by the time I have breakfasted, fed my birds and my squirrels, and dressed, there is an auction ready. In short, Madam, this was my life last week, and is I think every week, with the addition of forty episodes."

Of course, this confession was not intended to be read quite seriously. It is to be taken with two grains of allowance, one for humour, the other for affectation. It was the writer's pleasure to overact the part of an idle fine gentleman. But we may fairly conclude from the last two extracts that five o'clock was the dinner-hour of extreme fashion at this time. It would seem that the customary hour was three even with people of rank, and that in the greatest houses it was usual to serve supper. When Horace could escape from the loo-table in Upper Grosvenor Street, had no engagement to supper, and was not forced to pace Whitehall Terrace with a belated spinster till two in the morning, he was able to be at home and in bed—or at work with his books or his pen—by eleven o'clock.

CHAPTER V.

The Gout.—Visits to Paris.—Bath.—John Wesley.—Bad Weather.—English Summers.—Quitting Parliament.—Madame du Deffand.—Human Vanity.—The Banks of the Thames.—A Subscription Masquerade.—Extravagance of the Age.—The Pantheon.—Visiting Stowe with Princess Amelia.—George Montagu.—The Countess of Ossory.—Powder-Mills Blown up at Hounslow.—Distractions of Business and Pleasure.

WALPOLE'S acquaintance with the gout began before he had reached his fortieth year. Its earliest approaches he received without much discomposure. His chief reason, he said, for objecting to "this alderman distemper" was that he could show no title to it. "If either my father or mother had had it, I should not dislike it so much. I am herald enough to approve it if descended genealogically; but it is an absolute upstart in me, and what is more provoking, I had trusted to my great abstinence for keeping me from it: but thus it is, if I had any gentleman-like virtue, as patriotism or loyalty, I might have got something by them; I had nothing but that beggarly virtue temperance, and she had not interest enough to keep me from a fit of the gout." By degrees, however, the attacks of his enemy became too severe to be dismissed with pleasantries like these. In the summer of 1765, he was prostrated by a seizure which held him prisoner for several weeks. On recovering about the middle of September, he undertook a journey to Paris, partly to recruit his strength, and partly in execution of a long-formed design. He remained in the French capital till the following spring, mixing much in the society of the place, and doing ample justice to the wit and grace of Frenchwomen, but shrinking from and detesting the French philosophers.* During this period was formed his friendship with Madame du Deffand, his "dear old blind woman," as he often calls her, with whom, after his return to England, he maintained a weekly correspondence for the rest of her life. Altogether, he derived so much pleasure from his visit, that he repeated it every alternate summer down to that of 1771; and we find him in Paris again in 1775.

He had another illness in the middle of 1766, for which he tried the Bath waters; but Bath proved not at all to his taste, though he met the great Lord Chatham there, and many other persons of distinction. "These watering-places," he says, "that mimic a capital, and add vulgarisms and familiarities of their own, seem to me like abigails in cast gowns, and I am not young enough to take up with either." Finding

---

* "Their women are the first in the world in everything but beauty; sensible, agreeable, and infinitely informed. The *philosophes*, except Buffon, are solemn, arrogant, dictatorial coxcombs —I need not say superlatively disagreeable."—*Walpole to Mann*.

himself dull at Bath, he attended a Wesleyan service, of which he gives a somewhat flippant description:

"My health advances faster than my amusement. However, I have been at one opera, Mr. Wesley's. They have boys and girls with charming voices, that sing hymns, in parts, to Scotch ballad tunes; but indeed so long, that one would think they were already in eternity, and knew how much time they had before them. The chapel is very neat, with true Gothic windows (yet I am not converted); but I was glad to see that luxury is creeping in upon them before persecution: they have very neat mahogany stands for branches, and brackets of the same in taste. At the upper end is a broad *hautpas* of four steps, advancing in the middle: at each end of the broadest part are two of *my* eagles,* with red cushions for the parson and clerk. Behind them rise three more steps, in the midst of which is a third eagle for pulpit. Scarlet armed chairs to all three. On either hand, a balcony for elect ladies. The rest of the congregation sit on forms. Behind the pit, in a dark niche, is a plain table within rails; so you see the throne is for the apostle. Wesley is a lean elderly man, fresh-coloured, his hair smoothly combed, but with a *soupçon* of curl at the ends. Wondrous clean, but as evidently an actor as Garrick. He spoke his sermon, but so fast, and with so little accent, that I am sure he has often uttered it, for it was like a lesson. There were parts and eloquence in it; but towards the

* He alludes to his Roman Eagle at Strawberry Hill.

end he exalted his voice, and acted very ugly enthusiasm; decried learning, and told stories, like Latimer, of the fool of his college, who said, 'I *thanks* God for everything.' Except a few from curiosity, and *some honourable women*, the congregation was very mean. There was a Scotch Countess of Buchan, who is carrying a pure rosy vulgar face to heaven, and who asked Miss Rich, if that was *the author of the poets*. I believe she meant me and the Noble Authors."

Walpole was in a peevish humour about this time. He was out of health, and dispirited besides by an apprehension that the climate of Twickenham did not suit him. Thus he writes from Strawberry Hill: "What afflicts me most is, that I am persuaded that this place is too damp for me. I revive after being in London an hour, like a member of Parliament's wife. It will be a cruel fate, after having laid out so much money here, and building upon it as the nest of my old age, if I am driven from it by bad health." Unfavourable weather seems to have been in some measure the cause of these fears, and of the writer's disordered condition. Though the harvest-time of 1766 was fine, the crops, we are told, had been spoilt by previous rains, and the years which followed were a cycle of wet and cold seasons. Walpole grumbles at the weather with English vigour and French vivacity. Thus he writes to Montagu, in June, 1768:

" I perceive the deluge fell upon you before it reached us. It began here but on Monday last, and then rained near eight-and-forty hours without intermission. My poor hay has not a dry thread to its back. I have had a fire these three days. In short, every summer one lives in a state of mutiny and murmur, and I have found the reason: it is because we will affect to have a summer, and we have no title to any such thing. Our poets learnt their trade of the Romans, and so adopted the terms of their masters. They talk of shady groves purling streams, and cooling breezes, and we get sore throats and agues with attempting to realize these visions. Master Damon writes a song, and invites Miss Chloe to enjoy the cool of the evening, and never a bit have we of any such thing as a cool evening. Zephyr is a north-east wind, that makes Damon button up to the chin, and pinches Chloe's nose till it is red and blue; and then they cry, *This is a bad summer!* as if we ever had any other. The best sun we have is made of Newcastle coal, and I am determined never to reckon upon any other. We ruin ourselves with inviting over foreign trees, and making our houses clamber up hills to look at prospects. How our ancestors would laugh at us, who knew there was no being comfortable, unless you had a high hill before your nose, and a thick warm wood at your back! Taste is too freezing a commodity for us, and, depend upon it, will go out of fashion again.—There is indeed a natural warmth in this country, which, as you say, I am very glad not to enjoy any longer; I mean the hot-house in St. Stephen's chapel. My own sagacity makes me very vain, though there was very little merit in it. I had seen so much of all parties, that I had little esteem left for any; it is most indifferent to me who is in or who is out, or which is set in the pillory, Mr. Wilkes or my Lord Mansfield. I see the country going to ruin, and no man with brains enough to save it. That is mortifying; but what signifies who has the undoing it? I seldom suffer myself to think on this subject: *my* patriotism could do no good, and my philosophy can make me be at peace."

The concluding lines of the above extract refer to the writer's recent retirement from the House of Commons. In the spring of the preceding year, Walpole had announced that he should not again ask the suffrages of the Lynn burgesses, stating as his reasons the declining state of his health and his wish to withdraw from all public business; and though his health had improved in the interval, the General Election of 1768 found him fixed in his decision. Whatever may have been the real motives of his conduct, there is no indication in his Letters that he ever regretted the course he had taken. In June, 1769, he writes from Strawberry Hill: "I am come hither for two months, very busy with finishing my round tower, which has stood still these five years, and with an enchanting new cottage that I have built, and other little works. In August, I shall go to Paris for six weeks. In short, I am delighted with having bid adieu to Parliament and politics, and with doing nothing but what I like all the year round." But the season was again rainy. A few days later, we have a letter to Cole, who was then settled at Waterbeach, near Cambridge:

"Strawberry Hill, Monday, June 26, 1769.

"Oh! yes, yes, I shall like Thursday or Friday, 6th or 7th, exceedingly; I shall like your staying with me two days exceedinglier; and longer exceedingliest: and I will carry you back to Cambridge on our pilgrimage to Ely. But I should not at all like to be catched in the glories of an installation,* and find myself a doctor, before I knew where I was. It will be much more agreeable to find the whole *caput* asleep, digesting turtle, dreaming of bishoprics, and humming old catches of Anacreon, and scraps of Corelli. I wish Mr. Gray may not be set out for the north; which is rather the case than setting out for the summer. We have no summers, I think, but what we raise, like pine-apples, by fire. My hay is an absolute *water-souchy,* and teaches me how to feel for you. You are quite in the right to sell your fief in Marshland. I should be glad if you would take one step more, and quit Marshland. We live, at least, on terra firma in this part of the world, and can saunter out without stilts. *Item*, we do not wade into pools, and call it going upon the water, and get sore throats. I trust yours is better; but I recollect this is not the first you have complained of. Pray be not incorrigible, but come to shore."

At the end of August he is in Paris with Madame du Deffand. "My dear old woman," he writes, "is in better health than when I left her, and her spirits so

* The installation of the Duke of Grafton as Chancellor of the University of Cambridge. Gray wrote the Ode for the occasion.

increased, that I tell her she will go mad with age. When they ask her how old she is, she answers, 'J'ai soixante et mille ans.' " In a letter written to George Montagu a week afterwards, we have a description of this true Frenchwoman:

"Your two letters flew here together in a breath. I shall answer the article of business first. I could certainly buy many things for you here, that you would like, the reliques of the last age's magnificence; but since my Lady Holdernesse invaded the Custom-House with an hundred and fourteen gowns, in the reign of that two-penny monarch George Grenville, the ports are so guarded, that not a soul but a smuggler can smuggle anything into England; and I suppose you would not care to pay seventy-five per cent. on second-hand commodities. All I transported three years ago, was conveyed under the canon of the Duke of Richmond. I have no interest in our present representative; nor if I had, is he returning. Plate, of all earthly vanities, is the most impassable: it is not counterband in its metallic capacity, but totally so in its personal; and the officers of the Custom-House not being philosophers enough to separate the substance from the superficies, brutally hammer both to pieces, and return you—only the intrinsic; a compensation which you, who are no member of Parliament, would not, I trow, be satisfied with. Thus I doubt you must retrench your generosity to yourself, unless you can contract it into an Elzevir size, and be content with anything one can bring in one's pocket.

"My dear old friend was charmed with your mention of her, and made me vow to return you a thousand compliments. She cannot conceive why you will not step hither. Feeling in herself no difference between the spirits of twenty-three and seventy-three, she thinks there is no impediment to doing whatever one will, but the want of eyesight. If she had that, I am persuaded no consideration would prevent her making me a visit at Strawberry Hill. She makes songs, sings them, and remembers all that ever were made; and, having lived from the most agreeable to the most reasoning age, has all that was amiable in the last, all that is sensible in this, without the vanity of the former, or the pedant impertinence of the latter. I have heard her dispute with all sorts of people, on all sorts of subjects, and never knew her in the wrong. She humbles the learned, sets right their disciples, and finds conversation for everybody. Affectionate as Madame de Sévigné, she has none of her prejudices, but a more universal taste; and, with the most delicate frame, her spirits hurry her through a life of fatigue that would kill me, if I was to continue here. If we return by one in the morning from suppers in the country, she proposes driving to the Boulevard or to the Foire St. Ovide, because it is too early to go to bed. I had great difficulty last night to persuade her, though she was not well, not to sit up till between two and three for the comet; for which purpose she had appointed an astronomer to bring his telescopes to the president Henault's, as she thought it would amuse me. In short, her goodness to me is so excessive, that I feel unashamed at producing my withered person in a round of diversions, which I have quitted at home. I tell a story; I do feel ashamed, and sigh to be in my quiet castle and cottage; but it costs me many a pang, when I reflect that I shall probably never have resolution enough to take another journey to see this best and sincerest of friends, who loves me as much as my mother did! but it is idle to look forward—what is next year? —a bubble that may burst for her or me, before even the flying year can hurry to the end of its almanack! . . .

"Adieu, my t'other dear old friend! I am sorry to say, I see you almost as seldom as I do Madame du Deffand. However, it is comfortable to reflect that we have not changed to each other for some five-and-thirty years, and neither you nor I haggle about naming so ancient a term. I made a visit yesterday to the Abbess of Panthemont, General Oglethorpe's niece, and no chicken. I inquired after her mother, Madame de Mezieres, and thought I might to a spiritual votary to immortality venture to say, that her mother must be very old; she interrupted me tartly, and said, no, her mother had been married extremely young. Do but think of its seeming important to a saint to sink a wrinkle of her own through an iron grate! Oh! we are ridiculous animals; and if angels have any fun in them, how we must divert them."

Once more in England, he announces his return to the same friend:

"Strawberry Hill, Oct. 16, 1769.

"I arrived at my own Louvre last Wednesday night, and am now at my Versailles. Your last letter reached me but two days before I left Paris, for I have been an age at Calais and upon the sea. I could execute no commission for you, and, in truth, you gave me no explicit one; but I have brought you a bit of china, and beg you will be content with a little present, instead of a bargain. Said china is, or will be soon, in the Custom-House; but I shall have it, I fear, long before you come to London. . . .

"I feel myself here like a swan, that, after living six weeks in a nasty pool upon a common, is got back into its own Thames. I do nothing but plume and clean myself, and enjoy the verdure and silent waves. Neatness and greenth are so essential in my opinion to the country, that in France, where I see nothing but chalk and dirty peasants, I seem in a terrestrial purgatory that is neither town nor country. The face of England is so beautiful, that I do not believe Tempe or Arcadia were half so rural; for both lying in hot climates, must have wanted the turf of our lawns. It is unfortunate to have so pastoral a taste, when I want a cane more than a crook. We are absurd creatures; at twenty, I loved nothing but London."

The winter of 1769-70 Walpole spent as usual in London. He now moralizes on masquerades in the tone of an ancient:

"It is very lucky, seeing how much of the tiger enters

into the human composition, that there should be a good dose of the monkey too. If Æsop had not lived so many centuries before the introduction of masquerades and operas, he would certainly have anticipated my observation, and worked it up into a capital fable. As we still trade upon the stock of the ancients, we seldom deal in any other manufacture; and, though nature, after new combinations, lets forth new characteristics, it is very rarely that they are added to the old fund; else how could so striking a remark have escaped being made, as mine, on the joint ingredients of tiger and monkey? In France the latter predominates, in England the former; but, like Orozmades and Arimanius, they get the better by turns. The bankruptcy in France, and the rigours of the new Comptroller-General, are half forgotten, in the expectation of a new opera at the new theatre. Our civil war* has been lulled to sleep by a Subscription Masquerade, for which the House of Commons literally adjourned yesterday. Instead of Fairfaxes and Cromwells, we have had a crowd of Henry the Eighths, Wolseys, Vandykes, and Harlequins; and because Wilkes was not mask enough, we had a man dressed like him, with a visor, in imitation of his squint, and a Cap of Liberty on a pole. In short, sixteen or eighteen young lords have given the town a Masquerade; and politics, for the last fortnight, were forced to give way to habit-makers. The ball was last night at Soho; and, if possible, was more magnifi-

---

* The proceedings of the House of Commons against Wilkes had just produced a Ministerial crisis.

cent than the King of Denmark's. The Bishops opposed: he of London formally remonstrated to the King, who did not approve it, but could not help him. The consequence was, that four divine vessels belonging to the holy fathers, alias their wives, were at this Masquerade. Monkey again! A fair widow,* who once bore my whole name, and now bears half of it, was there, with one of those whom the newspapers call *great personages*—he dressed like Edward the Fourth, she like Elizabeth Woodville, in grey and pearls, with a black veil. Methinks it was not very difficult to find out the meaning of those masks.

"As one of my ancient passions, formerly, was Masquerades, I had a large trunk of dresses by me. I dressed out a thousand young Conways† and Cholmondeleys,‡ and went with more pleasure to see them pleased than when I formerly delighted in that diversion myself. It has cost me a great headache, and I shall probably never go to another. A symptom appeared of the change that has happened in the people.

"The mob was beyond all belief: they held flambeaux to the windows of every coach, and demanded to have the masks pulled off and put on at their pleasure, but with extreme good-humour and civility. I was with my Lady Hertford and two of her daughters, in their coach: the mob took me for Lord Hertford, and

* Maria Walpole, Countess Dowager of Waldegrave, who had now secretly married William Henry, Duke of Gloucester.
† Sons of Francis, Earl of Hertford, Mr. Walpole's cousin-german.
‡ Mr. Walpole's nephews.

huzzaed and blessed me! One fellow cried out, 'Are you for Wilkes?' another said, 'You fool, what has Wilkes to do with a Masquerade?'

"In good truth, that stock is fallen very low. The Court has recovered a majority of seventy-five in the House of Commons; and the party has succeeded so ill in the Lords, that my Lord Chatham has betaken himself to the gout, and appears no more. What Wilkes may do at his enlargement in April, I don't know, but his star is certainly much dimmed. The distress of France, the injustice they have been induced to commit on public credit, immense bankruptcies, and great bankers hanging and drowning themselves, are comfortable objects in our prospect; for one tiger is charmed if another tiger loses his tail."

Again, he descants on the extravagance of the age:

"What do you think of a winter-Ranelagh* erecting in Oxford Road, at the expense of sixty thousand pounds? The new Bank, including the value of the ground, and of the houses demolished to make room for it, will cost three hundred thousand; and erected, as my Lady Townley† says, *by sober citizens too!* I have touched before to you on the incredible profusion of our young men of fashion. I know a younger brother who literally gives a flower-woman half a guinea every morning for a bunch of roses for the nosegay in his button-hole. There has lately been an auction of stuffed birds; and,

* The Pantheon.
† In the comedy of "The Provoked Husband."

as natural history is in fashion, there are physicians and others who paid forty and fifty guineas for a single Chinese pheasant: you may buy a live one for five. After this, it is not extraordinary that pictures should be dear. We have at present three exhibitions. One West,* who paints history in the taste of Poussin, gets three hundred pounds for a piece not too large to hang over a chimney. He has merit, but is hard and heavy, and far unworthy of such prices. The rage to see these exhibitions is so great, that sometimes one cannot pass through the streets where they are. But it is incredible what sums are raised by mere exhibitions of anything—a new fashion; and to enter at which you pay a shilling or half-a-crown. Another rage is for prints of English portraits: I have been collecting them above thirty years, and originally never gave for a mezzotinto above one or two shillings. The lowest are now a crown; most, from half a guinea to a guinea. Lately, I assisted a clergyman [Granger] in compiling a catalogue of them; since the publication, scarce heads in books, not worth threepence, will sell for five guineas. Then we have Etruscan vases, made of earthenware, in Staffordshire, [by Wedgwood] from two to five guineas; and *or moulu*, never made here before, which succeeds so well, that a teakettle, which the inventor offered for one hundred guineas, sold by auction for one hundred and thirty. In short, we are at the height of extravagance and improvements, for we do improve rapidly in taste as well as in the former. I cannot say so much for our

* Benjamin West, afterwards, at Sir Joshua's death, President of the Royal Academy of Arts.

genius. Poetry is gone to bed, or into our prose; we are like the Romans in that too. If we have the arts of the Antonines,—we have the fustian also."

Our ancestors seem to have been much impressed with the splendour of the London Pantheon. Walpole recurs to the subject: " If we laugh at the French, they stare at us. Our enormous luxury and expense astonish them. I carried their Ambassador and a Comte de Levi the other morning to see the new winter-Ranelagh [the Pantheon] in Oxford Road, which is almost finished. It amazed me myself. Imagine Balbec in all its glory! The pillars are of artificial *giallo antico*. The ceilings, even of the passages, are of the most beautiful stuccos in the best taste of grotesque. The ceilings of the ball-rooms, and the panels, painted like Raphael's *loggias* in the Vatican. A dome like the Pantheon, glazed. Monsieur de Guisnes said to me, ' Ce n'est qu'à Londres qu'on peut faire tout cela.' " What a sermon would our moralist have preached, could he have foreseen that, in the reign of George III's granddaughter, this English Balbec would become a repository for cheap wines!

In July, 1770, Walpole received a command to attend the Princess Amelia on a visit to Stowe. He describes what occurred to George Montagu:

" The party passed off much better than I expected. A Princess at the head of a very small set for five days together did not promise well. However, she was very good-humoured and easy, and dispensed with a large quantity of etiquette. Lady Temple is good-nature itself, my Lord was very civil, Lord Besborough is made to suit all sorts of people, Lady Mary Coke respects royalty too much not to be very condescending, Lady Anne Howard* and Mrs. Middleton filled up the drawing-room, or rather made it out, and I was so determined to carry it off as well as I could, and happened to be in such good spirits, and took such care to avoid politics, that we laughed a great deal, and had not a cloud the whole time.

"We breakfasted at half an hour after nine; but the Princess did not appear till it was finished; then we walked in the garden, or drove about it in cabriolets, till it was time to dress; dined at three, which, though properly proportioned to the smallness of company to avoid ostentation, lasted a vast while, as the Princess eats and talks a great deal; then again into the garden till past seven, when we came in, drank tea and coffee, and played at pharaoh till ten, when the Princess retired, and we went to supper, and before twelve to bed. You see there was great sameness and little vivacity in all this. It was a little broken by fishing, and going round the park one of the mornings; but, in reality, the number of buildings and variety of scenes in the garden, made each day different from the rest, and my meditations on so historic a spot prevented my being tired. Every acre brings to one's mind some instance of the parts or pedantry, of the taste or want

---

* Lady Anne Howard, daughter of Henry, fourth Earl, and sister of Frederick, fifth Earl of Carlisle.

of taste, of the ambition or love of fame, or greatness or miscarriages, of those that have inhabited, decorated, planned, or visited the place. Pope, Congreve, Vanbrugh, Kent, Gibbs, Lord Cobham, Lord Chesterfield, the mob of nephews, the Lytteltons, Grenvilles, Wests, Leonidas Glover, and Wilkes, the late Prince of Wales, the King of Denmark, Princess Amelia, and the proud monuments of Lord Chatham's services, now enshrined there, then anathematised there, and now again commanding there, with the Temple of Friendship,* like the Temple of Janus, sometimes open to war, and sometimes shut up in factious cabals—all these images crowd upon one's memory, and add visionary personages to the charming scenes, that are so enriched with fanes and temples, that the real prospects are little less than visions themselves.

"On Wednesday night, a small Vauxhall was acted for us at the grotto in the Elysian fields, which was illuminated with lamps, as were the thicket and two little barks on the lake. With a little exaggeration, I could make you believe that nothing ever was so delightful. The idea was really pretty; but, as my feelings have lost something of their romantic sensibility, I did not quite enjoy such an entertainment *al fresco* so much as I should have done twenty years ago. The evening was more than cool, and the destined spot anything but dry. There were not half lamps enough, and

---

* The Temple of Friendship, like the ruins in the Campo Vaccino, is reduced to a single column at Stowe.—*Walpole to Crauford, 6th March,* 1766.

no music but an ancient militia-man, who played cruelly on a squeaking tabor and pipe. As our procession descended the vast flight of steps into the garden, in which was assembled a crowd of people from Buckingham and the neighbouring villages to see the Princess and the show, the moon shining very bright, I could not help laughing as I surveyed our troop, which, instead of tripping lightly to such an Arcadian entertainment, were hobbling down by the balustrades, wrapped up in cloaks and great-coats, for fear of catching cold. The Earl, you know, is bent double, the Countess very lame; I am a miserable walker, and the Princess, though as strong as a Brunswick lion, makes no figure in going down fifty stone stairs. Except Lady Anne, and by courtesy Lady Mary, we were none of us young enough for a pastoral. We supped in the grotto, which is as proper to this climate as a sea-coal fire would be in the dog-days at Tivoli.

"But the chief entertainment of the week, at least what was so to the Princess, is an arch, which Lord Temple has erected to her honour in the most enchanting of all picturesque scenes. It is inscribed on one side, 'AMELIÆ SOPHIÆ, AUG.,' and has a medallion of her on the other. It is placed on an eminence at the top of the Elysian fields, in a grove of orange-trees. You come to it on a sudden, and are startled with delight on looking through it: you at once see, through a glade, the river winding at the bottom; from which a thicket rises, arched over with trees, but opened, and discovering a hillock full of hay-cocks, beyond which in front is the Palladian bridge, and again over that a larger hill crowned with the castle. It is a tall landscape framed by the arch and the overbowering trees, and comprehending more beauties of light, shade, and buildings, than any picture of Albano I ever saw.

"Between the flattery and the prospect, the Princess was really in Elysium: she visited her arch four and five times every day, and could not satiate herself with it. The statues of Apollo and the Muses stand on each side of the arch. One day she found in Apollo's hand the following lines, which I had written for her, and communicated to Lord Temple."

We spare our readers the verses. The letter from which we have been quoting is one of the last of Walpole's letters to Montagu. A coolness arose the same year between the two friends, either without a cause, or for some cause which has not been explained, and continued until Montagu's death in 1780.* That Walpole regretted the breach his tone in referring to it shows, and his readers have reason to regret it likewise, for his letters to Montagu display more warmth of feeling and

---

* 'He dropped me, partly from politics and partly from caprice, for we never had any quarrel; but he was grown an excessive humourist, and had shed almost all his friends as well as me. He had parts, and infinite vivacity and originality till of late years; and it grieved me much that he had changed towards me after a friendship of between thirty and forty years.' This is Walpole's account written to Cole the day after Montagu's death. But Montagu's last letter to Walpole, dated October 6, 1770, is cordial and even affectionate in tone; while in Walpole's preceding letter there are some signs of pique, and the letter from Horace which ends the correspondence is both short and cold.

simplicity of style than any others in his published correspondence. A few months before Montagu drops out of sight, Lady Ossory appears in the list of the ladies to whom Walpole addressed sprightly letters in a strain of oddly mingled ceremony and familiarity. He had been on terms of friendship with her before her divorce from the Duke of Grafton; in his letters of that period he frequently refers to her as his Duchess, and speaks of following her and loo all over the kingdom. There can be no doubt that he often wrote to her at that time, but the first of his published letters to her is dated after her marriage with Lord Ossory. Here are two letters to her, one describing the damage done to his castle by an explosion of powder-mills at Hounslow, the other the sea of troubles into which he was plunged when his nephew, Lord Orford, was seized with insanity. The first letter was begun in London on the 5th January, 1772:

"I was waked very early this morning, by half an hour after nine; (I mean this for flattery, for Mr. Crauford says your ladyship does not rise till one); by the way, I was in the middle of a charming dream. I thought I was in the King's Library in Paris, and in a gallery full of books of prints, containing nothing but *fêtes* and decorations of scenery. I took down a long Roll, on which was painted, on vellum, all the ceremonies of the present reign: there was the young King walking to his coronation; the Regent before, who I thought was alive. I said to him, your Royal Highness has a great air; he seemed extremely flattered, when the house shook as if the devil were come for him. I had scarce recovered my vexation at being so disturbed, when the door of my room shook so violently that I thought somebody was breaking it open, though I knew it was not locked. It was broad daylight, but I did not know that housebreaking might not be still improving. I cried out 'Who is there?' Nobody answered. In less than another minute, the door rattled and shook still more robberaceously. I call again—no reply. I rung: the housemaid ran in as pale as white ashes, if you ever saw such, and cried, 'Goodness! Sir, I am frightened out of my wits: there has been an earthquake!' Oh! I believed her immediately. Philip [his valet] came in, and, being a Swiss philosopher, insisted it was only the wind. I sent him down to collect opinions in the street. He returned, and owned every body in this and the neighbouring streets were persuaded their houses had been breaking open; or had ran out of them, thinking there was an earthquake. Alas! it was much worse; for you know, Madam, our earthquakes are as harmless as a new-born child. At one, came in a courier from Margaret [his housekeeper] to tell me that five powder-mills had been blown up at Hounslow, at half an hour after nine this morning, had almost shook Mrs. Clive, and had broken parts or all of eight of my painted windows, besides other damage. This is a cruel misfortune: I don't know how I shall repair it! I shall go down to-morrow, and on Thursday will finish my report.

"Wednesday, 8th.

"Well! Madam, I am returned from my poor shattered castle, and never did it look so Gothic in its born days. You would swear it had been besieged by the Presbyterians in the Civil Wars, and that, finding it impregnable, they had vented their holy malice on the painted glass. As this gunpowder-army passed on, it demolished Mr. Hindley's fine bow-window of ancient Scripture histories; and only because your ladyship is my ally, broke the large window over your door, and wrenched off a lock in your kitchen. Margaret sits by the waters of Babylon, and weeps over Jerusalem. I shall pity those she shows the house to next summer, for her story is as long and deplorable as a chapter of casualties in 'Baker's Chronicle;' yet she was not taken quite unprepared, for one of the Bantam hens crowed on Sunday morning, and the chandler's wife told her three weeks ago, when the barn was blown down, that ill-luck never comes single. She is, however, very thankful that the China Room has escaped, and says, Heaven has always been the best creature in the world to her. I dare not tell her how many churches I propose to rob, to repair my losses."

The second is dated:

"Strawberry Hill, past midnight, June 11, 1773.

"Unless I borrow from my sleep, I can certainly have no time to please myself. I am this minute arrived here, Madam, and being the flower of chivalry, I sacrifice, like a true knight, the moments I steal from my rest to gallantry. Save me, or I shall become a solicitor in Chancery, unless business and fatigue overset my head, and reduce me to my poor nephew's state. Indeed, I am half hurried out of my senses. Think of me putting queries to lawyers, up to the ears in mortgages, wills, settlements, and contingent remainders. My lawyer is sent away that I may give audience to the Honourable Mr. Manners, the genuine, if not the legitimate son of Lord William. He came civilly yesterday morning to ask me if he might not seize the pictures at Houghton, which he heard were worth threescore thousand pounds, for nine thousand he has lent Lord Orford. The vulture's throat gaped for them all—what a scene is opened! Houghton will be a rookery of harpies—I doubt there are worse scenes to follow, and black transactions! What occupation chalked out for an end of a life that I had calculated for tranquillity, and which gout and law are to divide between them!

"In the midst of this prospect must I keep up the tone of the world, go shepherdising with Macaronies, sit up at loo with my Lady Hertford, be witness to Miss Pelham's orgies, dine at villas, and give dinners at my own. 'Tis well my spirits and resolution have survived my youth: you have heard how my mornings pass—now for the rest. Consultations of physicians, letters to Lady Orford, sent for to my brother, decent visits to *my* Court,* sup at Lady Powis's on Wednesday, drink tea with all the fashionable world at Mr. Fitzroy's farm on Thursday, blown by a north wind there into the house, and whisk back to Lady Hertford's; this morning to my brother's to hear of new bills, away to dine at ——, Muswell Hill, with the Beauclerks, and

* He means Gloucester House.

florists and natural historians, Banks and Solanders; return to town, step to ask a friend whether reversions of jointures can be left away, into my chaise and hither. To-morrow come two Frenchmen to dinner—on Monday, a man to sell me two acres immensely dear as a favour,—Philip [his valet], I cannot help it, you must go and put him off; I have not a minute, I must go back to-morrow night to meet the lawyers at my brother's on Sunday morning. Margaret [his housekeeper] comes in. ' Sir, Lady Bingham desires you will dine with her at Hampton Court on Tuesday;' I cannot. ' Sir, Captain What-d'ye-call'm has sent twice for a ticket to see the house'—Don't plague me about tickets. ' Sir, a servant from Isleworth brought this parcel.' What on earth is in it?—only printed proposals for writing the lives of all British writers, and a letter to tell me I could do it better than anybody, but as I may not have time, Dr. Berkenhout proposes to do it, and will write mine into the bargain, if I will but be so good as to write it first and send it him, and give him advice for the conduct of his work, and point out materials, and furnish him with anecdotes.

"My dear madam, what if you should send him this letter as a specimen of my life! Alas, alas! I have already lost my lilac tide. I have heard but one nightingale this year, and my farmer cut my hay last Tuesday morning without telling me, just as I was going to London. Is it to be borne? O for the *sang-froid* of an Almackian, who pursues his delights,

'Though in the jaws of ruin and codille!'"

CHAPTER VI.

Lord Nuneham.—Madame de Sévigné.—Charles Fox.—Mrs. Clive and Cliveden.—Goldsmith and Garrick.—Dearth of News.—Madame de Trop.—A Bunch of Grapes.—General Election.—Perils by Land and Water.—Sir Horace Mann.—Lord Clive.—The History of Manners.—A Traveller from Lima.—The Sçavoir Vivre Club.—Reflections on Life.—The Pretender's Happiness.—Paris Fashions.—Madame Du Deffand ill.—Growth of London.—Sir Joshua Reynolds.—Change in Manners.—Our Climate.

THE following letter is a specimen ot Horace's gossiping style at its best. It is addressed to Lord Nuneham, who was in Ireland with his father, Simon Earl Harcourt, the then Lord-Lieutenant. Elsewhere Walpole salutes his correspondent as "Your O'Royal Highness":

"Strawberry Hill, Dec. 6, 1773.

"I wanted an excuse for writing to you, my dear Lord, and your letter gives me an opportunity of thanking you; yet that is not all I wanted to say. I would, if I had dared, have addressed myself to Lady Nuneham, but I had not confidence enough, especially on so unworthy a subject as myself. Lady Temple, my friend, as well as that of Human Nature, has shown me some verses; but alas! how came such charming poetry to be thrown away on so unmeritorious a topic? I don't know whether I ought to praise the lines most, or censure the object most. Voltaire makes the excellence of French poetry consist in the number of difficulties it vanquishes. Pope, who celebrated Lord Bolingbroke, could not have succeeded, did not succeed, better; and yet I hope that, though a meaner subject, I am not so bad an one! Well! with all my humility, I cannot but be greatly flattered. Madame de Sévigné spread her leaf-gold over all her acquaintance, and made them shine; I should not doubt of the same glory, when Lady Nuneham's poetry shall come to light, if my own works were but burnt at the same time; but alas! Coulanges' verses were preserved, and so may my writings too. Apropos, my Lord, I have got a new volume of that divine woman's letters. Two are entertaining; the rest, not very divine. But there is an application, the happiest, the most exquisite, that even she herself ever made! She is joking with a President de Provence, who was hurt at becoming a grandfather. She assures him there is no such great misfortune in it; 'I have experienced the case,' says she, 'and, believe me, *Pæte, non dolet*.' If you are not both transported with *this*, ye are not the Lord and Lady Nuneham I take ye to be. There are besides some twenty letters of Madame de Simiane, who shows she would not have degenerated totally, if she had not lived in the country, or had anything to say. At the end are reprinted Madame de Sévigné's letters on Fouquet's Trial, which are very interesting.

"I do not know how you like your new subjects, but I hear they are extremely content with their Prince and Princess. I ought to wish your Lordship joy of all your prosperities, and of Mr. Fludd's baptism into the Catholic or Universal Faith; but I reserve public felicities for your old *Drawing-Room* in Leicester Fields. Private news we have little but Lord Carmarthen's and Lord Cranborne's marriages, and the approaching one of Lady Bridget Lane and Mr. Tall-Match. Lord Holland has given Charles Fox a draught of an hundred thousand pounds, and it pays all his debts, but a trifle of thirty thousand pounds, and those of Lord Carlisle, Crewe, and Foley, who being only friends, not Jews, may wait. So now any younger son may justify losing his father's and elder brother's estate on precedent.*

"Neither Lord nor Lady Temple are well, and yet they are both gone to Lord Clare's, in Essex, for a week. Lord Temple had a very bad fall in the Park, and lost his senses for an hour. Yet, though the horse is a vicious one, he has been upon it again. In short, there are no right-headed people but the Irish!

"As it is ancient good breeding not to conclude a

---

* 'I went to the House of Commons the other day to hear Charles Fox, contrary to a resolution I had made of never setting my foot there again. It is strange how disuse makes one awkward. I felt a palpitation, as if I were going to speak there myself. The object answered: Fox's abilities are amazing at so very early a period, especially under the circumstances of such a dissolute life. He was just arrived from Newmarket, had sat up drinking all night, and had not been in bed. How such talents make one laugh at Tully's rules for an orator, and his indefatigable application! His laboured orations are puerile in comparison with this boy's manly reason.'—*Walpole to Mann, April* 9, 1772.

letter without troubling the reader with compliments, and as I have none to send, I must beg your Lordship not to forget to present my respects to the Countesses of Barrymore and Massareene, my dear Sisters in Loo. You may be sure I am charged with a large parcel from Cliveden,* where I was last night. Except being extremely ill, Mrs. Clive is extremely well; but the tax-gatherer is gone off, and she must pay her window-lights over again; and the road before her door is very bad, and the parish won't mend it, and there is some suspicion that Garrick is at the bottom of it; so if you please to send a shipload of the Giant's Causey by next Monday, we shall be able to go to Mr. Rofey's rout at Kingston. The Papers said she was to act at Covent Garden, and she has printed a very proper answer in the *Evening Post*. Mr. Raftort† told me, that formerly, when he played Luna in 'The Rehearsal,' he never could learn to dance the Hays, and at last he went to the Man that teaches grown gentlemen.

"Miss Davis‡ is the admiration of all London, but of me, who do not love the perfection of what anybody can do, and wish she had less top to her voice and more bottom. However, she will break Millico's heart, which will not break mine. Fierville has sprained his leg, and there is another man who sprains his mouth with smiling on himself—as I have heard, for I have

---

* Walpole's playful name for Little Strawberry Hill, a cottage near his villa, and belonging to him, which he gave to Mrs. Clive, the actress, for her life.

† Mrs. Clive's brother, who lived with her.

‡ A new singer who attained great celebrity.

not seen him yet, nor a fat old woman and her lean daughter, who dance with him. London is very dull, so pray come back as soon as you can. Mason is up to the ears in 'Gray's Life;' you will like it exceedingly, which is more than you will do this long letter. Well! you have but to go into Lady Nuneham's dressing-room, and you may read something ten thousand times more pleasing. No, no! you are not the most to be pitied of any human being, though in the midst of Dublin Castle."

Next to the above, Walpole's liveliest letters about this date were written to Lady Ossory. Sometimes he has to lament the want of news: "Pray, Madam, where is the difference between London and the country, when everybody is in the country and nobody in town? The houses do not marry, intrigue, talk politics, game, or fling themselves out of window. The streets do not all run to the Alley, nor the squares mortgage themselves over head and ears. The play-houses do not pull themselves down; and all summer long, when nobody gets about them, they behave soberly and decently as any Christian in the parish of Marylebone. The English of this preface is that I have not the Israelitish art of making bricks without straw. I cannot invent news when nobody commits it." He has nothing better to tell than an anecdote of Goldsmith, who died a few months later, and Garrick: "I dined and passed Saturday at Beauclerk's, with the Edgecombes, the Garricks, and Dr. Goldsmith, and was most thoroughly tired, as I knew I should be, I who hate the playing off a butt. Goldsmith is a fool, the more wearying for having some sense. It was the night of a new comedy, called 'The School for Wives,'* which was exceedingly applauded, and which Charles Fox says is execrable. Garrick has at least the chief hand in it. I never saw anybody in a greater fidget, nor more vain when he returned, for he went to the play-house at half-an-hour after five, and we sat waiting for him till ten, when he was to act a speech in 'Cato' with Goldsmith! that is, the latter sat in t'other's lap, covered with a cloak, and while Goldsmith spoke, Garrick's arms that embraced him, made foolish actions. How could one laugh when one had expected this for four hours?" On Christmas night 1773, he writes: "This has been a very barren half-year. The next, I hope, will reinstate my letters in their proper character of newspapers."

The event, however, belied his hopes. In June, 1774, he writes to his Countess:

"Offended at you, Madam! I have crossed myself forty times since I read the impious words, never to be pronounced by human lips,—nay, and to utter them, when I am seemingly to blame!—yet, believe me, my silence is not owing to negligence, or to that most wicked of all sins, inconstancy. I have thought on you waking or sleeping, whenever I have thought at all, from the moment I saw you last; and if there was an echo in the neighbourhood besides Mr. Cambridge, I

* A comedy by Hugh Kelly.

should have made it repeat your Ladyship's name, till the parish should have presented it for a nuisance. I have begun twenty letters, but the naked truth is, I found I had absolutely nothing to say. You yourself owned, Madam, that I am grown quite lifeless, and it is very true. I am none of your Glastonbury thorns that blow at Christmas. I am a remnant of the last age, and have nothing to do with the present. I am an exile from the sunbeams of drawing-rooms; I have quitted the gay scenes of Parliament and the Antiquarian Society; I am not of Almack's; I don't understand horse-races; I never go to reviews; what can I have to talk of? I go to no *fêtes champêtres*, what can I have to think of? I know nothing but about myself, and about myself I know nothing. I have scarce been in town since I saw you, have scarce seen anybody here, and don't remember a tittle but having scolded my gardener twice, which, indeed, would be as important an article as any in Montaigne's Travels, which I have been reading, and if I was tired of his Essays, what must one be of these! What signifies what a man thought, who never thought of anything but himself; and what signifies what a man did, who never did anything?"

In August, hearing that Lady Ossory had again been disappointed of a son, he tells her: "I don't design to acknowledge Anne III.; I shall call her *Madame de Trop*, as they named one of the late King of France's daughters. A *dauphin!* a *dauphin!* I will repeat it as often as the *Graces*." A month later he is informed that *Madame de Trop* has received the name of Gertrude:

"MADAM,—'Methinks an Æsop's fable you relate,' as Dryden says in the 'Hind and Panther.' A mouse that wraps itself in a French cloak and sleeps on a couch; and a goldfinch that taps at the window and swears it will come in to quadrille at eleven o'clock at night! no, no, these are none of Æsop's cattle; they are too fashionable to have lived so near the creation. The mouse is neither Country Mouse nor City Mouse; and whatever else he may be, the goldfinch must be a Macaroni, or at least of the *Sçavoir vivre*. I do not deny but I have some skill in expounding types and portents; and could give a shrewd guess at the identical persons who have travestied themselves into a quadruped and biped; but the truth is, I have no mind, Madam, to be Prime Minister. King Pharaoh is mighty apt on emergencies to send for us soothsayers, and put the whole kingdom into our hands, if his butler or baker, with whom he is wont to gossip, does but tell him of a cunning man.

"I have no ambition to supplant Lord North—especially as the season approaches when I dread the gout; and I should be very sorry to be fetched out of my bed to pacify America. To be sure, Madam, you give me a fair field for uttering oracles: however, all I will unfold is, that the emblematic animals have no views on Lady Louisa.* The omens of her fortune are in herself; and I will burn my books, if beauty, sense,

---

* Lady Louisa Fitzpatrick, Lord Ossory's sister, afterwards married to the Earl of Shelburne.

and merit, do not bestow all the happiness on her they prognosticate. . . .

"I like the blue eyes, Madam, better than the denomination of Lady Gertrude Fitzpatrick, which, all respectable as it is, is very harsh and rough sounding; pray let her change it with the first goldfinch that offers. Nay, I do not even trust to the blueth of the eyes. I do not believe they last once in twenty times. One cannot go into any village fifty miles from London without seeing a dozen little children with flaxen hair and eyes of sky-blue. What becomes of them all? One does not see a grown Christian with them twice in a century, except in poetry.

"The Strawberry Gazette is very barren of news. Mr. Garrick has the gout, which is of more consequence to the metropolis than to Twitnamshire. Lady Hertford dined here last Saturday, brought her loo party, and stayed supper; there were Lady Mary Coke, Mrs. Howe, and the Colonels Maude and Keene. This was very heroic, for one is robbed every hundred yards. Lady Hertford herself was attacked last Wednesday on Hounslow Heath at three in the afternoon, but she had two servants on horseback, who would not let her be robbed, and the highwayman decamped.

"The greatest event I know was a present I received last Sunday, just as I was going to dine at Lady Blandford's, to whom I sacrificed it. It was a bunch of grapes as big—as big—as that the two spies carried on a pole to Joshua; for spies in those days, when they robbed a vineyard, were not at all afraid of being overtaken. In good truth, this bunch weighed three pounds and a half, *côte rôtie* measure; and was sent to me by my neighbour Prado, of the tribe of Issachar, who is descended from one of foresaid spies, but a good deal richer than his ancestor. Well, Madam, I carried it to the Marchioness of Blandford, but gave it to the *maître d'hôtel*, with injunctions to conceal it till the dessert. At the end of dinner, Lady Blandford said, she had heard of three immense bunches of grapes at Mr. Prado's, at a dinner he had made for Mr. Welbore Ellis. I said those things were always exaggerated. She cried, Oh! but Mrs. Ellis told it, and it weighed I don't know how many pounds, and the Duke of Argyll had been to see the hothouse, and she wondered, as it was so near, I would not go and see it. Not I, indeed, said I; I dare to say there is no curiosity in it. Just then entered the gigantic bunch. Everybody screamed There, said I, I will be shot if Mr. Prado has such a bunch as yours. In short, she suspected Lady Egremont, and the adventure succeeded to admiration. If you will send the Bedfordshire waggon, Madam, I will beg a dozen grapes for you. . . .

"Pray, Madam, is not it Farming-Woods' tide?* Who is to have the care of the dear mouse in your absence? I wish I could spare Margaret [his housekeeper], who loves all creatures so well that she would have been happy in the Ark, and sorry when the Deluge ceased; unless people had come to see Noah's old

* The period of the year when Lady Ossory left Ampthill for Farming Woods.

house, which she would have liked still better than cramming his menagerie."

The dearth of news was presently relieved by a General Election, about which and other topics Walpole writes to Mann:

"Strawberry Hill, Oct. 6, 1774.

"It would be unlike my attention and punctuality, to see so large an event as an irregular dissolution of Parliament, without taking any notice of it to you. It happened last Saturday, six months before its natural death, and without the design being known but the Tuesday before, and that by very few persons. The chief motive is supposed to be the ugly state of North America, and the effects that a cross winter might have on the next elections Whatever were the causes, the first consequences, as you may guess, were such a ferment in London as is seldom seen at this dead season of the year. Couriers, despatches, post-chaises, post-horses, hurrying every way! Sixty messengers passed through one single turnpike on Friday. The whole island is by this time in equal agitation; but less wine and money will be shed than have been at any such period for these fifty years. . . .

"The first symptoms are not favourable to the Court; the great towns are casting off submission, and declaring for popular members. London, Westminster, Middlesex, seem to have no monarch but Wilkes, who is at the same time pushing for the Mayoralty of London, with hitherto a majority on the poll. It is strange how this man, like a phœnix, always revives from his embers! America, I doubt, is still more unpromising. There are whispers of their having assembled an armed force, and of earnest supplications arrived for succours of men and ships. A civil war is no trifle; and how we are to suppress or pursue in such a vast region, with a handful of men, I am not an Alexander to guess; and for the fleet, can we put it upon casters and wheel it from Hudson's Bay to Florida? But I am an ignorant soul, and neither pretend to knowledge nor foreknowledge. All I perceive already is, that our Parliaments are subjected to America and India, and must be influenced by their politics; yet I do not believe our senators are more universal than formerly.

"It would be quite unfashionable to talk longer of anything but elections; and yet it is the topic on which I never talk or think, especially since *I took up my freedom.** . . .

" In the midst of this combustion, we are in perils by land and water. It has rained for this month without intermission. There is a sea between me and Richmond, and Sunday was se'nnight I was hurried down to Isleworth in the ferryboat by the violence of the current, and had great difficulty to get to shore. Our roads are so infested by highwaymen, that it is dangerous stirring out almost by day. Lady Hertford was attacked on Hounslow Heath at three in the afternoon. Dr. Eliot was shot at three days ago, without having resisted; and the day before yesterday we were near losing our

* His quitting Parliament.

Prime Minister, Lord North; the robbers shot at the postilion, and wounded the latter. In short, all the freebooters, that are not in India, have taken to the highway. The Ladies of the Bedchamber dare not go to the Queen at Kew in an evening. The lane between me and the Thames is the only safe road I know at present, for it is up to the middle of the horses in water. Next week I shall not venture to London even at noon, for the Middlesex election is to be at Brentford, where the two demagogues, Wilkes and Townshend, oppose each other; and at Richmond there is no crossing the river. How strange all this must appear to you Florentines; but you may turn to your Machiavelli and Guicciardini, and have some idea of it. I am the quietest man at present in the whole island; not but I might take some part, if I would. I was in my garden yesterday, seeing my servants lop some trees; my brewer walked in and pressed me to go to Guildhall for the nomination of members for the county. I replied, calmly, 'Sir, when I would go no more to my own election, you may be very sure I will go to that of nobody else.' My old tune is,

"'Suave mari magno turbantibus æquora ventis,' &c.

"Adieu!

"P.S. Arlington Street, 7th.

"I am just come to town, and find your letter. . . . The approaching death of the Pope will be an event of no consequence. That old mummery is near its conclusion, at least as a political object. The history of the latter Popes will be no more read than that of the last Constantinopolitan Emperors. Wilkes is a more conspicuous personage in modern story than the Pontifex Maximus of Rome. The poll for Lord Mayor ended last night; he and his late Mayor had above 1,900 votes, and their antagonists not 1,500. It is strange that the more he is opposed, the more he succeeds!"

The foregoing is an average sample of the bulk of Walpole's Letters to Sir Horace Mann. It was to these Macaulay referred when he said, sneeringly, that Walpole "left copies of his private letters, with copious notes, to be published after his decease." There can be no doubt that their author regarded them as a valuable contribution to the history of his times. And such, in truth, they were. Many of them contain full details of some political movement, written by one who, if not himself engaged in the struggle, was in close communication with the actors on one side at least. Hence, though these letters may be loaded with bias, they are often of solid substance. If they are not equally important for our present purpose, this is because they deal almost entirely with public matters and with the general news of the day. " Nothing is so pleasant in a letter," writes Walpole to Lady Ossory, "as the occurrences of society. I am always regretting in my correspondence with Madame du Deffand and Sir Horace Mann, that I must not make use of them, as the one has never lived in England, and the other not these fifty years; and so, my private stories would want notes as much as Petronius. Sir Horace and I have no acquaintance in common but the Kings and Queens of Europe."

In a letter to Mann, dated November 24, 1774, Walpole returns to the subject of the new Parliament:

"A great event happened two days ago—a political and moral event; the sudden death of that second Kouli Khan, Lord Clive. There was certainly illness in the case; the world thinks more than illness. His constitution was exceedingly broken and disordered, and grown subject to violent pains and convulsions. He came unexpectedly to town last Monday, and they say, ill. On Tuesday his physician gave him a dose of laudanum, which had not the desired effect. On the rest, there are two stories; one, that the physician repeated the dose; the other, that he doubled it himself, contrary to advice.* In short, he has terminated at fifty a life of so much glory, reproach, art, wealth, and ostentation! He had just named ten members for the new Parliament.†

"Next Tuesday that Parliament is to meet—and a deep game it has to play! few Parliaments a greater. The world is in amaze here that no account is arrived from America of the result of their General Congress—if any is come, it is very secret; and *that* has no favourable aspect. The combination and spirit there seem to

* Lord Clive, in fact, cut his throat, as Walpole, correcting himself, mentions in a postscript to this letter.

† In 1760, Walpole wrote: "General Clive is arrived, all over estates and diamonds. If a beggar asks charity, he says, 'Friend, I have no small brilliants about me.'"

be universal, and is very alarming. I am the humble servant of events, and you know never meddle with prophecy. It would be difficult to descry good omens, be the issue what it will.

"The old French Parliament is restored with great *éclat*. Monsieur de Maurepas, author of the revolution, was received one night at the Opera with boundless shouts of applause. It is even said that the mob intended, when the King should go to hold the *lit de justice*, to draw his coach. How singular it would be if Wilkes's case should be copied for a King of France! Do you think Rousseau was in the right, when he said that he could tell what would be the manners of any capital city, from certain given lights? I don't know what he may do on Constantinople and Pekin—but Paris and London! I don't believe Voltaire likes these changes. I have seen nothing of his writing for many months; not even on the poisoning Jesuits.* For our part, I repeat it, we shall contribute nothing to the *Histoire des Mœurs*, not for want of materials, but for want of writers. We have comedies without novelty, gross satires without stings, metaphysical eloquence, and antiquarians that discover nothing.

"' Bœotûm in crasso jurares aere natos !'

"Don't tell me I am grown old and peevish and supercilious—name the geniuses of 1774, and I submit. The next Augustan age will dawn on the other side of the Atlantic. There will, perhaps, be a Thucydides at Boston, a Xenophon at New York, and, in time, a

They poisoned Pope Ganganelli.—WALPOLE.

Virgil at Mexico, and a Newton at Peru. At last, some curious traveller from Lima will visit England, and give a description of the ruins of St. Paul's, like the editions of Balbec and Palmyra; but am I not prophesying, contrary to my consummate prudence, and casting horoscopes of empires like Rousseau? Yes; well, I will go and dream of my visions."

More than one writer has cited Walpole's traveller from Lima as the original of Lord Macaulay's traveller from New Zealand, who, in the midst of a vast solitude, takes his stand on a broken arch of London Bridge to sketch the ruins of St. Paul's. Others have traced the passage in the celebrated Review of Ranke's "History of the Popes," to Volney, Mrs. Barbauld, Kirke White, and Shelley; while others again have pointed out that, from whatsoever source derived, the idea expressed in this passage had been twice before employed by Macaulay, once, in 1824, in a Review of Mitford's "Greece," and the second time, in 1829, in his Review of Mill's "Essay on Government." The picture of the New Zealander, however, resembles the less ambitious, but equally graphic, figure of the traveller from Lima more closely than it does any of the other passages referred to.* What is remarkable is,

* "Who knows but that hereafter some traveller like myself will sit down upon the banks of the Seine, the Thames, or the Zuyder Zee? . . . Who knows but that he will sit down solitary amid silent ruins?" etc.—Volney's *Ruins*.

"When London shall be an habitation of bitterns, when St. Paul's and Westminster Abbey shall stand, shapeless and nameless ruins, in the midst of an unpeopled marsh; . . . some Transatlantic that the Review of Ranke's "History" appeared in October, 1840, whereas the later portion of Walpole's correspondence with Mann, to which the above extract belongs, was first published from the original manuscripts in 1843. How then could Macaulay know anything of the Peruvian stranger?*

The following was also addressed to Sir H. Mann. It is dated in May, 1775:

"You have not more Masquerades in Carnival than we have; there is one at the Pantheon to-night, another on Monday; and in June is to be a pompous one on the water, and at Ranelagh. This and the first are given by the Club called the *Sçavoir Vivre*, who till now have only shone by excess of gaming. The leader is that fashionable orator Lord Lyttelton,† of whom I need not tell *you* more. I have done with these diversions, and enjoy myself here. Your old acquaintance, Lord and Lady Dacre, and your old friend, Mr. Chute, dined with me to-day: poor Lord Dacre‡ is carried about,

---

commentator will be weighing . . . the respective merits of the Bells and the Fudges, and their historians."—Shelley, *Dedication to Peter Bell the Third*.

The rest are still more remote.

* Walpole, as well as Macaulay, repeats himself: "Nations at the acme of their splendour, or at the eve of their destruction, are worth observing. When they grovel in obscurity afterwards, they furnish neither events nor reflections; strangers visit the vestiges of the Acropolis, or may come to dig for capitals among the ruins of St. Paul's; but nobody studies the manners of the pedlars and banditti that dwell in mud huts within the precincts of a demolished temple." —*Letter to Mason, dated May* 12, 1778, *first published in* 1851.

† Thomas, second Lord Lyttelton; he had been at Florence.

‡ Thomas Lennard Barret; his wife was sister of Lord Camden.

though not worse than he has been these twenty years. Strawberry was in great beauty; what joy I should have in showing it to you! Is this a wish I must never indulge? Alas!

"I have had a long chain of thoughts since I wrote the last paragraph. They ended in smiling at the word *never*. How one pronounces it to the last moment! Would not one think I counted on a long series of years to come? Yet no man has the termination of all his views more before his eyes, or knows better the idleness of framing visions to one's self. One passes away so soon, and worlds succeed to worlds, in which the occupiers build the same castles in the air. What is ours but the present moment? And how many of mine are gone! And what do I want to show you? A plaything-vision, that has amused a poor transitory mortal for a few hours, and that will pass away like its master! Well, and yet is it not as sensible to conform to common ideas, and to live while one lives? Perhaps the wisest way is to cheat one's self. Did one concentre all one's thoughts on the nearness and certainty of dissolution, all the world would lie eating and sleeping like the savage Americans. Our wishes and views were given us to gild the dream of life, and if a Strawberry Hill can soften the decays of age, it is wise to embrace it, and due gratitude to the Great Giver to be happy with it. The true pain is the reflection on the numbers that are not so blessed; yet I have no doubt but the real miseries of life—I mean those that are unmerited and unavoidable,—will be compensated to the sufferers.

Tyrants are a proof of an hereafter. Millions of men cannot be formed for the sport of a cruel child.

"How happy is the Pretender in missing a Crown! When dead, he will have all the advantage that other Kings have, the being remembered; and that greater advantage, which Kings who die in their childhood have, historians will say, he would have been a great King if he had lived to reign; and that greatest advantage which so very few of them have, his reign will be stained with no crimes and blunders. If he is at Florence, pray recommend me to him for his historian; you see I have all the qualities a Monarch demands, I am disposed to flatter him. You may tell him too what I have done for his uncle Richard III. The mischief is in it, if I am not qualified for a Royal Historiographer, when I have whitewashed one of the very few whom my brethren, so contrary to their custom, have agreed to traduce."

In the autumn of 1775, Walpole was in Paris, whence he sends, for the benefit of Conway's daughter, this important piece of information: "Tell Mrs. Damer, that the fashion now is to erect the *toupée* into a high detached tuft of hair, like a cockatoo's crest; and this *toupée* they call *la physionomie*—I don't guess why." And in giving George Selwyn an account of the modish French ladies whom he met, he adds a description suited to the humour of that facetious gentleman: "With one of them," he says, "you would be delighted, a Madame de Marchais. She is not perfectly young, has a face like a Jew pedlar, her person is about four feet, her head about six, and her *coiffure* about ten. Her forehead, chin, and neck are whiter than a miller's; and she wears more festoons of natural flowers than all the *figurantes* at the Opera. Her eloquence is still more abundant, her *attentions* exuberant. She talks volumes, writes folios—I mean in *billets;* presides over the Académie, inspires passions. . . . She has a house in a nut-shell, that is fuller of invention than a fairy tale; her bed stands in the middle of the room, because there is no other space that would hold it; it is surrounded by a perspective of looking-glasses. . . ." In reference to the rage for *billets*, he mentions " a collection that was found last winter at Monsieur de Pondeveyllc's: there were sixteen thousand from one lady, in a correspondence of only eleven years. For fear of setting the house on fire if thrown into the chimney, the executors crammed them into the oven." " There have been known," he adds, " persons here who wrote to one another four times a day; and I was told of one couple, who being always together, and the lover being fond of writing, he placed a screen between them, and then wrote to Madam on t'other side, and flung them over." Of his " dear old friend," he reports:

" Madame du Deffand has been so ill, that the day she was seized I thought she would not live till night. Her Herculean weakness, which could not resist strawberries and cream after supper, has surmounted all the *ups* and *downs* which followed her excess; but her impatience to go everywhere and to do everything has been attended with a kind of relapse, and another kind of giddiness; so that I am not quite easy about her, as they allow her to take no nourishment to recruit, and she will die of inanition, if she does not live upon it. She cannot lift her head from the pillow without *étourdissemens*; and yet her spirits gallop faster than anybody's, and so do her repartees. She has a great supper to-night for the Duc de Choiseul, and was in such a passion yesterday with her cook about it, and that put Tonton* into such a rage, that *nos dames de Saint Joseph* thought the devil or the philosophers were flying away with their convent! As I have scarce quitted her, I can have had nothing to tell you. If she gets well, as I trust, I shall set out on the 12th; but I cannot leave her in any danger—though I shall run many myself, if I stay longer. I have kept such bad hours with this *malade*, that I have had alarms of gout; and bad weather, worse inns, and a voyage in winter, will ill suit me. . . .

"I must repose a great while after all this living in company; nay, intend to go very little into the world again, as I do not admire the French way of burning one's candle to the very snuff in public."

At the end of 1775, Sir Horace Mann's elder brother died, the family estate came to the Ambassador, and Walpole flattered himself "that a regular correspon-

* The lady's dog, which, on her death, passed into the care of Walpole.

dence of thirty-four years will cease, and that I shall see him again before we meet in the Elysian fields." He was disappointed. In February, 1776, he writes to his old friend: "You have chilled me so thoroughly by the coldness of your answer, and by the dislike you express to England, that I shall certainly press you no more to come. I thought at least it would have cost you a struggle." Again, a little later: "Pray be assured, I acquiesce in all you say on your own return, though grieved at your resolution, and more so at the necessity you find in adhering to it. It is not my disposition to prefer my own pleasure to the welfare of my friends. Your return might have opened a warm channel of affection which above thirty years could not freeze; but I am sure you know my steadiness too well to suspect me of cooling to you, because we are both grown too old to meet again. I wished that meeting as a luxury beyond what old age often tastes; but I am too well prepared for parting with everything to be ill-humouredly chagrined because one vision fails." In July, 1776, we find the following, also addressed to Mann :

"I did flatter myself with being diverted at your surprise from so general an alteration of persons, objects, manners, as you would have found; but there is an end of all that pleasing vision! I remember when my father went out of place, and was to return visits, which Ministers are excused from doing, he could not guess where he was, finding himself in so many new streets and squares. This was thirty years ago. They have been building ever since, and one would think they had imported two or three capitals. London could put Florence into its fob-pocket; but as they build so slightly, if they did not rebuild, it would be just the reverse of Rome, a vast circumference of city surrounding an area of ruins. As its present progress is chiefly north, and Southwark marches south, the metropolis promises to be as broad as long. Rows of houses shoot out every way like a polypus; and, so great is the rage of building everywhere, that, if I stay here a fortnight, without going to town, I look about to see if no new house is built since I went last. America and France must tell us how long this exuberance of opulence is to last! The East Indies, I believe, will not contribute to it much longer. Babylon and Memphis and Rome, probably, stared at their own downfall. Empires did not use to philosophise, nor thought much but of themselves. Such revolutions are better known now, and we ought to expect them—I do not say we do. This little island will be ridiculously proud some ages hence of its former brave days, and swear its capital was once as big again as Paris, or—what is to be the name of the city that will then give laws to Europe?—perhaps New York or Philadelphia."

At the close of 1776, Walpole had another severe illness. It is first mentioned in a letter to Lady Ossory:

" It is not from being made Archbishop of York, that

I write by a secretary [Kirgate], Madam; but because my right hand has lost its cunning. It has had the gout ever since Friday night, and I am overjoyed with it, for there is no appearance of its going any farther. I came to town on Sunday in a panic, concluding I should be bedrid for three months, but I went out last night, and think I shall be able in a few days to play upon the guitar if I could play upon it at all. . . .

"I have seen the picture of 'St. George,' and approve the Duke of Bedford's head, and the exact likeness of Miss Vernon,* but the attitude is mean and foolish, and expresses silly wonderment. But of all, delicious is a picture of a little girl of the Duke of Buccleuch, who is overlaid with a long cloak, bonnet, and muff, in the midst of the snow, and is perishing blue and red with cold, but looks so smiling, and so good-humoured, that one longs to catch her up in one's arms and kiss her till she squalls.

"My hand has not a word more to say."

The attack proved obstinate, and we have again complaints of the English climate, mixed with lamentations over the change in English manners. Thus in February, 1777, he writes:

* This picture, by Sir Joshua Reynolds, was painted for Mr. Rigby. The attitude of Miss Vernon is, as Walpole here says, affected. That of Lord William Russell illustrates the genius of Sir Joshua. The story is told, that the boy was unwilling to stand still for his portrait, and running about the room, crouched in a corner to avoid it. Sir Joshua, at once seizing the possibility of painting him so, said, "Well, stay there, my little fellow,' and drew him in a natural position of fear at the dragon.—R. VERNON SMITH (afterwards LORD LYVEDEN).

"Everything is changed; as always must happen when one grows old, and is prejudiced to one's old ways. I do not like dining at nearly six, nor beginning the evening at ten at night. If one does not conform, one must live alone; and that is more disagreeable and more difficult in town than in the country, where old useless people ought to live. Unfortunately, the country does not agree with me; and I am sure it is not fancy; for my violent partiality to Strawberry Hill cannot be imposed upon. I am persuaded that it is the dampness of this climate that gives me so much gout; and London, from the number of fires and inhabitants, must be the driest spot in the nation."

The following, written to Lord Nuneham in July, is in a gayer tone:

"Now I have taken this liberty, my dear Lord, I must take a little more; you know my old admiration and envy are your garden. I do not grudge Pomona or Sir James Cockburn their hot-houses, nor intend to ruin myself by raising sugar and water in tanner's bark and peach skins. The Flora Nunehamica is the height of my ambition, and if your Linnæus should have any disciple that would condescend to look after my little flower-garden, it would be the delight of my eyes and nose, provided the cataracts of heaven are ever shut again! Not one proviso do I make, but that the pupil be not a Scot. We had peace and warm weather before the inundation of that northern people, and therefore I beg to have no Attila for my gardener.

"Apropos, don't your Lordship think that another set of legislators, the Maccaronis and Maccaronesses, are very wise? People abuse them for turning days, nights, hours and seasons topsy-turvy; but surely it was upon mature reflection. We had a set of customs and ideas borrowed from the continent that by no means suited our climate. Reformers bring back things to their natural course. Notwithstanding what I said in spite in the paragraph above, we are in truth but Greenlanders, and ought to conform to our climate. We should lay in store of provisions and candles and masquerades and coloured lamps for ten months in the year, and shut out our twilight and enjoy ourselves. In September and October, we may venture out of our ark, and make our hay, and gather in our corn, and go to horse-races, and kill pheasants and partridges for stock for our winter's supper. I sailed in a skiff and pair this morning to Lady Cecilia Johnston, and found her, like a good housewife, sitting over her fire, with her cats and dogs and birds and children. She brought out a dram to warm me and my servants, and we were very merry and comfortable. As Lady Nuneham has neither so many two-footed or four-footed cares upon her hands, I hope her hands have been better employed.

"I wish I could peep over her shoulder one of these wet mornings!"

CHAPTER VII.

The American War.—Irish Discontent.—Want of Money.—The Houghton Pictures Sold.—Removal to Berkeley Square.—Ill-health.—A Painting by Zoffani.—The Rage for News.—The Duke of Gloucester.—Wilkes.—Fashions, Old and New.—Mackerel News.—Pretty Stories.—Madame de Sévigné's Cabinet.—Picture of his Waldegrave Nieces.—The Gordon Riots.—Death of Madame du Deffand.—The Blue Stockings.

HUMOURIST as he was, and too often swayed by prejudice, no man had a sounder judgment than Walpole when he gave his reason fair play. In his estimate of public events, he sometimes displayed unusual sagacity. Though his dislike of Lord Chatham led him to disparage the efforts of the old man eloquent to avert the American War—efforts which filled Franklin with admiration—he yet foresaw quite as clearly as Chatham the disastrous results of that contest. The celebrated speeches which fell dead on the ear of Parliament had no more effect upon Walpole; but Walpole did not need to be moved by them, for he was convinced already. "This interlude," he writes to Conway, who was then in Paris, "would be entertaining, if the scene was not so totally gloomy. The Cabinet have determined on civil war. . . . There is food for meditation!

Will the French you converse with be civil and keep their countenances? Pray remember it is not decent to be dancing at Paris, when there is a civil war in your own country. You would be like the country squire, who passed by with his hounds as the battle of Edgehill began." The letter in which these words occur is dated January 22, 1775. Three weeks later, the writer adds: "The war with our Colonies, which is now declared, is a proof how much influence jargon has on human actions. A war on our own trade is *popular!** Both Houses are as eager for it as they were for conquering the Indies—which acquits them a little of rapine, when they are as glad of what will impoverish them as of what they fancied was to enrich them." His sympathy, as well as his judgment, was on the side of the Colonies On September 7th 1775, he writes to Mann: "You will not be surprised that I am what I always was, a zealot for liberty in every part of the globe, and consequently that I most heartily wish success to the Americans. They have hitherto not made *one* blunder; and the Administration have made a thousand, besides the two capital ones, of first provoking, and then of uniting the Colonies. The latter seem to have as good heads as hearts, as we want both." And on the 11th: "The

---

* 'I forgot to tell you that the town of Birmingham has petitioned the Parliament to enforce the American Acts, that is, make war; for they have a manufacture of swords and muskets.'—WALPOLE to MANN, Jan. 27th, 1775.

'Is it credible that five or six of the great *trading* towns have presented addresses against the Americans?'—SAME to SAME, Oct. 10, 1775. The writer tries to persuade himself that these addresses were procured by 'those boobies, the country gentlemen.'

Parliament is to meet on the 20th of next month, and vote twenty-six thousand seamen! What a paragraph of blood is there! With what torrents must liberty be preserved in America! In England what can save it? . . . What prospect of comfort has a true Englishman? Why, that Philip II. miscarried against the boors of Holland, and that Louis XIV. could not replace James II. on the throne!" And when Fortune declared herself on the side of the Colonists, Horace, unmoved by the reverses of his country, steadily preserved the same tone. "We have been horribly the aggressors," he wrote at the end of 1777, "and I must rejoice that the Americans are to be free, as they had a right to be, and as I am sure they have shown they deserve to be." But the calamities and disgraces of the time weighed heavily on his spirits. His correspondence throughout 1777 and the two following years is full of the American War. He recurs to the subject again and again, and harps upon it continually. It does not fall within our plan to quote his criticisms and reflections on the conduct of Lord North and his opponents. They are generally as acute and sensible as they are always vigorous and lively. The chief mistake one remarks in them is, that they assume the victory of America to mean the ruin of England's Empire. The writer saw British troops everywhere defeated, retreating, laying down their arms; France allying herself with the rebellious Colonies, and threatening England with invasion; Spain joining in the hostile league; and Ireland showing fresh signs of disaffection: what wonder if he was tempted to predict that we should "moulder piecemeal into our insignificant islandhood?" In May, 1779, he writes: "Our oppressive partiality to two or three manufacturing towns in England has revolted the Irish, and they have entered into combinations against purchasing English goods in terms more offensive than the first associations of the Colonies. In short, we have for four or five years displayed no alacrity or address, but in provoking our friends and furnishing weapons of annoyance to our enemies; and the unhappy facility with which the Parliament has subscribed to all these oversights has deceived the Government into security, and encouraged it to pull almost the whole fabric on its own head. We can escape but by concessions and disgrace; and when we attain peace, the terms will prove that Parliamentary majorities have voted away the wisdom, glory, and power of the nation."

Before the date of this extract, the pressure of the war had made itself felt in English society. In the preceding summer, Horace had written to Mason, then engaged on his poem of "The English Garden":

"Distress is already felt; one hears of nothing but of the want of money; one sees it every hour. I sit in my Blue window, and miss nine in ten of the carriages that used to pass before it. Houses sell for nothing, which, two years ago, nabobs would have given lacs of diamonds for. Sir Gerard Vanneck's house and beautiful terrace on the Thames, with forty acres of ground, and valued by his father at twenty thousand pounds, was bought in last week at six thousand. Richmond is deserted; an hundred and twenty coaches used to be counted at the church-door—there are now twenty. I know nobody that grows rich but Margaret. This Halcyon season has brought her more customers than ever, and were anything to happen to her, I have thoughts, like greater folk, of being my own minister, and showing my house myself. I don't wonder *your Garden* has grown in such a summer, and I am glad it has, that our taste in gardening may be immortal in verse, for I doubt it has seen its best days! Your poem may transplant it to America, whither our best works will be carried now, as our worst used to be. Do not you feel satisfied in knowing you shall be a classic in a free and rising empire? Swell all your ideas, give a loose to all your poetry; your lines will be repeated on the banks of the Orinoko; and which is another comfort, Ossian's ' Dirges ' will never be known there. Poor Strawberry must sink *in fœce Romuli ;* that melancholy thought silences me."

Besides being vexed at the state of public affairs, Walpole suffered much about this time from the gout, and from family troubles. His nephew, Lord Orford, having recovered from a second attack of insanity, resolved on selling the pictures at Houghton. In February, 1779, Horace writes to Lady Ossory: " The pictures at Houghton, I hear, and I fear, are sold: what can I say? I do not like even to think on it. It is the most signal mortification to my idolatry for my father's memory, that it could receive. It is stripping the temple of his glory and of his affection. A madman excited by rascals has burnt his Ephesus. I must never cast a thought towards Norfolk more; nor will hear my nephew's name if I can avoid it. Him I can only pity; though it is strange he should recover any degree of sense, and never any of feeling!" The transaction was not, in fact, at that moment concluded. In the course of the same year, however, the whole gallery was sold to the Empress of Russia for a little more than forty thousand pounds. Walpole did not think the bargain a bad one, though he would rather, he said, the pictures were sold to the Crown of England than to that of Russia, where they would be burnt in a wooden palace on the first insurrection, while in England they would still be Sir Robert Walpole's Collection. "But," he added, "my grief is that they are not to remain at Houghton, where he placed them and wished them to remain."

While grieving over his father's pictures, Horace found himself involved in a Chancery suit. The lease of his town house in Arlington Street running out about this time, he had bought a larger house in Berkeley Square. Difficulties, however, hindered the completion of the purchase, and the affair went into Chancery. Fortunately, under Walpole's management, the suit became a friendly one. "I have persisted in complimenting and flattering my parties, till by dint of complaisance and respect I have brought them to pique themselves on equal attentions; so that, instead of a lawsuit, it has more the air of a treaty between two little German princes who are mimicking their betters only to display their titular dignities. His Serene Highness, Colonel Bishopp, is the most obsequious and devoted servant of my Serenity the Landgrave of Strawberry." The judge was equally agreeable. " Yesterday I received notice from my attorney that the Master of the Rolls has, with epigrammatic despatch, heard my cause, and pronounced a decree in my favour. Surely, the whip of the new driver, Lord Thurlow, has pervaded all the hard wheels of the law, and set them galloping. I must go to town on Monday, and get my money ready for payment,—not from impatience to enter on my premises, but though the French declare they are coming to burn London, bank-bills are still more combustible than houses, and should my banker's shop be reduced to ashes, I might have a mansion to pay for, and nothing to pay with. If both were consumed, at least I should not be in debt." The purchase-money paid, and possession taken, the next step was to remove to Berkeley Square. In October, 1779, he writes to Lady Ossory, whose sister-in-law,* the newly-married Countess of Shelburne, was just established in the same square:

" My constitution, which set out under happy stars, seems to keep pace with the change of constellations, and fail like the various members of the empire. I am now confined with the rheumatism in my left arm, and find no benefit from our woollen manufacture, which I flattered myself would always be a resource. On

* The Lady Louisa Fitzpatrick before referred to.—*See p.* 131.

Monday I shall remove to Shelburne Square, and watch impatiently the opening of the Countess's windows; though with all her and her Earl's goodness to me, I doubt I shall profit little of either. I do not love to be laughed at or pitied, and dread exposing myself to numbers of strange servants and young people, who wonder what Methuselah does out of his coffin. Lady Blandford is gone; her antediluvian dowagers dispersed; amongst whom I was still reckoned a lively young creature. Wisdom I left forty years ago to Welbore Ellis, and must not pretend to rival him now, when he is grown so rich by the semblance of it. Since I cannot then act old age with dignity, I must keep myself out of the way, and weep for England in a corner."

The Lady Blandford mentioned in this passage was a widow who had lived within a few miles of Horace, at Sheen, and had recently died. During her illness, Walpole, in writing to Lady Ossory, had dwelt on the Roman fortitude with which the sick lady supported her sufferings, and on the devotion shown to her by her friend, Miss Stapylton. He added in his usual strain. "Miss Stapylton has £30,000, and Lady Blandford nothing. I wish we had some of these exalted characters in breeches! These two women shine like the last sparkles in a piece of burnt paper, which the children call the parson and clerk. Alas! the rest of our old ladies are otherwise employed; they are at the head of fleets and armies." Walpole at this moment was altogether out of heart. "I see myself a poor invalid, threatened with a painful and irksome conclusion, and mortified at seeing the decay of my country more rapid than my own." But he could still keep up a tone of gaiety. In November he wrote to Mann:

"I went this morning to Zoffani's to see his picture or portrait of the 'Tribune at Florence;' and, though my letter will not put on its boots these three days, I must write while the subject is fresh in my head. The first thing I looked for, was *you*—and I could not find you. At last I said, 'Pray, who is *that* Knight of the Bath?'—'Sir Horace Mann.'—'Impossible!' said I. My dear Sir, how you have left me in the lurch!—you are grown fat, jolly, young; while I am become the skeleton of Methuselah. . . .

"Well! but are you really so portly a personage as Zoffani has represented you? I envy you. Everybody can grow younger and plump, but I. My brother, Sir Edward Walpole, is as sleek as an infant, and, though seventy-three, is still quite beautiful. He has a charming colour, and not a wrinkle. I told him, when Lord Orford* was in danger, that he might think what he would, but I would carry him into the Court of Chancery, and put it to the consciences of the judges, which of us two was the elder by eleven years?"

And two days later we have the followin amusing letter to Lady Ossory:

"Berkeley Square, Nov. 14, 1779.

"I must be equitable; I must do the world justice; there are really some hopes of its amendment; I have

* Horace's nephew, the mad earl.

not heard one lie these four days; but then, indeed, I have heard nothing. Well, then, why do you write? Stay, Madam; my letter is not got on horseback yet; nor shall it mount till it has something to carry. It is my duty, as your gazetteer, to furnish you with news, true or false, and you would certainly dismiss me if I did not, at least, tell you something that was impossible. The whole nation is content with hearing anything new, let it be ever so bad. Tell the first man you meet that Ireland has revolted; away he runs, and tells everybody he meets,—everybody tells everybody, and the next morning they ask for more news. Well, Jamaica is taken; oh, Jamaica is taken. Next day, what news? Why, Paul Jones is landed in Rutlandshire, and has carried off the Duchess of Devonshire, and a squadron is fitting out to prevent it; and I am to have a pension for having given the earliest intelligence; and there is to be a new farce called *The Rutlandshire Invasion*, and the King and Queen will come to town to see it, and the Prince of Wales will not, because he is not old enough to understand pantomimes.*

"Well, Madam; having despatched the nation and its serious affairs, one may chat over private matters. I have seen Lord Macartney, and do affirm that he is shrunk, and has a *soupçon* of black that was not wont to reside in his complexion. . . .

"Mr. Beauclerk has built a library in Great Russell Street, Bloomsbury, that reaches half-way to Highgate.

* The Prince was now in his eighteenth year, having been born on the 12th of August, 1762.

Everybody goes to see it ; it has put the Museum's nose quite out of joint.

"Now I return to politics. Sir Ralph Payne and Dr. Johnson are answering General Burgoyne, and they say the words are to be so long that the reply must be printed in a pamphlet as long as an atlas, but in an Elzevir type, or the first sentence would fill twenty pages in octavo. You may depend upon the truth of it, for Mr. Cumberland told it in confidence to one with whom he is not at all acquainted, who told it to one whom I never saw; so you see, Madam, there is no questioning the authority.

"I will not answer so positively for what I am going to tell you, as I had it only from the person himself. The Duke of Gloucester was at Bath with the Margrave of Anspach. Lord Nugent came up and would talk to the Duke, and then asked if he might take the liberty of inviting his Royal Highness to dinner? I think you will admire the quickness and propriety of the answer: —the Duke replied, 'My Lord, I make no acquaintance but in London,' where you know, Madam, he only has levees. The Irishman continued to talk to him even after that rebuff. He certainly hoped to have been very artful—to have made court there, and yet not have offended anywhere else* by not going in town, which would have been a gross affront to the Duke, had he accepted the invitation.

"I was at Blackheath t'other morning, where I was

* The Duke was in disgrace with the King on account of his marriage.

grieved. There are eleven Vander Werffs that cost an immense sum: half of them are spoiled since Sir Gregory Page's death by servants neglecting to shut out the sun. There is another room hung with the history of Cupid and Psyche, in twelve small pictures by Luca Giordano, that are sweet. There is, too, a glorious Claude, some fine Teniers, a noble Rubens and Snyders, two beautiful Philippo Lauras, and a few more,—and several very bad. The house is magnificent, but wounded me; it was built on the model of Houghton, except that three rooms are thrown into a gallery.

"Now I have tapped the chapter of pictures, you must go and see Zoffani's 'Tribune at Florence,' which is an astonishing piece of work, with a vast deal of merit.

"There too you will see a delightful piece of Wilkes looking—no, squinting tenderly at his daughter. It is a caricature of the Devil acknowledging Miss Sin in Milton. I do not know why, but they are under a palm-tree, which has not grown in a free country for some centuries.

"15th.

"With all my pretences, there is no more veracity in me than in a Scotch runner for the Ministry. Here must I send away my letter without a word in it worth a straw. All the good news I know is, that a winter is come in that will send armies and navies to bed, and one may stir out in November without fear of being tanned. I am heartily glad that we shall keep Jamaica and the East Indies another year, that one may have time to lay in a stock of tea and sugar for the rest of one's days. I think only of the necessaries of life, and do not care a rush for gold and diamonds, and the pleasure of stealing logwood. The friends of Government, who have thought of nothing but of reducing us to our islandhood, and bringing us back to the simplicity of ancient times, when we were the frugal, temperate, virtuous old English, ask how we did before tea and sugar were known. Better, no doubt; but as I did not happen to be born two or three hundred years ago, I cannot recollect precisely whether diluted acorns, and barley bread spread with honey, made a very luxurious breakfast.

"I was last night at Lady Lucan's to hear the Misses Bingham sing Jomelli's 'Miserere,' set for two voices. There were only the Duchess of Bedford, Lady Bute . . . and half a dozen Irish. . . . The Duchess told me, that a habit-maker returned from Ampthill is gone stark in love with Lady Ossory, on fitting her with the new dress—I think they call it a Levite—and says he never saw so glorious a figure. I know that; and so you would be in a hop-sack, Madam —but where is the grace in a man's nightgown bound round with a belt?

"Good-night, Lady! I hope I shall have something to tell you in my next, that my letter may be shorter.

"Codicil to my to-day's :—viz. Nov. 15, 1779.

"I enclosed the above to Lord Ossory, because it was not worth sixpence, and had sent it to the post, and then went to Bedford House, where, lo! enters Lady Shelburne, looking as fresh and ripe as Pomona. N.B. Her windows were not open yesterday, and to-day there was such a mist, ermined with snow, that I could not see. I find it was not a habit-maker that was smitten with your Ladyship as a pig in a poke, but somebody else; but as her Grace's mouth has lost one tooth, and my ear, I suspect, another, I have not found out who the unfortunate man is.

"Next enters your Ladyship's letter. I have seen my dignity of Minister to Spain*—many a fair castle have I erected in that country, but truly never resided there. . . . This is long enough for a codicil, in which one has nothing more to give."

In the same lively mood, he writes about the same time to Mason:

"Berkeley Square, Nov. I don't know what day.

"If you can be content with anything but news as fresh as mackerel, I will tell you as pretty a story as a gentleman can hear in a winter's day, though it has not a grain of novelty in it but to those who never heard it, which was my case till yesterday.

"When that philosophic tyrant the Czarina (who murdered two emperors for the good of their people, to the edification of Voltaire, Diderot, and D'Alembert) proposed to give a code of laws that should serve all her subjects as much or as little as she pleased, she

* Referring to a rumour that he had been appointed ambassador to Spain.

ordered her various states to send deputies who should specify their respective wants. Amongst the rest came a representative of the Samoieds; he waited on the marshal of the diet of legislation, who was Archbishop of Novgorod. 'I am come,' said the savage, 'but I do not know for what.' 'My clement mistress,' said his Grace, 'means to give a body of laws to all her dominions.'—'Whatever laws the Empress shall give us,' said the Samoied, 'we shall obey, but we want no laws.'—'How,' said the Prelate, 'not want laws! why, you are men like the rest of the world, and must have the same passions, and consequently must murder, cheat, steal, rob, plunder,' &c., &c., &c.

'It is true,' said the savage, 'we have now and then a bad person among us, but he is sufficiently punished by being shut out of all society.'

"If you love nature in its *naturalibus*, you will like this tale. I think one might make a pretty 'Spectator' by inverting the hint: I would propose a general jail delivery, not only from all prisons, but madhouses, as not sufficiently ample for a quarter of the patients and candidates; and to save trouble, and yet make as impartial distinction, to confine the virtuous and the few that are in their senses. But I am digressing, and have not yet told you the story I intended; at least, only the first part.

"One day Count Orlow, the Czarina's accomplice in more ways than one, exhibited himself to the Samoied in the robes of the order, and refulgent with diamonds. The savage surveyed him attentively, but silently.

'May I ask,' said the favourite, 'what it is you admire?'—'Nothing,' replied the Tartar: 'I was thinking how ridiculous you are.'—'Ridiculous,' cried Orlow, angrily; 'and pray in what?'—'Why, you shave your beard to look young, and powder your hair to look old!'

"Well! as you like my stories, I will tell you a third, but it is prodigiously old, yet it is the only new trait that I have found in that ocean *Bibliothèque des Romans*, which I had almost abandoned; for I am out of patience with novels and sermons, that have nothing new, when the authors may say what they will without contradiction.

"My history is a romance of the Amours of Eleanor of Aquitaine, Queen of our Henry the Second. She is in love with somebody who is in love with somebody else. She puts both in prison. The Count falls dangerously ill, and sends for the Queen's Physician. Eleanor hears it, calls for the Physician, and gives him a bowl, which she orders him to prescribe to the Count. The Doctor hesitates, doubts, begs to know the ingredients.—'Come,' says her Majesty, 'your suspicions are just—it is poison; but remember, it is a crime I want from you, not a lecture; go and obey my orders; my Captain of the guard and two soldiers shall accompany you, and see that you execute my command, and give no hint of my secret; go, I will have no reply:' the Physician submits, finds the prisoner in bed, his mistress sitting by. The Doctor feels his pulse, produces the bowl, sighs, and says, 'My dear friend, I cannot cure your disorder, but I have a remedy here for myself,' and swallows the poison.

"Is not this entirely new? it would be a fine *coup de théâtre*, and yet would not do for a tragedy, for the Physician would become the hero of the piece, would efface the lovers; and yet the rest of the play could not be made to turn on him.

"As all this will serve for a letter at any time, I will keep the rest of my paper for something that will not bear postponing.

"20th.

"Come, my letter shall go, though with only one new paragraph. Lord Weymouth has resigned, as well as Lord Gower. I believe that little faction flattered themselves that their separation would blow up Lord North, and yet I am persuaded that sheer cowardice has most share in Weymouth's part. There is such universal dissatisfaction, that when the crack is begun, the whole edifice perhaps may tumble, but where is the architect that can repair a single story? The nation stayed till everything was desperate, before it would allow that a single tile was blown off."

At the close of the year, he is cheered by the sight of a precious relic:

"You are to know, Madam, that I have in my custody the individual ebony cabinet in which Madame de Sévigné kept her pens and paper for writing her matchless letters. It was preserved near Grignan by an old man who mended her pens, and whose descendant gave it last year to Mr. Selwyn, as truly worthy of such a sacred relic. It wears, indeed, all the outward and visible signs of such venerable preciousness, for it is clumsy, cumbersome, and shattered, and inspires no more idea of her spirit and *légèreté*, than the mouldy thigh-bone of a saint does of the unction of his sermons. I have full powers to have it repaired and decorated as shall seem good in my own eyes, though I had rather be authorised to inclose and conceal it in a shrine of gold and jewels."

Towards the end of May, 1780, he writes: "Sir Joshua has begun a charming picture of my three fair nieces, the Waldegraves, and very like. They are embroidering and winding silk; I rather wished to have them drawn like the Graces, adorning a bust of the Duchess as the Magna Mater; but my ideas are not adopted." We hear no more of this picture for some time. Attention was almost immediately engrossed by the Gordon riots. Walpole writes to Lady Ossory:

"Berkeley Square, June 3, 1780.

" I know that a governor or gazetteer ought not to desert their posts, if a town is besieged, or a town is full of news; and therefore, Madam, I resume my office. I smile to-day—but I trembled last night; for an hour or more I never felt more anxiety. I knew the bravest of my friends were barricaded into the House of Commons, and every avenue to it impossible. Till I heard the Horse and Foot Guards were gone to their rescue, I expected nothing but some dire misfortune; and the first thing I heard this morning was that part of the town had had a fortunate escape from being burnt after ten last night. You must not expect order, Madam; I must recollect circumstances as they occur; and the best idea I can give your Ladyship of the tumult will be to relate it as I heard it.

"I had come to town in the morning on a private occasion, and found it so much as I left it, that though I saw a few blue cockades here and there, I only took them for new recruits. Nobody came in; between seven and eight I saw a hack and another coach arrive at Lord Shelburne's, and thence concluded that Lord George Gordon's trumpet had brayed to no purpose. At eight I went to Gloucester House; the Duchess told me, there had been a riot, and that Lord Mansfield's glasses had been broken, and a bishop's, but that most of the populace were dispersed. About nine his Royal Highness and Colonel Heywood arrived; and then we heard a much more alarming account. The concourse had been incredible, and had by no means obeyed the injunctions of their apostle, or rather had interpreted the spirit instead of the letter. The Duke had reached the House with the utmost difficulty, and found it sunk from the temple of dignity to an asylum of lamentable objects. There were the Lords Hillsborough, Stormont, Townshend, without their bags, and with their hair dishevelled about their ears, and Lord Willoughby without his periwig, and Lord Mansfield, whose glasses had been broken, quivering on the woolsack like an aspen. Lord Ashburnham had been torn out of his chariot, the Bishop of Lincoln ill-treated, the Duke of Northumberland had lost his watch in the holy hurly-burly, and Mr. Mackenzie his snuff-box and spectacles. Alarm came that the mob had thrown down Lord Boston, and were trampling him to death; which they almost did. They had diswigged Lord Bathurst on his answering them stoutly, and told him he was the pope, and an old woman; thus splitting Pope Joan into two. Lord Hillsborough, on being taxed with negligence, affirmed that the Cabinet had the day before empowered Lord North to take precautions; but two Justices that were called denied having received any orders. Colonel Heywood, a very stout man, and luckily a very cool one, told me he had thrice been collared as he went by the Duke's order to inquire what was doing in the other House; but though he was not suffered to pass, he reasoned the mob into releasing him,—yet, he said, he never saw so serious an appearance and such determined countenances.

"About eight the Lords adjourned, and were suffered to go home; though the rioters declared that if the other House did not repeal the Bill,* there would at night be terrible mischief. Mr. Burke's name had been given out as the object of resentment. General Conway I knew would be intrepid and not give way; nor did he, but inspired the other House with his own resolution.

* An Act passed in 1778 relaxing the penal laws against Roman Catholics.

Lord George Gordon was running backwards and forwards, from the windows of the Speaker's Chamber denouncing all that spoke against him to the mob in the lobby. Mr. Conway tasked him severely both in the House and aside, and Colonel Murray told him he was a disgrace to his family. Still the members were besieged and locked up for four hours, nor could divide, as the lobby was crammed. Mr. Conway and Lord Frederick Cavendish, with whom I supped afterwards, told me there was a moment when they thought they must have opened the doors and fought their way out sword in hand. Lord North was very firm, and at last they got the Guards and cleared the pass.

"Blue banners had been waved from tops of houses at Whitehall as signals to the people, while the coaches passed, whom they should applaud or abuse. Sir George Savile's and Charles Turner's coaches were demolished. Ellis, whom they took for a Popish gentleman, they carried prisoner to the Guildhall in Westminster, and he escaped by a ladder out of a window. Lord Mahon harangued the people from the balcony of a coffee-house, and begged them to retire."

In a letter to Mann he continues the story:

"This tumult, which was over between nine and ten at night, had scarce ceased before it broke out in two other quarters. Old Haslang's* chapel was broken open and plundered; and, as he is a Prince of

* Count Haslang, Minister from the Elector of Bavaria: he had been here from the year 1740.

Smugglers as well as Bavarian Minister, great quantities of run tea and contraband goods were found in his house. This one cannot lament; and still less, as the old wretch has for these forty years usurped a hired house, and, though the proprietor for many years has offered to remit his arrears of rent, he will neither quit the house nor pay for it.

"Monsieur Cordon, the Sardinian Minister, suffered still more. The mob forced his chapel, stole two silver lamps, demolished everything else, threw the benches into the street, set them on fire, carried the brands into the chapel, and set fire to that; and, when the engines came, would not suffer them to play, till the Guards arrived, and saved the house and probably all that part of the town. Poor Madame Cordon was confined by illness. My cousin, Thomas Walpole, who lives in Lincoln's Inn Fields, went to her rescue, and dragged her, for she could scarce stand with terror and weakness, to his own house."

Of the events of Black Wednesday, Horace was an eye-witness. His letters to his Countess form a sort of journal:

"Wednesday, five o'clock, June 7, 1780.

"I am heartily glad I am come to town, though never was a less delicious place; but there was no bearing to remain philosophically in the country, and hear the thousand rumours of every hour, and not know whether one's friends and relations were not destroyed. Yesterday Newgate was burnt, and other houses, and Lord Sandwich near massacred. At Hyde Park Corner, I saw Guards at the Lord President's door, and in Piccadilly, met George Selwyn and the Signorina,* whom I wondered he ventured there. He came into my chaise in a fury, and told me Lord Mansfield's house is in ashes, and that five thousand men were marched to Caen Wood—it is true, and that one thousand of the Guards are gone after them. A camp of ten thousand is forming in Hyde Park as fast as possible, and the Berkshire militia is just arrived. Wedderburn and Lord Stormont are threatened, and I do not know who. The Duchess of Beaufort sent an hour ago to tell me Lord Ashburnham had just advertised her that he is threatened, and was sending away his poor bedridden Countess and children; and the Duchess begged to know what I proposed to do. I immediately went to her, and quieted her, and assured her we are as safe as we can be anywhere, and as little obnoxious; but if she was alarmed, I advised her to remove to Notting Hill, where Lady Mary Coke is absent. The Duchess said the mob were now in Saville Row; we sent thither, and so they are, round Colonel Woodford's, who gave the Guards orders to fire at Lord Mansfield's, where six at least of the rioters were killed.

"The mob are now armed, having seized the stores in the Artillery Ground.

"If anything can surprise your Ladyship, it will be what I am going to tell you. Lord George Gordon

* Mademoiselle Fagniani, Selwyn's adopted daughter.

went to Buckingham House this morning, and asked an audience of the King. Can you be more surprised still? —He was refused.

"I must finish, for I am going about the town to learn, and see, and hear. Caen Wood is saved; a regiment on march met the rioters.

"It will probably be a black night: I am decking myself with blue ribbons, like a May-day garland. Horsemen are riding by with muskets. I am sorry I did not bring the armour of Francis I. to town, as I am to guard a Duchess Dowager and an heiress. Will it not be romantically generous if I yield the latter to my nephew?

"From my garrison in Berkeley Square.

"Wednesday night, past two in the morning, June 7, 1780.

"As it is impossible to go to bed (for Lady Betty Compton has hoped I would not this very minute, which, next to her asking the contrary, is the thing not to be refused), I cannot be better employed than in proving how much I think of your Ladyship at the most horrible moment I ever saw. You shall judge.

"I was at Gloucester House between nine and ten. The servants announced a great fire; the Duchess, her daughters, and I went to the top of the house, and beheld not only one but two vast fires, which we took for the King's Bench and Lambeth; but the latter was the New Prison, and the former at least was burning at midnight. Colonel Heywood came in and acquainted his Royal Highness that nine houses in Great Queen

Street had been gutted, and the furniture burnt; and he had *seen* a great Catholic distiller's at Holborn Bridge broken open and all the casks staved; and since, the house had been set on fire.

"At ten I went to Lord Hertford's, and found him and his sons charging muskets. Lord Rockingham has two hundred soldiers in his house, and is determined to defend it. Thence I went to General Conway's, and in a moment a servant came in and said there was a great fire just by. We went to the street-door and thought it was St. Martin's Lane in flames, but it is either the Fleet Prison or the distiller's. I forgot that in the court of Gloucester House I met Colonel Jennings, who told me there had been an engagement at the Royal Exchange to defend the Bank, and that the Guards had shot sixty of the mob; I have since heard seventy, for I forgot to tell your Ladyship that at a *great* council, held this evening at the Queen's House, at which Lord Rockingham and the Duke of Portland were present, military execution was ordered, for, in truth, the Justices dare not act.

"After supper I returned to Lady Hertford, finding Charing Cross, and the Haymarket, and Piccadilly, illuminated from fear, though all this end of the town is hitherto perfectly quiet, lines being drawn across the Strand and Holborn, to prevent the mob coming westward. Henry and William Conway arrived, and had seen the populace break open the toll-houses on Blackfriars Bridge, and carry off bushels of halfpence, which fell about the streets, and then they set fire to the toll-houses. General Conway's porter had seen five distinct conflagrations.

"Lady Hertford's cook came in, white as this paper. *He is a German Protestant.* He said his house had been attacked, his furniture burnt; that he had saved one child, and left another with his wife, whom he could not get out; and that not above ten or twelve persons had assaulted his house. I could not credit this, at least was sure it was an episode that had no connection with the general insurrection, and was at most some pique of his neighbours. I sent my own footman to the spot in Woodstock Street; he brought me word there had been eight or ten apprentices who made the riot, that two Life Guardsmen had arrived and secured four of the enemies. It seems the cook had refused to illuminate like the rest of the street. To-morrow I suppose his Majesty King George Gordon will order their release; they will be inflated with having been confessors, and turn heroes.

"On coming home I visited the Duchess Dowager and my fair ward; and am heartily tired with so many expeditions, for which I little imagined I had youth enough left.

"We expect three or four more regiments to-morrow, besides some troops of horse and militia already arrived. We are menaced with counter-squadrons from the country. There will, I fear, be much blood spilt before peace is restored. The Gordon has already surpassed Masaniello, who I do not remember set his own capital on fire. Yet I assure your ladyship there is no panic.

Lady Aylesbury has been at the play in the Haymarket, and the Duke and my four nieces at Ranelagh, this evening. For my part, I think the *common* diversions of these last four-and-twenty hours are sufficient to content any moderate appetite; and as it is now three in the morning, I shall wish you good night, and try to get a little sleep myself, if Lord George Macbeth has not murdered it all. I own I shall not soon forget the sight I saw from the top of Gloucester House.

" Thursday morning, after breakfast.

" I do not know whether to call the horrors of the night greater or less than I thought. My printer, who has been out all night, and on the spots of action, says, not above a dozen were killed at the Royal Exchange, some few elsewhere; at the King's Bench, he does not know how many; but in other respects the calamities are dreadful. He saw many houses set on fire, women and children screaming, running out of doors with what they could save, and knocking one another down with their loads in the confusion. Barnard's Inn is burnt, and some houses, mistaken for Catholic. Kirgate* says most of the rioters are apprentices, and plunder and drink have been their chief objects, and both women and men are still lying dead drunk about the streets: brandy is preferable to enthusiasm. I trust many more troops will arrive to-day. What families ruined! What wretched wives and mothers! What public disgrace! —ay! and where, and when, and how will all this con-

* Walpole's printer.

fusion end! and what shall we be when it is concluded? I remember the Excise and the Gin Act, and the rebels at Derby, and Wilkes's interlude, and the French at Plymouth; or I should have a very bad memory; but I never till last night saw London and Southwark in flames!

"After dinner.

"It is a moment, Madam, when to be surprised is not surprising. But what will you say to the House of Commons meeting by twelve o'clock to-day, and adjourning, ere fifty members were arrived, to Monday se'nnight! So adieu all government but the sword!

"Will your Ladyship give me credit when I heap contradictions on absurdities — will you believe such confusion and calamities, and yet think there is no consternation? Well, only hear. My niece, Mrs. Keppel, with her three daughters, drove since noon over Westminster Bridge, through St. George's Fields, where the King's Bench is smoking, over London Bridge, passed the Bank, and came the whole length of the City! They have been here, and say the people *look* very unquiet; but can one imagine that they would be smiling? Old Lady Albemarle, who followed me in a few minutes from Gloucester House, was robbed at Mrs. Keppel's door in Pall Mall, between ten and eleven, by a horseman. Sparrow, one of the delivered convicts, who was to have been hanged this morning, is said to have been shot yesterday as he was spiriting up the rioters. Kirgate has just heard in the Park, that the Protestant Association disavow the seditious, and will take up arms against them. If we are saved, it will be so as by fire.

"I shall return to my own castle to-morrow: I had not above four hours' sleep last night, and must get some rest. General Conway is enraged at the adjournment, and will go away too. Many coaches and chaises did leave London yesterday. My intelligence will not be so good nor so immediate; but you will not want correspondents. Disturbances are threatened again for to-night; and some probably will happen, but there are more troops, and less alacrity in the outlaws.

"Berkeley Square, June 9, at noon, 1780.

"All has been quiet to-night, as far as we know in this region; but not without blood being spilt yesterday. The rioters attacked the Horse Guards about six in Fleet Street, and, not giving them time to load, were repelled by the bayonet. Twenty fell, thirty-five were wounded and sent to the hospital, where two died directly. Three of the Guards were wounded, and a young officer named Marjoribank. Mr. Conway's footman told me he was on a message at Lord Amherst's when the Guards returned, and that their bayonets were steeped in blood.

"I heard, too, at my neighbour Duchess's, whither I went at one in the morning, that the Protestant Associators, disguised with blue cockades as friends, had fallen on the rioters in St. George's Fields, and killed many. I do not warrant the truth, but I did hear often in the evening that there had been slaughter in the Borough, where a great public-house had been destroyed, and a house at Redriffe, and another at Islington. Zeal has entirely thrown off the mask, and owned its name—plunder. Its offspring have extorted money from several houses with threats of firing them as Catholic. Apprentices and Irish chairmen, and all kinds of outlaws, have been the most active. Some hundreds are actually dead about the streets, with the spirits they plundered at the distiller's; the low women knelt and sucked them as they ran from the staved casks.

"It was reported last night that the primate, George Gordon, is fled to Scotland: for aught I know he may not be so far off as Grosvenor Place. All is rumour and exaggeration; and yet it would be difficult to exaggerate the horrors of Wednesday night; a town taken by storm could alone exceed them.

"I am going to Strawberry this instant, exhausted with fatigue, for I have certainly been on my feet longer these last eight-and-forty hours than in forty days before. . . .

"Adieu! Madam; allow my pen a few holidays, unless the storm recommences."

On hearing that Lord George Gordon had been arrested, he writes again:

"Strawberry Hill, Saturday night, late.

"Was not I cruelly out of luck, Madam, to have been

fishing in troubled waters for two days for your Ladyship's entertainment, and to have come away very few hours before the great pike was hooked? Well, to drop metaphor, here are Garth's lines reversed,

> 'Thus little villains oft submit to fate,
> That great ones may enjoy the world in state.'

Four convicts on the eve of execution are let loose from Newgate, and Lord George Gordon is sent to the Tower. If he is hanged, the old couplet will recover its credit, for Mr. Wedderburn is Chief Justice.

"I flatter myself I shall receive a line from your Ladyship to-morrow morning: I am impatient to hear what you think of *black Wednesday*. I know how much you must have been shocked, but I long to read your own expressions; when you answer, then one is conversing. My sensations are very different from what they were. While in the thick of the conflagration, I was all indignation and a thousand passions. Last night, when sitting silently alone, horror rose as I cooled; and grief succeeded, and then all kinds of gloomy presages. For some time people have said, where will all this end? I as often replied, where will it begin? It is now begun, with a dreadful overture; and I tremble to think what the chorus may be! The sword reigns at present, and saved the capital! What is to depose the sword?—Is it not to be feared, on the other hand, that other swords may be lifted up?—What probability that everything will subside quietly into the natural channel?—Nay, how narrow will that channel be, whenever the prospect is cleared by peace? What a dismal fragment of an empire! yet would that moment were come when we are to take a survey of our ruins! That moment I probably shall not see. When I rose this morning, I found the exertions I had made with such puny powers, had been far beyond what I could bear; I was too sick to go on with dressing myself. This evening I have been abroad, and you shall hear no more of it. I have been with Lady Di, at Richmond, where I found Lady Pembroke, Miss Herbert, and Mr. Brudenell. Lord Herbert is arrived. They told me the melancholy position of Lady Westmorland. She is sister of Lord George Gordon, and wife of Colonel Woodford, who is forced to conceal himself, having been the first officer who gave orders to the soldiers to fire, on the attack of Lord Mansfield's house. How many still more deplorable calamities from the tragedy of this week that one shall never hear of! I will change my style, and, like an epilogue after a moving piece, divert you with a *bon-mot* of George Selwyn. He came to me yesterday morning from Lady Townshend, who, terrified by the fires of the preceding night, talked the language of the Court, instead of Opposition. He said she put him in mind of removed tradesmen, who hang out a board with, 'Burnt out from over the way.' Good-night, Madam, till I receive your letter.

"Monday morning, the 12th.

"Disappointed! disappointed! not a line from your Ladyship; I will not send away this till I hear from you. Last night, at Hampton Court, I heard of two Popish chapels demolished at Bath, and one at Bristol. My coachman has just been in Twickenham, and says half Bath is burnt; I trust this is but the natural progress of lies, that increase like a chairman's legs by walking. Mercy on us! we seem to be plunging into the horrors of France, in the reigns of Charles VI. and VII.!—yet, as extremes meet, there is at this moment amazing insensibility. Within these four days I have received five applications for tickets to see my house! One from a set of company who fled from town to avoid the tumults and fires. I suppose Æneas lost Creüsa by her stopping at Sadlers' Wells.

"13th.

"The letter I have this moment received is so kind, Madam, that it effaces all disappointment. Indeed, my impatience made me forget that no post comes in here on Mondays. To-day's letters from town mention no disturbance at Bristol or anywhere else. Every day gained is considerable, at least will be so when there has been time for the history of last week to have spread, and intelligence from the distant counties to be returned. All I have heard to-day is of some alteration to be made to the Riot Act, that Lord George cannot be tried this month, and that the King will go to the House on Monday. I will now answer what is necessary in your Ladyship's and take my leave, for, as you observe, the post arrives late, and I have other letters that I must answer. Mr. Williams interrupted me, and has added a curious anecdote,—and a horrible one, to my collection of the late events. One project of the diabolical incendiaries was to let loose the lions in the Tower, and the lunatics in Bedlam. The latter might be from a fellow-feeling in Lord George, but cannibals do not invite wild beasts to their banquets. The Princess Daskiou will certainly communicate the thought to her mistress and accomplice, the Legislatress of Russia.

" P.S. I like an ironic sentence in yesterday's *London Courant*, which says, all our grievances are *red-dressed*."

To complete the misfortunes of these years, Walpole lost his "blind old woman" in the autumn of 1780. Under date October 9th, he writes from Strawberry Hill to Mann:

" I have heard from Paris of the death of my dear old friend Madame du Deffand, whom I went so often thither to see. It was not quite unexpected, and was softened by her great age, eighty-four, which forbad distant hopes; and, by what I dreaded more than her death, her increasing deafness, which, had it become, like her blindness, total, would have been living after death. Her memory only *began* to impair; her amazing sense and quickness, not at all. I have written to her once a week for these last fifteen years, as correspondence and conversation could be her only pleasures. You see that I am the most faithful letter-writer in the world—and, alas! never see those I am so constant to! One is forbidden common-place reflections on these misfortunes, because they *are* common-place; but is not that, because they are natural? But your never having known that dear old woman is a better reason for not making you the butt of my concern."

Three weeks later we have the following from London to Lady Ossory:

"As I have been returned above a fortnight, I should have written had I had a syllable to tell you; but what could I tell you from that melancholy and very small circle at Twickenham Park, almost the only place I do go to in the country, partly out of charity, and partly as I have scarce any other society left which I prefer to it; for, without entering on too melancholy a detail, recollect, Madam, that I have outlived most of those to whom I was habituated, Lady Hervey, Lady Suffolk, Lady Blandford — my dear old friend [Madame du Deffand], I should probably never have seen again — yet that is a deeper loss, indeed! She has left me all her MSS. — a compact between us — in one word I had, at her earnest request, consented to accept them, on condition she should leave me nothing else. She had, indeed, intended to leave me her little all, but I declared I would never set foot in Paris again (this was ten years ago) if she did not engage to retract that destination. To satisfy her, I at last agreed to accept her papers, and one thin gold box with the portrait of her dog. I have written to beg her dog itself, which is so cross, that I am sure nobody else would treat it well; and I have ordered her own servant, who read all letters to her, to pick out all the letters of living persons, and restore them to the several writers without my seeing them."

Walpole's liking for accomplished French women like Madame du Deffand was equalled by his dislike of the English "Blue-stockings." At the beginning of 1781, he seems to have been a good deal in company with the latter, and we have some amusing passages: "I met Mrs. Montagu t'other night at a visit. She said she had been alone the whole preceding day, *quite hermetically sealed*—I was very glad she was uncorked, or I might have missed that piece of learned nonsense. . . . I was much diverted with your setting Mrs. Montagu on her head, which indeed she does herself without the help of Hermes. She is one of my principal entertainments at Mrs. Vesey's, who collects all the graduates and candidates for fame, where they vie with one another, till they are as unintelligible as the good folks at Babel."

"Mr. Gilpin* talks of my researches, which makes me smile; I know, as Gray would have said, how little I have *researched*, and what slender pretensions are mine to so pompous a term. Apropos to Gray, Johnson's 'Life,' or rather criticism on his Odes, is come out; a most wretched, dull, tasteless, *verbal* criticism—yet, timid too. But he makes amends, he admires Thom-

---

* Author of an "Essay on Prints," the third edition of which he dedicated to Horace Walpole.

son and Akenside, and Sir Richard Blackmore, and has reprinted Dennis's 'Criticism on Cato,' to save time, and swell his pay. In short, as usual, he has proved that he has no more ear than taste. Mrs. Montagu and all her Mænades intend to tear him limb from limb for despising their moppet Lord Lyttelton."

" I saw Dr. Johnson last night at Lady Lucan's, who had assembled a *blue-stocking* meeting in imitation of Mrs. Vesey's Babels. It was so blue, it was quite Mazarine-blue. Mrs. Montagu kept aloof from Johnson, like the West from the East. There were Soame Jenyns, *Persian* Jones, Mr. Sherlocke, the new court with Mr. Courtenay, besides the out-pensioners of Parnassus. Mr. Wraxall* was not, I wonder why, and so will he, for he is popping into every spot where he can make himself talked of, by talking of himself; but I hear he will come to an untimely beginning in the House of Commons."

* Afterwards Sir Nathaniel William Wraxall, Bart., known by his " Memoirs of His Own Life."

CHAPTER VIII.

Walpole in his Sixty-fourth Year.—The Royal Academy.—Tonton.—Charles Fox.—William Pitt.—Mrs. Hobart's *Sans Souci.*—Improvements at Florence.—Walpole's Dancing Feats.—No Feathers at Court.—Highwaymen.—Loss of the *Royal George.*—Mrs. Siddons.—Peace.—Its Social Consequences.—The Coalition.—The Rivals.—Political Excitement.—The Westminster Election.—Political Caricatures.—Conway's Retirement.—Lady Harrington.—Balloons.—Illness.—Recovery.

"I NEVER remonstrate against the behests of Dame Prudence, though a lady I never got acquainted with till near my grand climacteric." So wrote Horace soon after passing the mystic period, compounded of seven and nine, which was once regarded as the topmost round in the ladder of human life. He would have his correspondents believe that his attention to the dame's commands was not very regular at first. In the spring of 1781, he is able to report to Conway, " My health is most flourishing for me." Accordingly, he goes about a good deal, and enjoys a sort of rejuvenescence. Of course, he visits the Exhibition of the Royal Academy at Somerset House, where Reynolds's picture of the Ladies Waldegrave was shown. " The Exhibition," he writes to Mason, "is much inferior to last year's;* nobody shines there but Sir Joshua and Gainsborough. The head of the former's Dido is very fine; I do not admire the rest of the piece. His Lord Richard Cavendish is bold and stronger than he ever coloured. The picture of my three nieces is charming. Gainsborough has two pieces with land and sea, so free and natural that one steps back for fear of being splashed. The back front of the Academy is handsome, but like the other to the street, the members are so heavy, that one cannot stand back enough to see it in any proportion, unless in a barge moored in the middle of the Thames." The same day, May 6, he writes to Conway from Strawberry Hill:

"Though it is a bitter north-east, I came hither to-day to look at my lilacs, though *à la glace;* and to get from pharaoh, for which there is a rage. I doated on it above thirty years ago; but it is not decent to sit up all night now with boys and girls. My nephew, Lord Cholmondeley, the banker *à la mode*, has been demolished. He and his associate, Sir Willoughby Aston, went early t'other night to Brooks's, before Charles Fox and Fitzpatrick, who keep a bank there, were come; but they soon arrived, attacked their rivals, broke their bank, and won above four thousand pounds. 'There,' said Fox, 'so should all usurpers be served!' He did still better; for he sent for his tradesmen, and paid as far as the money would go. In the

* This was the second Exhibition at Somerset House. The first was in May, 1780.

mornings he continues his war on Lord North, but cannot break *that* bank. . . .

"I told you in my last that Tonton was arrived. I brought him this morning to take possession of his new villa, but his inauguration has not been at all pacific. As he has already found out that he may be as despotic as at St. Joseph's, he began with exiling my beautiful little cat; upon which, however, we shall not quite agree. He then flew at one of my dogs, who returned it by biting his foot till it bled, but was severely beaten for it. I immediately rung for Margaret to dress his foot; but in the midst of my tribulation could not keep my countenance; for she cried, 'Poor little thing, he does not understand my language!' I hope she will not recollect, too, that he is a Papist!"

We have a further anecdote of Charles Fox told a few days later, also in a letter to Conway:

"I had been to see if Lady Aylesbury was come to town: as I came up St. James's Street, I saw a cart and porters at Charles's door; coppers and old chests of drawers loading. In short, his success at faro has awakened his host of creditors; but unless his bank has swelled to the size of the Bank of England, it could not have yielded a sop apiece for each. Epsom, too, had been unpropitious; and one creditor has actually seized and carried off his goods, which did not seem worth removing. As I returned full of this scene, whom should I find sauntering by my own door but Charles? He came up, and talked to me at the coach-window on the Marriage Bill,* with as much *sang-froid* as if he knew nothing of what had happened. I have no admiration for insensibility to one's own faults, especially when committed out of vanity. Perhaps the whole philosophy consisted in the commission. If *you* could have been as much to blame, the last thing you would bear well would be your own reflections. The more marvellous Fox's parts are, the more one is provoked at his follies, which comfort so many rascals and blockheads, and make all that is admirable and amiable in him only matter of regret to those who like him as I do.†

* On the 7th of June, Mr. Fox moved for leave to bring in a bill to amend the Act of the 26th of George II., for preventing clandestine marriages. The bill passed the Commons, but was rejected by the Lords.

† "Mr. Fox never had much intimate intercourse with Horace Walpole; did not, I think, like him at all; had no opinion of his judgment or conduct; probably had imbibed some prejudice against him, for his ill-usage of his father; and certainly entertained an unfavourable, and even unjust, opinion of his abilities as a writer." So says Lord Vassall-Holland in one of the passages from his pen printed in Russell's Memorials of Fox. See vol. i., p. 276. It may be mentioned here, that Lord Holland's Collections for the Life of Fox, which are contained in the work just referred to, include numerous extracts from manuscript papers of Horace Walpole. "These papers, the property of Lord Waldegrave, were lent to me," says Lord Holland, "and have been long in my possession." That the manuscripts to which Lord Holland thus had access comprised the portion of Walpole's correspondence with Mann, which was first published in 1843, appears by several passages which his lordship quotes from these letters. Is it possible that this circumstance may furnish a solution of the ethnological question, to which we have adverted on p. 141, as to the descent of Macaulay's New Zealander from Walpole's Peruvian? From 1831 Macaulay had been an *habitué* of Holland House. Trevelyan's "Life of Lord Macaulay," vol. i. p. 176, et seq.

"I did intend to settle at Strawberry on Sunday; but must return on Thursday, for a party made at Marlborough House for Princess Amelia. I am continually tempted to retire entirely; and should, if I did not see how very unfit English tempers are for living quite out of the world. We grow abominably peevish and severe on others, if we are not constantly rubbed against and polished by them. I need not name friends and relations of yours and mine as instances. My prophecy on the short reign of faro is verified already. The bankers find that all the calculated advantages of the game do not balance pinchbeck *parolis* and debts of honourable women. The bankers, I think, might have had a previous and more generous reason, the very bad air of holding a bank:—but this country is as hardened against the *petite morale*, as against the greater.— What should I think of the world if I quitted it entirely?"

Again a few days, and we come upon an early mention of the youthful William Pitt: "The young William Pitt has again displayed paternal oratory. The other day, on the Commission of Accounts, he answered Lord North, and tore him limb from limb. If Charles Fox could feel, one should think such a rival, with an unspotted character, would rouse him. What if a Pitt and Fox should again be rivals!" Some time later, Walpole asks Lady Ossory: "Apropos of *bon-mots*, has our lord told you that George Selwyn calls Mr. Fox and Mr. Pitt 'the idle and the industrious apprentices'? If he has not, I am sure you will thank me, Madam."

In the summer of 1781, Horace has a touch of rheumatism, but still he keeps up his juvenile tone. Witness the two following letters to Lady Ossory:

"Strawberry Hill, July 7, 1781.

" You must be, or will be, tired of my letters, Madam ; every one is a contradiction to the last ; there is alternately a layer of complaints, and a layer of foolish spirits. To-day the wind is again in the dolorous corner. For these four days I have been confined with a pain and swelling in my face. The apothecary says it is owing to the long drought ; but as I should not eat grass were there ever such plenty, and as my cows, though starving, have no swelled cheeks, I do not believe him. I humbly attribute my frequent disorders to my longevity, and to that Proteus the gout, who is not the less himself for being incog. Excuses I have worn out, and, therefore, will not make any for not obeying your kind invitation again to Ampthill. I can only say, I go nowhere, even when Tonton is invited— except to balls—and yet though I am the last Vestris that has appeared, Mrs. Hobart did not invite me to her *Sans Souci* last week, though she had all my other juvenile contemporaries, Lady Berkeley, Lady Fitzroy, Lady Margaret Compton, and Mrs. French, etc. Perhaps you do not know that the lady of the *fête*, having made as many conquests as the King of Prussia, has borrowed the name of that hero's villa for her hut on

Ham Common, where she has built two large rooms of timber under a cabbage. Her field officers, General French, General Compton, etc., were sweltered in the ball-room, and then frozen at supper in tents on the grass. She herself, as intrepid as King Frederic, led the ball, though dying of the toothache, which she had endeavoured to drown in laudanum; but she has kept her bed ever since the campaign ended.

"This is all I know in the world, for the war seems to have taken laudanum too, and to keep its bed.

"I have received a letter to-day from Sir Horace Mann, who tells me the Great-Duke has been making *wondrous improvements* at Florence. He has made a passage through the Tribune, and built a brave new French room of stucco in white and gold, and placed the Niobe in it; but as everybody is tired of her telling her old story, she and all the Master and Miss Niobes are orderly disposed round the chamber, and if anybody asks who they are, I suppose they answer, Francis Charles Ferdinand Ignatius Neopomucenus, or Maria Theresa Christina Beatrice, etc. Well, Madam, have I any cause to sigh that the pictures at Houghton are transported to the North Pole, if the Tribune at Florence is demolished by Vandals, and Niobe and her progeny dance a *cotillon?* O sublunary grandeur, short-lived as a butterfly! We smile at a clown who graves the initials of his name, or the shape of his shoe, on the leads of a church, in hopes of being remembered, and yet he is as much known as king I don't know whom, who built the Pyramids to eternise his memory. Methinks Anacreon was the only sensible philosopher. If I loved wine, and should look well in a chaplet of roses, I would crown myself with flowers, and go tipsy to bed every night *sans souci*.

"July 25, 1781.

" Poor human nature, what a contradiction it is! to-day it is all rheumatism and morality, and sits with a death's head before it: to-morrow it is dancing!—Oh! my Lady, my Lady, what will you say, when the next thing you hear of me after my last letter is, that I have danced three country-dances with a whole set, forty years younger than myself! Shall not you think I have been chopped to shreds and boiled in Medea's kettle? Shall not you expect to see a print of Vestris teaching me?—and Lord Brudenell dying with envy? You may stare with all your expressive eyes, yet the fact is true. Danced—I do not absolutely say, *danced*—but I swam down three dances very gracefully, with the air that was so much in fashion after the battle of Oudenarde, and that was still taught when I was fifteen, and that I remember General Churchill practising before a glass in a gouty shoe.

" To be sure you die with impatience to know the particulars. You must know then—for all my revels must out—I not only went five miles to Lady Aylesford's ball last Friday, but my nieces, the Waldegraves, desired me there to let them come to me for a few days, as they had been disappointed about a visit they were to make at another place; but that is neither here nor there. Well, here they are, and last night we went to

Lady Hertford at Ditton. Soon after, Lady North and her daughters arrived, and besides Lady Elizabeth and Lady Bell Conways, there were their brothers Hugh and George. All the *jeunesse* strolled about the garden. We ancients, with the Earl and Colonel Keene, retired from the dew into the drawing-room. Soon after, the two youths and seven nymphs came in, and shut the door of the hall. In a moment, we heard a burst of laughter, and thought we distinguished something like the scraping of a fiddle. My curiosity was raised, I opened the door, and found four couples and a half standing up, and a miserable violin from the ale-house. 'Oh,' said I, 'Lady Bell shall not want a partner;' I threw away my stick, and *me voilà dansant comme un charme!* At the end of the third dance, Lord North and his son, in boots, arrived. 'Come,' said I, 'my Lord, you may dance, if I have'—but it ended in my *resigning my place* to his son.

"Lady North has invited us for to-morrow, and I shall reserve the rest of my letter for the second volume of my regeneration; however, I declare I will not *dance*. I will not make myself too cheap; I should have the Prince of Wales sending for me three or four times a week to hops in Eastcheap. As it is, I feel I shall have some difficulty to return to my old dowagers, at the Duchess of Montrose's, and shall be humming the Hempdressers, when they are scolding me for playing in flush.

"Friday, the 27th.

"I am not only a prophet, but have more command

of my passions than such impetuous gentry as prophets are apt to have. We found the fiddles as I foretold; and yet I kept my resolution and did *not* dance, though the Sirens invited me, and though it would have shocked the dignity of old Tiffany Ellis, who would have thought it an indecorum. The two younger Norths and Sir Ralph Payne supplied my place. I played at cribbage with the matrons, and we came away at midnight. So if I now and then do cut a colt's tooth, I have it drawn immediately. I do not know a paragraph of news—the nearer the minister, the farther from politics.

"P.S. My next jubilee dancing shall be with Lady Gertrude."

Not long after the date of these letters, Mann sends news of further improvements at Florence. Walpole answers:

"The decree* you sent me against high heads diverted me. It is as necessary here, but would not have such expeditious effect. The Queen has never admitted feathers at Court; but, though the nation has grown excellent courtiers, Fashion remained in opposition, and not a plume less was worn anywhere else. Some centuries ago, the Clergy preached against monstrous head-dresses; but Religion had no more power than our Queen. It is better to leave the Mode to its own vagaries; if she is not contradicted, she seldom remains long in the same mood. She is very despotic; but

* An ordinance of the Great-Duke against high head-dresses.

though her reign is endless, her laws are repealed as fast as made."

The frequency of highway robberies only a century ago sounds surprising to the present generation. Horace recounts to Lady Ossory an adventure of this kind which befell him and his friend and neighbour, Lady Browne, in the autumn of this jovial 1781:

"The night I had the honour of writing to your Ladyship last, I was robbed—and, as if I were a sovereign or a nation, have had a discussion ever since whether it was not a *neighbour* who robbed me—and should it come to the ears of the newspapers, it might produce as ingenious a controversy amongst our anonymous wits as any of the noble topics I have been mentioning. *Voici le fait.* Lady Browne and I were, as usual, going to the Duchess of Montrose at seven o'clock. The evening was very dark. In the close lane under her park-pale, and within twenty yards of the gate, a black figure on horseback pushed by between the chaise and the hedge on my side. I suspected it was a highwayman, and so I found did Lady Browne, for she was speaking and stopped. To divert her fears, I was just going to say, Is not that the apothecary going to the Duchess? when I heard a voice cry 'Stop!' and the figure came back to the chaise. I had the presence of mind, before I let down the glass, to take out my watch and stuff it within my waistcoat under my arm. He said, 'Your purses and watches!' I replied, 'I have no watch.' 'Then your purse!' I gave it to him; it had nine guineas. It was so dark that I could not see his hand, but felt him take it. He then asked for Lady Browne's purse, and said, 'Don't be frightened; I will not hurt you.' I said, 'No; you won't frighten the lady?' He replied, 'No; I give you my word I will do you no hurt.' Lady Browne gave him her purse, and was going to add her watch, but he said, 'I am much obliged to you! I wish you good-night!' pulled off his hat, and rode away. 'Well,' said I, 'Lady Browne, you will not be afraid of being robbed another time, for you see there is nothing in it.' 'Oh! but I am,' said she, 'and now I am in terrors lest he should return, for I have given him a purse with only bad money that I carry on purpose.' 'He certainly will not open it directly,' said I, 'and at worst he can only wait for us at our return; but I will send my servant back for a horse and a blunderbuss,' which I did. The next distress was not to terrify the Duchess, who is so paralytic and nervous. I therefore made Lady Browne go into the parlour, and desired one of the Duchess's servants to get her a glass of water, while I went into the drawing-room to break it to the Duchess. 'Well,' said I, laughing to her and the rest of the company, 'you won't get much from us to-night.' 'Why,' said one of them, 'have you been robbed?' 'Yes, a little,' said I. The Duchess trembled; but it went off. Her groom of the chambers said not a word, but slipped out, and Lady Margaret and Miss Howe having servants there on horseback, he gave them pistols and despatched them different ways. This was exceedingly clever, for he knew the Duchess would not have suffered it, as lately he had detected a man who had robbed her garden, and she would not allow him to take up the fellow. These servants spread the story, and when my footman arrived on foot, he was stopped in the street by the ostler of the 'George,' who told him the highwayman's horse was then in the stable; but this part I must reserve for the second volume, for I have made this no story so long and so tedious that your Ladyship will not be able to read it in a breath; and the second part is so much longer and so much less, contains so many examinations of witnesses, so many contradictions in the depositions, which I have taken myself, and, I must confess, with such abilities and shrewdness that I have found out nothing at all, that I think to defer the prosecution of my narrative till all the other inquisitions on the anvil are liquidated, lest your Ladyship's head, strong as it is, should be confounded, and you should imagine that Rodney or Ferguson was the person who robbed us in Twickenham Lane. I would not have detailed the story at all, if you were not in a forest, where it will serve to put you to sleep as well as a newspaper full of lies; and I am sure there is as much dignity in it as in the combined fleet, and ours, popping in and out alternately, like a man and woman in a weather-house."

A few months later he writes to his Countess:

"Strawberry Hill, Aug. 31, 1782.

"It is very strange indeed, Madam, that you should make me excuses for writing, or think that I have anything better, or even more urgent, to do than to read your letters. It is very true that the Duchess de la Vallière, in a hand which I could not decypher, has recommended Count Soltikoff and his wife to me: but, oh! my shame, I have not yet seen them. I did mean to go to town to-day on purpose, but I have had the gout in my right eyelid, and it was swelled yesterday as big as a walnut; being now shrunk to less than a pistachio, I propose in two or three days to make my appearance. Luckily the Countess was born in England, the daughter of the former Czernichew, and she is in such terrors of highwaymen, that I shall be quit for a breakfast; so it is an ill highwayman that blows nobody good. In truth, it would be impossible, in this region, to amass a set of company for dinner to meet them. The Hertfords, Lady Holdernesse, and Lady Mary Coke did dine here on Thursday, but were armed as if going to Gibraltar; and Lady Cecilia Johnston would not venture even from Petersham—for in the town of Richmond they rob even before dusk—to such perfection are all the arts brought! Who would have thought that the war with America would make it impossible to stir from one village to another? yet so it literally is. The Colonies took off all our commodities down to highwaymen. Now being forced to mew, and then turn them out, like pheasants, the roads are stocked with them, and they are so tame that they even come into houses.

"I have just been reading a most entertaining book, which I will recommend to you, as you are grown antiquaries: I don't know whether it is published yet, for the author sent it to me. Part was published some time ago in the 'Archæologia,' and is almost the only paper in that mass of rubbish that has a grain of common sense. It is 'Mr. E. King on ancient Castles.' You will see how comfortably and delectably our potent ancestors lived, when in the constant state of war to which we are coming. Earls, barons, and their fair helpmates lived pell-mell in dark dungeons with their own soldiers, as the poorest cottagers do now with their pigs. I shall repent decking Strawberry so much, if I must turn it into a garrison.

"Mr. Vernon was your Ladyship's informant about the Soltikoffs; but he gave me more credit for my intended civilities than I deserved. The French do not conceive, when they address strangers to us, that we do not at all live in their style. It is no trouble to them, who have miscellaneous dinners or suppers, to ask one or two more; nor are they at any expense in language, as everybody speaks French. In the private way in which I live, it is troublesome to give a formal dinner to foreigners, and more so to find company for them in a circle of dowagers, who would only jabber English scandal out of the *Morning Post*. . . .

"Just this moment I hear the shocking loss of the *Royal George!* Admiral Kempenfelt is a loss indeed; but I confess I feel more for the hundreds of poor babes who have lost their parents! If one grows ever so indifferent, some new calamity calls one back to this deplorable war! If one is willing to content one's self, in a soaking autumn, with a match broken, or with the death of a Prince Duodecimus, a clap of thunder awakens one, and one hears that Britain herself has lost an arm or a leg. I have been expecting a deluge, and a famine, and such casualties as enrich a Sir Richard Baker; but we have all King David's options at once! and what was his option before he was anointed, freebooting too?

"Drowned as we are, the country never was in such beauty; the herbage and leafage are luxurious. The Thames gives itself Rhone airs, and almost foams; it is none of your home-brewed rivers that Mr. Brown makes with a spade and a watering-pot. Apropos, Mr. Duane,* like a good housewife, in the middle of his grass-plot, has planted a pump and a watering-trough for his cow, and I suppose on Saturdays dries his towels and neckcloths on his orange-trees; but I must have done, or the post will be gone."

At the end of 1782, Mrs. Siddons was the talk of the town. Prejudiced as Walpole was apt to be in his judgments of actors, as of authors, his impressions of this famous actress will be read with interest:

"I have been for two days in town, and seen Mrs. Siddons. She pleased me beyond my expectation, but not up to the admiration of the *ton*, two or three of whom were in the same box with me. . . . Mr. Crawford asked me if I did not think her the best actress I

---

* A neighbour at Twickenham.

ever saw? I said, 'By no means; we old folks were apt to be prejudiced in favour of our first impressions.' She is a good figure, handsome enough, though neither nose nor chin according to the Greek standard, beyond which both advance a good deal. Her hair is either red, or she has no objection to its being thought so, and had used red powder. Her voice is clear and good; but I thought she did not vary its modulations enough, nor ever approach enough to the familiar—but this may come when more habituated to the awe of the audience of the capital. Her action is proper, but with little variety; when without motion, her arms are not genteel. Thus you see all my objections are very trifling; but what I really wanted, but did not find, was originality, which announces genius, and without both which I am never intrinsically pleased. All Mrs. Siddons did, good sense or good instruction might give. I dare to say, that were I one-and-twenty, I should have thought her marvellous; but alas! I remember Mrs. Porter and the Dumesnil—and remember every accent of the former in the very same part. Yet this is not entirely prejudice: don't I equally recollect the whole progress of Lord Chatham and Charles Townshend, and does it hinder my thinking Mr. Fox a prodigy?—Pray don't send him this paragraph too."

Again:

"Mrs. Siddons continues to be the mode, and to be modest and sensible. She declines great dinners, and says her business and the cares of her family take up her whole time. When Lord Carlisle carried her the tribute-money from Brooks's, he said she was not *maniérée* enough. 'I suppose she was grateful,' said my niece, Lady Maria. Mrs. Siddons was desired to play ' Medea ' and ' Lady Macbeth.'—' No,' she replied ' she did not look on them as female characters.' She was questioned about her transactions with Garrick: she said, ' He did nothing but put her out; that he told her she moved her right hand when it should have been her left. In short,' said she, ' I found I must not shade the tip of his nose.' "

The war was now over. Lord North had fallen; his successor, Lord Rockingham, was dead; and Lord Shelburne, who had grasped the helm in spite of Fox, had to meet the demands of the victorious Colonists and their French allies, with the certainty that whatever he arranged would be distasteful to his countrymen, and bitterly opposed by the partisans both of his rival and of North. With the first weeks of 1783 came news of peace. Horace writes about it, in almost the same words, to Mann and Lady Ossory, his two chief correspondents at this time: " Peace is arrived. I cannot express how glad I am. I care not a straw what the terms are, which I believe I know more imperfectly than anybody in London. I am not apt to love details—my wish was to have peace, and the next to see America secure of its liberty. Whether it will make good use of it, is another point. It has an opportunity that never occurred in the world before, of being able to select the best parts of every known constitution; but I suppose it will not, as too prejudiced against royalty to adopt it, even as a corrective of aristocracy and democracy." He anticipates that highway robberies will grow more daring on the disbanding of troops, and that there will be an inundation of French visitors. In less than six months he was able to boast that both his prophecies had been fulfilled. In June, he describes how, on a dark and rainy night, Strawberry Hill was invaded by the French Ambassador at the head of a large party:

"Of all houses upon earth, mine, from the painted glass and over-hanging trees, wants the sun the most; besides the Star Chamber and passage being obscured on purpose to raise the Gallery. They ran their foreheads against Henry VII., and took the grated door of the Tribune for the dungeon of the castle. I mustered all the candlesticks in the house, but before they could be lighted up, the young ladies, who, by the way, are extremely natural, agreeable, and civil, were seized with a panic of highwaymen, and wanted to go. I laughed, and said, I believed there was no danger, for that I had not been robbed these two years. However, I was not quite in the right; they were stopped in Knightsbridge by two footpads, but Lady Pembroke having lent them a servant besides their own, they escaped."

Shortly afterwards he writes to Mann:

"We have swarms of French daily; but they come as if they had laid wagers that there is no such place as England, and only wanted to verify its existence, or that they had a mind to dance a minuet on English ground; for they turn on their heel the moment after landing. Three came to see this house last week, and walked through it literally while I wrote eight lines of a letter; for I heard them go up the stairs, and heard them go down, exactly in the time I was finishing no longer a paragraph. It were happy for me had nobody more curiosity than a Frenchman; who is never struck with anything but what he has seen every day at Paris. I am tormented all day and every day by people that come to see my house, and have no enjoyment of it in summer. It would be even in vain to say that the plague is here. I remember such a report in London when I was a child, and my uncle, Lord Townshend, then Secretary of State, was forced to send guards to keep off the crowd from the house in which the plague was said to be; they would go and *see* the plague!"

Walpole apologises to his diplomatic correspondent for dwelling on such trifling topics. "The Peace," he says, "has closed the chapter of important news, which was all our correspondence lived on." The period of dulness and inaction, however, came to an end with the close of the Parliamentary vacation. The Coalition Government of Fox and Lord North, which had superseded Lord Shelburne in the spring, was now fairly brought to the bar of public opinion. Walpole, who had offended Fox's adherents by the part he had played in the intrigues[*]

[*] There can be no doubt that Horace about this time, as on former occasions, had dreamed of seeing Conway in the position of

which followed on the death of Lord Rockingham, sought to retrieve his character by an eager support of the new Administration. He was loud in his praises of Fox's masterly eloquence and strong sense. He now disparages Fox's chief opponent. "His competitor, Mr. Pitt," says Horace, "appears by no means an adequate rival. Just like their fathers, Mr. Pitt has brilliant language, Mr. Fox solid sense; and such luminous powers of displaying it clearly, that mere Eloquence is but a Bristol stone, when set by the diamond Reason." The country at this moment was agitated by the debates on Fox's celebrated India Bill. This measure was being carried by triumphant majorities through the Lower House, and, as Walpole thought, the Opposition did not expect to succeed even in the House of Lords. He goes so far as to add, " Mr. Pitt's reputation is much sunk ; nor, though he is a much more correct logician than his father, has he the same firmness and perseverance. It is no wonder that he was dazzled by his own premature fame ; yet his late checks may be of use to him, and teach him to appreciate his strength better, or to wait till it is confirmed. Had he listed under Mr. Fox, who loved and courted

---

Prime Minister. The General had taken a prominent part in the last attacks upon Lord North, and when the latter gave place to Lord Rockingham's second Administration, the services of the former were requited by the office of Commander-in-Chief, with a seat in the Cabinet. But Walpole's illusion about his friend was finally dispelled when, in the search for a leader which went on during and after Lord Rockingham's last illness, it appeared that Conway's name occurred to no one but himself.—*See Walpole to Mason, May* 7, 1882, *and to Mann, July* 1, 1782.

him, he would not only have discovered modesty, but have been more likely to succeed him, than by commencing his competitor." This was written on the 5th of December, 1783. Ten days later the India Bill was defeated in the House of Lords; the King at once dismissed the Coalition; and before the end of the year Pitt was installed as head of the Government, a position which he retained for the rest of Walpole's life. The struggle which the new Ministry had to maintain for several weeks against an adverse majority in the House of Commons is matter of familiar history which needs not here be dwelt upon.

The intense excitement which these events created throughout the country is faithfully reflected in Walpole's correspondence. We find them producing a rupture between him and his correspondent of many years' standing, the poet Mason, which was not healed till shortly before the deaths of the parties. And in writing to Mann, Walpole several times refers to the general ferment. Thus he says: "Politics have engrossed all conversation, and stifled other events, if any have happened. Indeed our ladies, who used to contribute to enliven correspondence, are become politicians, and, as Lady Townley says, 'squeeze a little too much lemon into conversation.' They have been called back a little to their own profession—dress, by a magnificent ball which the Prince of Wales gave two nights ago to near six hundred persons, to which the Amazons of both parties were invited; and not a scratch was given or received." Again, in announcing the dissolution of Parliament: "All the island will be a scene of riot, and probably of violence. The parties are not separated in gentle mood: there will, they say, be contested elections everywhere: consequently vast expense and animosities... We have no private news at all. Indeed, politics are all in all. I question whether any woman will have anything to do with a man of a different party. Little girls say, 'Pray, Miss, of which side are you?' I heard of one that said, 'Mama and I cannot get Papa over to our side!'.. To the present drama, Elections, I shall totally shut my ears. I hated elections forty years ago; and, when I went to White's, preferred a conversation on Newmarket to one on elections: for the language of the former I did not understand, and, consequently, did not listen to; the other, being uttered in common phrase, made me attend, whether I would or not. When such subjects are on the tapis, they make me a very insipid correspondent. One cannot talk of what one does not care about; and it would be jargon to you, if I did: however, do not imagine but I allow a sufficient quantity of dulness to my time of life. I have kept up a correspondence with you with tolerable spirit for three-and-forty years together, without our once meeting. Can you wonder that my pen is worn to the stump? You see it does not abandon you; nor, though conscious of its own decay, endeavour to veil it by silence. The Archbishop of Gil Blas has long been a lesson to me to watch over my own ruins; but I do not extend that jealousy of vanity to commerce with an old friend. You knew me in my days of folly and riotous spirit; why should I hide my dotage from you, which is not equally my fault and reproach?

In the middle of the elections, Horace writes once more:

"The scene is wofully changed for the Opposition, though not half the new Parliament is yet chosen. Though they still contest a very few counties and some boroughs, they own themselves totally defeated. They reckoned themselves sure of two hundred and forty members; they probably will not have an hundred and fifty; and, amongst them, not some capital leaders,—perhaps not the Commander-in-Chief, Mr. Fox, certainly not the late Commander-in-Chief of the Army, General Conway. In short, between the industry of the Court and the India Company, and that momentary frenzy that sometimes seizes a whole nation, as if it were a vast animal, such aversion to the Coalition and such a detestation of Mr. Fox have seized the country, that, even where omnipotent gold retains its influence, the elected pass through an ordeal of the most virulent abuse. The great Whig families, the Cavendishes, Rockinghams, Bedfords, have lost all credit in their own counties; nay, have been tricked out of seats where the whole property was their own; and in some of those cases a *royal* finger has too evidently tampered, as well as singularly and revengefully towards Lord North and Lord Hertford; the latter of whom, however, is likely to have six of his own sons* in the House of Commons—an extraordinary instance. Such a proscription, however, must have sown so deep resentment as it was not wise to provoke; considering that permanent fortune is a jewel that in no crown is the most to be depended upon!

"When I have told you these certain truths, and when you must be aware that this torrent of unpopularity broke out in the capital, will it not sound like a contradiction if I affirm that Mr. Fox himself is still struggling to be chosen for Westminster, and maintains so sturdy a fight, that Sir Cecil Wray, his antagonist, is not yet three hundred ahead of him, though the Court exerts itself against him in the most violent manner, by mandates, arts, etc.—nay, sent at once a body of two hundred and eighty of the Guards to give their votes as householders, which *is* legal, but which my father in the most quiet seasons would not have dared to do! At first, the contest threatened to be bloody: Lord Hood† being the third candidate, and on the side of the Court, a mob of three hundred sailors undertook to drive away the opponents; but the Irish chairmen,‡ being retained by Mr. Fox's party, drove them back to their element, and cured the tars of their ambition of a naval victory. In truth, Mr. Fox has all the popularity in Westminster; and, indeed, is so amiable and winning, that, could he have stood in person all over England, I question whether he would not have carried the Parliament.

* He did get but five of his sons into that Parliament. —WALPOLE
† Lord Hood was an admiral.
‡ Almost all the hackney-chairmen in London were Irish.

The beldams hate him; but most of the pretty women in London are indefatigable in making interest for him, the Duchess of Devonshire in particular.* I am ashamed to say how coarsely she has been received by some worse than tars! But me nothing has shocked so much as what I heard this morning: at Dover they roasted a poor *fox* alive by the most diabolic allegory!—a savage meanness that an Iroquois would not have committed. Base, cowardly wretches! how much nobler to have hurried to London and torn Mr. Fox himself piecemeal! I detest a country inhabited by such stupid barbarians. I will write no more to-night; I am in a passion!"

A fortnight later he adds:

"Most elections are over; and, if they were not, neither you nor I care about such details. I have no notion of filling one's head with circumstances of which, in six weeks, one is to discharge it for ever. Indeed, it is well that I live little in the world, or I should be obliged to provide myself with that viaticum for common conversation. Our ladies are grown such vehement politicians, that no other topic is admissible; nay, I do not know whether *you* must not learn our politics for the *conversationi* at Florence,—at least, if Paris gives the *ton* to Italy, as it used to do. There are

---

* "The fact of the Duchess having purchased the vote of a stubborn butcher by a kiss, is, we believe, undoubted. It was probably during the occurrence of these scenes that the well-known compliment was paid to her by an Irish mechanic: 'I could light my pipe at her eyes.' "—*Jesse's* "Selwyn," vol. iv., p. 118.

as warm parties for Mr. Fox or Mr. Pitt at Versailles and Amsterdam as in Westminster. At the first, I suppose, they exhale in epigrams; are expressed at the second by case-knives; at the last they vent themselves in deluges of satiric prints,* though with no more wit than there is in a case-knife. I was told last night that our engraved pasquinades for this winter, at twelvepence or sixpence a-piece, would cost six or seven pounds."

In the result, Fox was returned, but Conway lost his seat. Walpole congratulates the latter on his retirement from public life:

"Berkeley Square, Wednesday, May 5, 1784.

"Your cherries, for aught I know, may, like Mr. Pitt, be half ripe before others are in blossom; but at Twickenham, I am sure, I could find dates and pomegranates on the quickset hedges, as soon as a cherry in swaddling-clothes on my walls. The very leaves on the horse-chesnuts are little things, that cry and are afraid of the north wind, and cling to the bough as if *old poker* was coming to take them away. For my part, I have seen nothing like spring but a chimney-

* " Fox said that Sayers's caricatures had done him more mischief than the debates in Parliament, or the works of the press. The prints of Carlo Khan, Fox running away with the India House, Fox and Burke quitting Paradise when turned out of office, and many others of these publications, had certainly a vast effect on the public mind."—*Lord Chancellor Eldon,* "Life of Twiss," vol. i., p. 162. This very apt quotation is made by Mr. P. Cunningham in his valuable edition of Walpole's Letters.

sweeper's garland; and yet I have been three days in the country—and the consequence was, that I was glad to come back to town.

"I do not wonder that you feel differently; anything is warmth and verdure when compared to poring over memorials. In truth, I think you will be much happier for being out of Parliament. You could do no good there; you have no views of ambition to satisfy; and when neither duty nor ambition calls (I do not condescend to name avarice, which never is to be satisfied, nor deserves to be reasoned with, nor has any place in your breast), I cannot conceive what satisfaction an elderly man can have in listening to the passions or follies of others: nor is eloquence such a banquet, when one knows that, whoever the cooks are, whatever the sauces, one has eaten as good beef or mutton before, and, perhaps, as well dressed. It is surely time to live for one's self, when one has not a vast while to live; and you, I am persuaded, will live the longer for leading a country life. How much better to be planting, nay, making experiments on smoke* (if not too dear), than reading applications from officers, a quarter of whom you could not serve, nor content three quarters! You had not time for necessary exercise; and, I believe, would have blinded yourself. In short, if you will live in the air all day, be totally idle, and not read or write a line by candle-light, and retrench your suppers, I shall rejoice in your having nothing to do but that

---

* Alluding to some coke-ovens for which Conway obtained a patent.

dreadful punishment, pleasing yourself. Nobody has any claims on you; you have satisfied every point of honour; you have no cause for being particularly grateful to the Opposition; and you want no excuse for living for yourself. Your resolutions on economy are not only prudent, but just; and, to say the truth, I believe that if you had continued at the head of the Army, you would have ruined yourself. You have too much generosity to have curbed yourself, and would have had too little time to attend to doing so. I know by myself how pleasant it is to have laid up a little for those I love, for those that depend on me, and for old servants. . . .

"You seem to think that I might send you more news. So I might, if I would talk of elections; but those, you know, I hate, as, in general, I do all details. How Mr. Fox has recovered such a majority I do not guess; still less do I comprehend how there could be so many that had not voted, after the poll had lasted so long.* Indeed, I should be sorry to understand such mysteries. . . .

"P.S. The summer is come to town, but I hope is gone into the country too."

---

* Mr. Pitt says, in a letter to Mr. Wilberforce, on the 8th of April, "Westminster goes on well, in spite of the Duchess of Devonshire and the other women of the people; but when the poll will close is uncertain." At the close of it, on the 17th of May, the numbers were, for Hood, 6,694; Fox, 6,223; Wray, 5,998. Walpole, whose delicate health at this time confined him almost entirely to his house, went in a sedan-chair to give his vote for Mr. Fox.

The new Parliament having met, and disclosed a majority of more than two to one in favour of the Government, Walpole dismisses politics and returns to lighter topics. He writes to Conway:

"Strawberry Hill, June 30, 1784.

"Instead of coming to you, I am thinking of packing up and going to town for winter, so desperate is the weather! I found a great fire at Mrs. Clive's this evening, and Mr. Raftor hanging over it like a smoked ham. They tell me my hay will be all spoiled for want of cutting; but I had rather it should be destroyed by standing than by being mowed, as the former will cost me nothing but the crop, and 'tis very dear to make nothing but a water-souchy of it.

"You know I have lost a niece, and found another nephew: he makes the fifty-fourth, reckoning both sexes. We are certainly an affectionate family, for of late we do nothing but marry one another. Have not you felt a little twinge in a remote corner of your heart on Lady Harrington's death?* She dreaded death so extremely that I am glad she had not a moment to be sensible of it. I have a great affection for sudden deaths; they save one's self and everybody else a deal of ceremony.

"The Duke and Duchess of Marlborough breakfasted here on Monday, and seemed much pleased, though it

---

* The Lady Caroline Petersham of the frolic at Vauxhall, related in a former chapter. Conway in his youth had been enamoured of her.

rained the whole time with an Egyptian darkness. I should have thought there had been deluges enough to destroy all Egypt's other plagues: but the newspapers talk of locusts; I suppose relations of your beetles, though probably not so fond of green fruit; for the scene of their campaign is Queen Square, Westminster, where there certainly has not been an orchard since the reign of Canute.

"I have, at last, seen an air-balloon; just as I once did see a tiny review, by passing one accidentally on Hounslow Heath. I was going last night to Lady Onslow at Richmond, and over Mr. Cambridge's field I saw a bundle in the air not bigger than the moon, and she herself could not have descended with more composure if she had expected to find Endymion fast asleep. It seemed to 'light on Richmond Hill; but Mrs. Hobart was going by, and her *coiffure* prevented my seeing it alight. The papers say, that a balloon has been made at Paris representing the castle of Stockholm, in compliment to the King of Sweden; but that they are afraid to let it off: so, I suppose, it will be served up to him in a dessert. No great progress, surely, is made in these airy navigations, if they are still afraid of risking the necks of two or three subjects for the entertainment of a visiting sovereign. There is seldom a *feu de joie* for the birth of a Dauphin that does not cost more lives. I thought royalty and science never haggled about the value of blood when experiments are in the question.

"I shall wait for summer before I make you a visit.

Though I dare to say that you have converted your smoke-kilns into a manufactory of balloons, pray do not erect a Strawberry castle in the air for my reception, if it will cost a pismire a hair of its head. Goodnight! I have ordered my bed to be heated as hot as an oven, and Tonton and I must go into it."

The recent invention of balloons was at this time exciting general interest. "This enormous capital," says Walpole, "that must have some occupation, is most innocently amused with those philosophic playthings, air-balloons. An Italian, one Lunardi, is the first *airgonaut* that has mounted into the clouds in this country. He is said to have bought three or four thousand pounds in the stocks, by exhibiting his person, his balloon, and his dog and cat, at the Pantheon for a shilling each visitor. Blanchard, a Frenchman, is his rival; and I expect that they will soon have an air-fight in the clouds, like a stork and a kite."

This year ended for our author with a severe attack of gout. He replies to inquiries from Lady Ossory:

"Berkeley Square, Dec. 27, 1784.

"I am told that I am in a prodigious fine way; which, being translated into plain English, means that I have suffered more sharp pain these two days than in all the moderate fits together that I have had for these last nine years: however, Madam, I have one great blessing, there is drowsiness in all the square hollows of the red-hot bars of the gridiron on which I lie, so that I scream and fall asleep by turns, like a babe that is cutting its first teeth. I can add nothing to this exact account, which I only send in obedience to your Ladyship's commands, which I received just now: I did think on Saturday that the worst was over."

On his recovery, he writes:

"I am always thanking you, Madam, I think, for kind inquiries after me; but it is not my fault that I am so often troublesome! I would it were otherwise!—however, I do not complain. I have attained another resurrection, and was so glad of my liberty, that I went out both Saturday and Sunday, though so snowy a day and so rainy a day never were invented. Yet I have not ventured to see Mrs. Jordan,* nor to skate in Hyde Park. We had other guess winters in my time!—fine sunny mornings, with now and then a mild earthquake, just enough to wake one, and rock one to sleep again comfortably. My recoveries surprise me more than my fits; but I am quite persuaded now that I know exactly how I shall end: as I am a statue of chalk, I shall crumble to powder, and then my inside will be blown away from my terrace, and hoary-headed Margaret will tell the people that come to see my house,—

'One morn we miss'd him on the 'custom'd hill.'

When that is the case, Madam, don't take the pains of inquiring more; as I shall leave no *body* to return to, even Cagliostro would bring me back to no purpose."

* At this time commencing her career as an actress.

CHAPTER IX.

Lady Correspondents.—Madame de Genlis.—Miss Burney and Hannah More.—Deaths of Mrs. Clive and Sir Horace Mann.—Story of Madame de Choiseul.—Richmond.—Queensberry House.—Warren Hastings.—Genteel Comedy.—St. Swithin.—Riverside Conceits.—Lord North.—The Theatre again.—Gibbon's History.—Sheridan.—Conway's Comedy.—A Turkish War.—Society Newspapers.—The Misses Berry.—Bonner's Ghost.—The Arabian Nights.—King's College Chapel.—Richmond Society.—New Arrivals.—The Berrys visit Italy.—A Farewell Letter.

No one who has looked through Walpole's published letters can have failed to observe that the great majority of those which belong to the last twelve or thirteen years of the writer's life are addressed to female correspondents. This is not an accidental circumstance. It is clear that, as his old friends dropped off, Horace supplied their places, in almost every instance, with women. The antiquary Pinkerton succeeds to the antiquary Cole,* but Montagu and Mason, Sir Horace Mann† and Lord Strafford,‡ had no successors of their own sex. Except when literary topics were on the carpet, Walpole, in his latter days, shrank from en-

---

* Cole died 16th December, 1782.
† See page 226.
‡ Lord Strafford died 10th March, 1791.

gaging in discussion with younger and more vigorous men. In several passages of his correspondence, he acknowledges this feeling of reserve and shyness. But with ladies of every class he was always at home and at ease. Old or young, grave or gay, English or French, they found him their devoted servant, full of nicely adjusted gallantry, never too busy to entertain with gossip and letters, ever ready to assist with advice, and when occasion required, with the contents of a well-stocked purse. Thus, from the year 1785 onwards, we have him generally in correspondence with ladies, and as often as not, about ladies. During the first part of this period especially, sketches of well-known women meet us, thrown off at frequent intervals by his practised pen. Here is an account of a visit from Madame de Genlis in July, 1785:

" You surprise me, Madam, by saying the newspapers mention my disappointment of seeing Madame de Genlis. How can such arrant trifles spread? It is very true, that as the hill would not go to see Madame de Genlis, she has come to see the hill. Ten days ago Mrs. Cosway sent me a note that *Madame* desired a ticket for Strawberry Hill. I thought I could not do less than offer her a breakfast, and named yesterday se'nnight. Then came a message that she must go to Oxford and take her Doctor's degree; and then another, that I should see her yesterday, when she did arrive with Miss Wilkes and Pamela, whom she did not even present to me, and whom she has educated to be very like herself in the face. I told her I could not attribute the honour of her visit but to my late dear friend Madame du Deffand. It rained the whole time, and was dark as midnight, so that she could scarce distinguish a picture; but you will want an account of her, and not of what she saw or could not see. Her person is agreeable, and she seems to have been pretty. Her conversation is natural and reasonable, not *précieuse* and affected, and searching to be eloquent, as I had expected. I asked her if she had been pleased with Oxford, meaning the buildings, not the wretched oafs that inhabit it. She said she had had little time; that she had wished to learn their plan of education, which, as she said sensibly, she supposed was adapted to our Constitution. I could have told her that it is directly repugnant to our Constitution, and that nothing is taught there but drunkenness and prerogative, or, in their language, Church and King. I asked if it is true that the new edition of Voltaire's works is prohibited: she replied, severely,—and then condemned those who write against religion and government, which was a little unlucky before her friend *Miss Wilkes*. She stayed two hours, and returns to France to-day *to her duty*. I really do not know whether the Duc de Chartres is in England or not. She did lodge in his house in Portland Place; but at Paris, I think, has an hotel where she educates his daughters."

A little later, he reports: " Dr. Burney and his daughter, Evelina-Cecilia, have passed a day and a half with me.* He is lively and agreeable; she half-and-half sense and modesty, which possess her so entirely, that not a cranny is left for affectation or pretension. Oh! Mrs. Montagu, you are not above half as accomplished." This was an unusual tribute from the fastidious Horace.

Here, too, we must introduce the name of another literary lady, whose acquaintance with our author, begun some time previously, ripened about this date into an occasional exchange of letters. Hannah More,† then one of the Vesey coterie in Clarges Street, which, however, she presently quitted, ranked, we conceive, in Walpole's estimation, about midway between Mrs. Montagu and Miss Burney. Writing to Hannah, not long after her retirement from London, he says: "The last time I saw her," that is Mrs. Vesey, "Miss Burney passed the evening there, looking quite recovered and

* Very shortly after this visit, Miss Burney was appointed one of the Keepers of the Queen's Robes in the room of Madame Haggerdorn, who retired.

† Born in 1745, at Stapleton, near Bristol, where her father had the care of the Charity School. Early in life, she joined her sisters in establishing a school for young ladies, which had great success. In 1773 she published a pastoral drama, called "The Search after Happiness," and in 1774 a tragedy founded on the story of Regulus. These works led to her introduction into London society. Her tragedy "Percy" was produced at Covent Garden on the 10th of December, 1777, and ran nineteen nights. About this time also she wrote "The Fatal Falsehood," and "Sacred Dramas." In 1786, when she was forty years of age, she withdrew from London, and settled at Cowslip Green, near her native place, in which district she spent the remainder of her life, devoting herself to works of charity, and the composition of religious books.

well, and so cheerful and agreeable, that the Court seems only to have improved the ease of her manner, instead of stamping more reserve on it, as I feared: but what slight graces it can give, will not compensate to us and the world for the loss of her company and her writings. Not but that *some young ladies* who can write, can stifle their talent as much as if they were under lock and key in the royal library. I do not see but *a cottage* is as pernicious to genius as the Queen's waiting-room."

Walpole had laughed at the "Blue-stockings," but he bows graciously to the authors of "Cecilia" and "Percy," and marks by an altered style of address his sense of the difference between the tone of these ladies and that of the Lady Ossorys and Kitty Clives with whom his youth and middle life had been spent. Poor Kitty's old age of cards came to an end before the close of 1785, and Cliveden, which she had occupied for more than thirty years, stood for awhile untenanted. Horace lamented the loss of his old friend and neighbour, but she was several years senior to himself, and her death was not unexpected. The pair had lived so much together that probably few letters passed between them: none have been preserved, and the removal of the lady makes no gap in the gentleman's correspondence. It is otherwise with the next name which was struck from Walpole's list of old familiar acquaintances. Shortly after losing a friend from whom he was never long parted, he lost the friend whom he never met. No long time had elapsed since Walpole had written to

Mann: "Shall we not be very venerable in the annals of friendship? What Orestes and Pylades ever wrote to each other for four-and-forty years without meeting? A correspondence of near half a century is not to be paralleled in the annals of the Post Office." Again, about the time of Mrs. Clive's death: "*Now* I think we are like Castor and Pollux; when one rises, t'other sets; when you can write, I cannot. I have got a very sharp attack of gout in my right hand. . . . . Your being so well is a great comfort to me." Despite this congratulation, however, the Ambassador was very near to his final setting. He died at Florence on the 16th of November, 1786, after a long illness, during the latter part of which he was apparently not in a condition to receive letters. Walpole's last letter to him is dated June 22, 1786. It makes the eight hundred and ninth in the collection, as printed, of Walpole's part of the correspondence between them.

But we must not suppose that Lady Ossory's gazetteer is all this time forgetful of his Countess. Here is an anecdote which he sends her in the early part of 1786:

"How do you like, Madam, the following story? A young Madame de Choiseul is inloved with by Monsieur de Coigny and Prince Joseph of Monaco. She longed for a parrot that should be a miracle of eloquence: every other shop in Paris sells mackaws, parrots, cockatoos, &c. No wonder one at least of the rivals soon found a Mr. Pitt, and the bird was immediately declared the nymph's first minister: but as she had two passions as well as two lovers, she was also enamoured of General Jackoo at Astley's. The unsuccessful candidate offered Astley ingots for his monkey, but Astley demanding a *terre* for life, the paladin was forced to desist, but fortunately heard of another miracle of parts of the Monomotapan race, who was not in so exalted a sphere of life, being only a *marmiton* in a kitchen, where he had learnt to pluck fowls with an inimitable dexterity. This dear animal was not invaluable, was bought, and presented to Madame de Choiseul, who immediately made him the *secretaire de ses commandemens.* Her caresses were distributed equally to the animals, and her thanks to the donors. The first time she went out, the two former were locked up in her bed-chamber. Ah! I dread to tell the sequel. When the lady returned and flew to her chamber, Jackoo the second received her with all the *empressement* possible—but where was Poll?—found at last under the bed, shivering and cowering—and without a feather, as stark as any Christian. Poll's presenter concluded that his rival had given the monkey with that very view, challenged him, they fought, and both were wounded; and an heroic adventure it was!"

Mrs. Clive being dead, and another sister-in-loo, Lady Browne, whom he often called his better-half, having left Twickenham, Walpole, when at Strawberry Hill, began to look across the water for society. He was attracted to Richmond by George Selwyn, who was now at times domesticated there with the Duke of

Queensberry, the "Old Q" of the caricaturists. In December, 1786, Horace writes:

"I went yesterday to see the Duke of Queensberry's palace at Richmond, under the conduct of George Selwyn, the *concierge*. You cannot imagine how noble it looks now all the Cornbury pictures from Amesbury are hung up there. The great hall, the great gallery, the eating-room, and the corridor, are covered with whole and half-lengths of royal family, favourites, ministers, peers, and judges, of the reign of Charles I. —not one an original, I think, at least not one fine, yet altogether they look very respectable; and the house is so handsome, and the views so rich, and the day was so fine, that I could only have been more pleased if (for half an hour) I could have seen the real palace that once stood on that spot, and the persons represented walking about!—A visionary holiday in old age, though it has not the rapture of youth, is a sedate enjoyment that is more sensible because one attends to it and reflects upon it at the time; and as new tumults do not succeed, the taste remains long in one's memory's mouth."

Walpole was late this year in removing to Berkeley Square. The political topic of the London season was the debates in the House of Commons on the charges against Warren Hastings; the social topic, in our author's circle at any rate, appears to have been some theatrical performances at the Duke of Richmond's house in Whitehall. Horace seems to have interested himself a good deal more in the latter subject than the former. Lady Ossory having urged him to read a pamphlet in favour of Mr. Hastings, he replies:

"The pamphlet I have read, Madam; but cannot tell you what would have been my opinion of it, because my opinion was influenced before I saw it. A lady-politician ordered me to read it, and to admire it, as the *chef-d'œuvre* of truth, eloquence, wit, argument, and impartiality; and she assured me that the *reasonings* in it were unanswerable. I believe she meant the *assertions*, for I know she uses those words as synonymous. I promised to obey her, as I am sure that ladies understand politics better than I do, and I hold it as a rule of faith—

"That all that they admire is sweet,
And all is sense that they repeat.

"How much ready wit they have! I can give you an instance, Madam, that I heard last night. After the late execution of the *eighteen* malefactors, a female was hawking an account of them, but called them *nineteen*. A gentleman said to her, 'Why do you say *nineteen*? there were but *eighteen* hanged.' She replied, 'Sir, I did not know *you* had been reprieved.'"

A week later, he writes again:

"Berkeley Square, Feb. 9, 1787.

"Though I sigh for your Ladyship's coming to town, I do not know whether I shall not be a loser, for what news don't you send me? That Lord Salisbury is a poet is nothing to your intelligence that *I* am going to turn player; nay, perhaps I should, if I were not too young for the company!—You tell me, too, that I snub and sneer; I protest, I thought I was the snubee. . . .

"For sneering, Heaven help me! I was guiltless. Every day I meet with red-hot politicians in petticoats, and told your Ladyship how I had been schooled by one of them, and how docile I was. If you yourself have any zeal for making converts, I should be very ready to be a proselyte, if I could get anything by it. It is very creditable, honourable, and fashionable; but, alas! I am so insignificant that I fear nobody would buy me; and one should look sillily to put one's self up to sale and not find a purchaser.

"In short, I doubt I shall never make my fortune by turning courtier or comedian; and therefore I may as well adhere to my old principles, as I have always done, since you yourself, Madam, would not be flattered in a convert that nobody would take off your hands. If you could bring over Mr. Sheridan, he would do something: he talked for five hours and a half on Wednesday, and turned everybody's head. One heard everybody in the streets raving on the wonders of that speech; for my part, I cannot believe it was so supernatural as they say—do you believe it was, Madam? I will go to my oracle, who told me of the marvels of the pamphlet, which assures us that Mr. Hastings is a prodigy of virtue and abilities; and, as you think so too, how should such a fellow as Sheridan, who has no diamonds to bestow, fascinate all the world?—Yet witchcraft, no doubt, there has been, for when did simple eloquence ever convince a majority? Mr. Pitt and 174 other persons found Mr. Hastings guilty last night,* and only sixty-eight remained thinking with *the pamphlet* and your Ladyship, that he is as white as snow. Well, at least there is a new crime, sorcery, to charge on the Opposition! and, till they are cleared of that charge, I will never say a word in their favour, nor think on politics more, which I would not have mentioned but in answer to your Ladyship's questions; and therefore I hope we shall drop the subject, and meet soon in Grosvenor Place in a perfect neutrality of good humour."

His remarks on the Duke's Theatre are contained in the following letter, written after his early return to Twickenham.

"Strawberry Hill, June 14, 1787.

"Though your Ladyship *gave me law* (a very proper synonyme for delay), I should have answered your letter incontinently, but I have had what is called a *blight* in one of my eyes, and for some days was forced to lie fallow, neither reading nor writing a line; which is a little uncomfortable when quite alone. I do begin to creep about my house, but have not recovered my feet enough to compass the whole circuit of my garden. Monday last was pleasant, and Tuesday very warm;

* That is, voted that the charge relating to the spoliation of the Begums of Oude contained matter for impeachment.

but we are relapsed into our east windhood, which has reigned ever since I have been here for this *green winter*, which, I presume, is the highest title due to this season, which in southern climes is positive *summer*, a name imported by our travellers, with grapes, peaches, and tuberoses. However, most of my senses have enjoyed themselves—my sight with verdure, my smell by millions of honeysuckles, my hearing by nightingales, and my feeling with good fires: tolerable luxury for an old cavalier in the north of Europe! Semiramis of Russia is not of my taste, or she would not travel half round the arctic circle; unless she means to conquer the Turks, and transfer the seat of her empire to Constantinople, like its founder. The ghost of Irene will be mighty glad to see her there, though a little surprised that the Grand Duke, her son, is still alive. I hear she has carried her grandchildren with her as hostages, or she might be dethroned, and not hear of it for three months.

"I am very far from tired, Madam, of encomiums on the performance at Richmond House, but I, by no means, agree with the criticism on it that you quote, and which, I conclude, was written by some player, from envy. Who should act genteel comedy perfectly, but people of fashion that have sense? Actors and actresses can only guess at the tone of high life, and can*not* be inspired with it. Why are there so few genteel comedies, but because most comedies are written by men not of that sphere? Etherege, Congreve, Vanbrugh, and Cibber wrote genteel comedy, because they lived in the best company; and Mrs. Oldfield played it so well, because she not only followed, but often set, the fashion. General Burgoyne has written the best modern comedy, for the same reason; and Miss Farren* is as excellent as Mrs. Oldfield, because she has lived with the best style of men in England: whereas Mrs. Abington can never go beyond *Lady Teazle*, which is a second-rate character, and that rank of women are always aping women of fashion, without arriving at the style. Farquhar's plays talk the language of a marching regiment in country quarters: Wycherley, Dryden, Mrs. Centlivre, etc., wrote as if they had only lived in the ' Rose Tavern ;'† but then the Court lived in Drury Lane, too, and Lady Dorchester and Nell Gwyn were equally good company. The Richmond Theatre, I imagine, will take root. I supped with the Duke at Mrs. Damer's, the night before I left London, and they were talking of improvements on *the local*, as the French would say."

A few weeks later, he has dismissed the talk of London, and is occupied with his neighbours on the Thames. The following is a letter to Lord Strafford:

"Strawberry Hill, July 28, 1787.

"Saint Swithin is no friend to correspondence, my dear Lord. There is not only a great sameness in his own proceedings, but he makes everybody else dull—I

---

* Miss Elizabeth Farren, afterwards Countess of Derby.
† A celebrated tavern adjoining Drury Lane Theatre.

mean in the country, where one frets at its raining every day and all day. In town he is no more minded than the proclamation against vice and immorality. Still, though he has all the honours of the quarantine, I believed it often rained for forty days long before St. Swithin was born, if ever born he was; and the proverb was coined and put under his patronage, because people observed that it frequently does rain for forty days together at this season. I remember Lady Suffolk telling me, that Lord Dysart's great meadow at Ham had never been mowed but once in forty years without rain. I said, 'All that that proved was, that rain was good for hay,' as I am persuaded the climate of a country and its productions are suited to each other. Nay, rain is good for haymakers too, who get more employment the oftener the hay is made over again. I do not know who is the saint that presides over thunder; but he has made an unusual quantity in this chill summer, and done a great deal of serious mischief, though not a fiftieth part of what Lord George Gordon did seven years ago, and happily he is fled.

"Our little part of the world has been quiet as usual. The Duke of Queensberry has given a sumptuous dinner to the Princesse de Lamballe—*et voilà tout.* I never saw her, not even in France. I have no particular *penchant* for sterling princes and princesses, much less for those of French plate.

"The only entertaining thing I can tell your Lordship from our district is, that old Madam French, who lives close by the bridge at Hampton Court, where, between her and the Thames, she has nothing but one grass-plot of the width of her house, has paved that whole plot with black and white marble in diamonds, exactly like the floor of a church; and this curious metamorphosis of a garden into a pavement has cost her three hundred and forty pounds:—a tarpaulin she might have had for some shillings, which would have looked as well, and might easily have been removed. To be sure, this exploit, and Lord Dudley's obelisk *below* a hedge, with his canal at right angles with the Thames, and a sham bridge no broader than that of a violin, and *parallel* to the river, are not preferable to the monsters in clipt yews of our ancestors. On the contrary, Mrs. Walsingham is making her house at Ditton (now baptized Boyle Farm*) very orthodox. Her daughter Miss Boyle, who has real genius, has carved three tablets in marble with boys, designed by herself. Those sculptures are for a chimney-piece; and she is painting panels in grotesque for the library, with pilasters of glass in black and gold. Miss Crewe, who has taste too, has decorated a room for her mother's house at Richmond, which was Lady Margaret Compton's, in a very pretty manner. How much more amiable the old women of the next age will be, than most of those we remember, who used to tumble at once from gallantry to devout scandal and cards, and revenge on the young of their own sex the desertion of ours! Now they are ingenious, they will not want amusement."

* Recently the seat of Lord St. Leonards.

In the autumn, he pays a visit to Lord North:

"I dined last Monday at Bushy (for you know I have more *penchant* for Ministers that are out than when they are in) and never saw a more interesting scene. Lord North's spirits, good humour, wit, sense, drollery, are as perfect as ever—the unremitting attention of Lady North and his children, most touching. Mr. North leads him about, Miss North sits constantly by him, carves meat, watches his every motion, scarce puts a bit into her own lips; and if one cannot help commending her, she colours with modesty and sorrow till the tears gush into her eyes. If ever loss of sight could be compensated, it is by so affectionate a family."

Not long after this, Walpole repeats a good-humoured jest of the blind old man on receiving a call from his *quondam* opponent, Colonel Barré, whose sight also was nearly gone. Lord North said: "Colonel Barré, nobody will suspect us of insincerity, if we say that we should always be overjoyed to see each other."

With the return of winter, the theatre comes up again. There was a stage at Ampthill as well as at Whitehall:

"Berkeley Square, Jan. 15, 1788.

"All joy to your Ladyship on the success of your theatric campaign. I do think the representation of plays as entertaining and ingenious, as choosing king and queen, and the gambols and mummeries of our ancestors at Christmas; or as making one's neighbours and all their servants drunk, and sending them home ten miles in the dark with the chance of breaking their necks by some comical overturn. I wish I could have been one of the audience; but, alas! I am like the African lamb, and can only feed on the grass and herbs that grow within my reach.

"I can make no returns yet from the theatre at Richmond House; the Duke and Duchess do not come till the birthday, and I have been at no more rehearsals, being satisfied with two of the play. Prologue or epilogue there is to be none, as neither the plays nor the performers, in general, are new. The 'Jealous Wife' is to succeed for the exhibition of Mrs. Hobart, who could have no part in 'The Wonder.'

"My histrionic acquaintance spreads. I supped at Lady Dorothy Hotham's with Mrs. Siddons, and have visited and been visited by her, and have seen and liked her much, yes, very much, in the passionate scenes of 'Percy;' but I do not admire her in cool declamation, and find her voice very hollow and defective. I asked her in which part she would most wish me to see her? She named Portia in the 'Merchant of Venice;' but I begged to be excused. With all my enthusiasm for Shakespeare, it is one of his plays that I like the least. The story of the caskets is silly, and, except the character of Shylock, I see nothing beyond the attainment of a mortal: Euripides, or Racine, or Voltaire, might have written all the rest. Moreover, Mrs. Siddons's warmest devotees do not hold her above a demigoddess in comedy. I have chosen 'Athenais,' in which she is to appear soon; her scorn is admirable. . . . .

"Puppet-shows are coming on, the birth-day, the Parliament, and the trial of Hastings and his imp, Elijah. They will fill the town, I suppose."

Walpole was as severe on professional authors as on professional actors. "Except," he says, "for such a predominant genius as Shakespeare and Milton, I hold authors cheap enough: what merit is there in pains, and study, and application, compared with the extempore abilities of such men as Mr. Fox, Mr. Sheridan, or Mr. Pitt?" But he made a further exception in favour of Gibbon. The following extract, besides an estimate of Gibbon's History, contains a reference to the celebrated Begum Speech delivered by Sheridan in Westminster Hall on the trial of Warren Hastings:

"I finished Mr. Gibbon a full fortnight ago, and was extremely pleased. It is a most wonderful mass of information, not only on history, but almost on all the ingredients of history, as war, government, commerce, coin, and what not. If it has a fault, it is in embracing too much, and consequently in not detailing enough, and in striding backwards and forwards from one set of princes to another, and from one subject to another; so that, without much historic knowledge, and without much memory, and much method in one's memory, it is almost impossible not to be sometimes bewildered: nay, his own impatience to tell what he knows, makes the author, though commonly so explicit, not perfectly clear in his expressions. The last chapter of the fourth volume, I own, made me recoil, and I could scarcely push through it. So far from being Catholic or heretic, I wished Mr. Gibbon had never heard of Monophysites, Nestorians, or any such fools! But the sixth volume made ample amends; Mahomet and the Popes were gentlemen and good company. I abominate fractions of theology and reformation.

"Mr. Sheridan, I hear, did not quite satisfy the passionate expectation that had been raised; but it was impossible he could, when people had worked themselves into an enthusiasm of offering fifty—ay, *fifty* guineas for a ticket to hear him. Well, we are sunk and deplorable in many points, yet not absolutely gone, when history and eloquence throw out such shoots! I thought I had outlived my country; I am glad not to leave it desperate!"

The next letter contains further references to the Begum Speech. It is addressed to Lord Strafford, and is one of the latest of Walpole's letters to that nobleman which have been preserved:

"Strawberry Hill, Tuesday night, June 17, 1788.

"I guess, my dear Lord, and only guess, that you are arrived at Wentworth Castle. If you are not, my letter will lose none of its bloom by waiting for you; for I have nothing fresh to tell you, and only write because you enjoined it. I settled in my Liliputian towers but this morning. I wish people would come into the country on May-day, and fix in town the first of November. But as they will not, I have made up my mind; and having so little time left, I prefer London, when my friends and society are in it, to living here alone, or with the weird sisters of Richmond and Hampton. I had additional reason now, for the streets are as green as the fields: we are burnt to the bone, and have not a lock of hay to cover our nakedness: oats are so dear, that I suppose they will soon be eaten at Brooks's and fashionable tables as a rarity. Though not resident till now, I have flitted backwards and forwards, and last Friday came hither to look for a minute at a ball at Mrs. Walsingham's at Ditton; which would have been very pretty, for she had stuck coloured lamps in the hair of all her trees and bushes, if the east wind had not danced a reel all the time by the side of the river.

"Mr. Conway's play,* of which your Lordship has seen some account in the papers, has succeeded delightfully, both in representation and applause. The language is most genteel, though translated from verse; and both prologue and epilogue are charming. The former was delivered most justly and admirably by Lord Derby, and the latter with inimitable spirit and grace by Mrs. Damer. Mr. Merry and Mrs. Bruce played excellently too. But General Conway, Mrs. Damer, and everybody else are drowned by Mr. Sheridan, whose renown has engrossed all Fame's tongues and trumpets. Lord

* A comedy called "False Appearances," translated from "L'Homme du Jour" of Boissy. It was first acted at the private theatre at Richmond House, and afterwards at Drury Lane.

Townshend said he should be sorry were he forced to give a vote directly on Hastings, before he had time to cool; and one of the Peers saying the speech had not made the same impression on him, the Marquis replied, A seal might be finely cut, and yet not be in fault for making a bad impression.

"I have, you see, been forced to send your Lordship what scraps I brought from town. The next four months, I doubt, will reduce me to my old sterility; for I cannot retail French Gazettes, though as a good Englishman bound to hope they will contain a civil war. I care still less about the double imperial campaign, only hoping that the poor dear Turks will heartily beat both Emperor and Empress. If the first Ottomans could be punished, they deserve it, but the present possessors have as good a prescription on their side as any people in Europe. We ourselves are Saxons, Danes, Normans; our neighbours are Franks, not Gauls; who the rest are, Goths, Gepidæ, Heruli, Mr. Gibbon knows; and the Dutch usurped the estates of herrings, turbots, and other marine indigenæ. Still, though I do not wish the hair of a Turk's beard to be hurt, I do not say that it would not be amusing to have Constantinople taken, merely as a lusty event; for neither could I live to see Athens revive, nor have I much faith in two such bloody-minded vultures, cock and hen, as Catherine and Joseph, conquering for the benefit of humanity; nor does my Christianity admire the propagation of the Gospel by the mouth of cannon. What desolation of peasants and their families by the episodes of forage and quarters! Oh! I wish Catherine and Joseph were brought to Westminster Hall and worried by Sheridan! I hope, too, that the poor Begums are alive to hear of his speech: it will be some comfort, though I doubt nobody thinks of restoring them a quarter of a lac!"

We must now find place for a letter to Miss More:

"Strawberry Hill, July 4, 1788.

"I am soundly rejoiced, my dear Madam, that the present summer is more favourable to me than the last; and that, instead of not answering my letters in three months, you open the campaign first. May not I flatter myself that it is a symptom of your being in better health? I wish, however, you had told me so in positive words, and that all your complaints have left you. Welcome as is your letter, it would have been ten times more welcome bringing me that assurance; for don't think I forget how ill you was last winter. As letters, you say, now keep their coaches, I hope those from Bristol will call often at my door.* I promise you I will never be denied to them.

"No botanist am I; nor wished to learn from *you*, of

---

* Meaning the establishment of the Mail-coach. Miss More, in her last letter, had said,—"Mail-coaches, which come to others, come not to me: letters and newspapers, now that they travel in coaches, like gentlemen and ladies, come not within ten miles of my hermitage; and while other fortunate provincials are studying the world and its ways, and are feasting upon elopements, divorces, and suicides, tricked out in all the elegancies of Mr. Topham's phraseology, I am obliged to be contented with village vices, petty iniquities, and vulgar sins."—*Memoirs*, vol. ii., p. 77.

all the Muses, that *piping* has a new signification. I had rather that *you* handled an oaten pipe than a carnation one; yet setting layers, I own, is preferable to reading newspapers, one of the chronical maladies of this age. Everybody reads them, nay, quotes them, though everybody knows they are stuffed with lies or blunders. How should it be otherwise? If any extraordinary event happens, who but must hear it before it descends through a coffee-house to the runner of a daily paper? They who are always wanting news, are wanting to hear they don't know what. A lower species, indeed, is that of the scribes you mention, who every night compose a journal for the satisfaction of such *illiterati*, and feed them with all the vices and misfortunes of every private family; nay, they now call it a *duty* to publish all those calamities which decency to wretched relations used in compassion to suppress, I mean self-murder in particular. Mr. Hesse's was detailed at length; and to-day that of Lord Saye and Sele. The pretence is, *in terrorem*, like the absurd stake and highway of our ancestors; as if there were a precautionary potion for madness, or the stigma of a newspaper were more dreadful than death. Daily journalists, to be sure, are most respectable magistrates! Yes, much like the cobblers that Cromwell made peers.

"I do lament your not going to Mr. Conway's play: both the author and actors deserved such an auditor as you, and you deserved to hear them. However, I do not pity *good* people who out of virtue lose or miss any pleasures. Those pastimes fleet as fast as those of the wicked; but, when gone, you saints can sit down and feast on your self-denial, and drink bumpers of satisfaction to the health of your own merit. So truly I don't pity you.

"You say you hear no news, yet you quote Mr. Topham;* therefore why should I tell you that the King is going to Cheltenham? or that the Baccelli lately danced at the Opera at Paris with a blue bandeau on her forehead, inscribed, *Honi soit qui mal y pense!*

"Well! would we committed nothing but follies! What do we not commit when the abolition of slavery hitches! Adieu!

> "Though Cato died, though Tully spoke,
> Though Brutus dealt the godlike stroke,
> Yet perish'd fated Rome.

"*You* have written; and I fear that even, if Mr. Sheridan speaks, trade, the modern religion, will predominate. Adieu!"

Our next extract contains an account of an incident which proved more fortunate for the writer than anything that happened to him during the remainder of

---

* Major Topham was the proprietor of the fashionable morning paper entitled *The World*. "In this paper," says Mr. Gifford, in his preface to the "Baviad," "were given the earliest specimens of those unqualified and audacious attacks on all private character, which the town first smiled at for their quaintness, then tolerated for their absurdity; and—now that other papers equally wicked and more intelligible have ventured to imitate it—will have to lament to the last hour of British liberty."

his life. It is from a letter to Lady Ossory, dated Strawberry Hill, October 11, 1788. Horace writes:

"I am sorry, for the third time of this letter, that I have no new village anecdotes to send your Ladyship, since they divert you for a moment. I have one, but some months old. Lady Charleville, my neighbour, told me three months ago, that, having some company with her, one of them had been to see Strawberry. 'Pray,' said another, 'who is that Mr. Walpole?' 'Who!' cried a third, 'don't you know the great epicure, Mr. Walpole?' 'Pho!' said the first, 'great epicure! you mean the antiquarian.' There, Madam, surely this anecdote may take its place in the chapter of local fame. If I have picked up no recent anecdotes on our Common, I have made a much more, to me, precious acquisition. It is the acquaintance of two young ladies of the name of Berry, whom I first saw last winter, and who accidentally took a house here with their father for the season. Their story is singular enough to entertain you. The grandfather,* a Scot, had a large estate in his own country, £5,000 a year it is said; and a circumstance I shall tell you makes it probable. The oldest son married for love a woman with no fortune. The old man was enraged, and would not see him. His wife died and left these two young ladies. The grandfather wished for an heir male and pressed the widower to remarry, but could not prevail; the son declaring he would consecrate himself to his daughters

* Walpole was mistaken here. It was their granduncle, not their grandfather, from whom Mr. Berry had expected to inherit.

and their education. The old man did not break with him again, but, much worse, totally disinherited him, and left all to his second son, who very handsomely gave up £800 a year to his elder brother. Mr. Berry has since carried his daughters for two or three years to France and Italy, and they are returned the best-informed and the most perfect creatures I ever saw at their age. They are exceedingly sensible, entirely natural and unaffected, frank, and, being qualified to talk on any subject, nothing is so easy and agreeable as their conversation, nor more apposite than their answers and observations. The eldest, I discovered by chance, understands Latin and is a perfect Frenchwoman in her language. The younger draws charmingly, and has copied admirably Lady Di's gipsies, which I lent, though for the first time of her attempting colours. They are of pleasing figures. Mary, the eldest, sweet, with fine dark eyes, that are very lively when she speaks, with a symmetry of face that is the more interesting from being pale; Agnes, the younger, has an agreeable sensible countenance, hardly to be called handsome, but almost. She is less animated than Mary, but seems, out of deference to her sister, to speak seldomer, for they dote on each other, and Mary is always praising her sister's talents. I must even tell you they dress within the bounds of fashion, though fashionably; but without the excrescences and balconies with which modern hoydens overwhelm and barricade their persons. In short, good sense, information, simplicity, and ease characterise the Berrys; and this is not particularly mine, who am apt to be prejudiced, but the universal voice of all who know them. The first night I met them I would not be acquainted with them, having heard so much in their praise that I concluded they would be all pretension. The second time, in a very small company, I sat next to Mary, and found her an angel both inside and out. Now, I do not know which I like best; except Mary's face, which is formed for a sentimental novel, but it is ten times fitter for a fifty times better thing, genteel comedy. This delightful family comes to me almost every Sunday evening, as our region is too *proclamatory* to play at cards on the seventh day. I forgot to tell you that Mr. Berry is a little merry man, with a round face, and you would not suspect him of so much feeling and attachment. I make no excuse for such minute details; for, if your Ladyship insists on hearing the humours of my district, you must for once indulge me with sending you two pearls that I found in my path."

At the date of the above extract, Mary Berry was in her twenty-sixth year, Agnes Berry in her twenty-fifth. The notice taken by Walpole of these ladies gave them a position in the best London society, which they enjoyed for upwards of sixty years; but this patronage, and any other benefits which he bestowed upon them, were much more than repaid by the grateful attention with which they sacrificed themselves to promote the comfort of his last years. The new acquaintance advanced rapidly. Here is one of the earliest of Walpole's letters to the sisters which has been published. Like many others of the series, it is addressed to the two jointly.

"February 2, 17—71* [1789].

"I am sorry, in the sense of that word before it meant, like a Hebrew word, glad or sorry, that I am engaged this evening; and I am at your command on Tuesday, as it is always my inclination to be. It is a misfortune that words are become so much the current coin of society, that, like King William's shillings, they have no impression left; they are so smooth, that they mark no more to whom they first belonged than to whom they do belong, and are not worth even the twelvepence into which they may be changed: but if they mean too little, they may seem to mean too much too, especially when an old man (who is often synonymous for a miser) parts with them. I am afraid of protesting how much I delight in your society, lest I should seem to affect being gallant; but if two negatives make an affirmative, why may not two ridicules compose one piece of sense? and therefore, as I am in love with you both, I trust it is a proof of the good sense of your devoted H. Walpole."

A few months later we have the following letter to Miss More:

* The date is thus put, alluding to his age, which, in 1789. was seventy-one.—MARY BERRY.

"Strawberry Hill, June 23, 1789.

"Madam Hannah,

"You are an errant reprobate, and grow wickeder and wickeder every day. You deserve to be treated like a *nègre*; and your favourite Sunday, to which you are so partial, that you treat the other poor six days of the week as if they had no souls to be saved, should, if I could have my will, 'shine no Sabbath-day for you.' Now, don't simper, and look as innocent as if virtue would not melt in your mouth. Can you deny the following charges?—I lent you the 'Botanic Garden,' and you returned it without writing a syllable, or saying where you were, or whither you was going; I suppose for fear I should know how to direct to you. Why, if I did send a letter after you, could not you keep it three months without an answer, as you did last year?

"In the next place, you and your *nine* accomplices, who, by the way, are too good in keeping you company, have clubbed the prettiest Poem imaginable,* and communicated it to Mrs. Boscawen, with injunctions not to give a copy of it; I suppose because you are ashamed of having written a panegyric. Whenever you *do* compose a satire, you are ready enough to publish it; at least, whenever you do, you will din one to death with it. But now, mind your perverseness: that very pretty novel poem, and I must own it is charming, have you gone and spoiled, flying in the faces of your best friends the Muses, and keeping no *measures* with them.

"Bishop Bonner's Ghost.

I'll be shot if they dictated two of the best lines with two syllables too much in each—nay, you have weakened one of them,

"' Ev'n Gardiner's mind'

is far more expressive than *steadfast* Gardiner's; and, as Mrs. Boscawen says, whoever knows anything of Gardiner, could not want that superfluous epithet; and whoever does not, would not be the wiser for your foolish insertion—Mrs. Boscawen did not call it foolish, but I do. The second line, as Mesdemoiselles the Muses handed it to you, Miss, was,

"' Have all be free and saved—'

not, 'All be free and all be saved:' the second *all be* is a most unnecessary tautology. The poem was perfect and faultless, if you could have let it alone. I wonder how your mischievous flippancy could help maiming that most new and beautiful expression, ' sponge of sins;' I should not have been surprised, as you love verses too full of feet, if you had changed it to 'that scrubbing-brush of sins.'

"Well! I will say no more now: but if you do not order me a copy of 'Bonner's Ghost' incontinently, never dare to look my printing-house in the face again. Or come, I'll tell you what; I will forgive all your enormities if you will let me print your poem. I like to filch a little immortality out of others, and the Strawberry press could never have a better opportunity. I will not haggle for the public; I will be content with printing only two hundred copies, of which you shall have half and I half. It shall cost you nothing but a yes. I only propose this in case you do not mean to print it yourself. Tell me sincerely which you like. But as to not printing it at all, charming and unexceptionable as it is, you cannot be so preposterous.

"I by no means have a thought of detracting from your own share in your own poem; but, as I do suspect that it caught some inspiration from your perusal of 'The Botanic Garden,' so I hope you will discover that *my* style is much improved by having lately studied 'Bruce's Travels.' There I dipped, and not in St. Giles's Pound, where one would think this author had been educated. Adieu! Your friend, or mortal foe, as you behave on the present occasion."

Before the date of the last, the Misses Berry had set out on a summer excursion. The following is in answer to a letter from the elder:

"Strawberry Hill, June 30, 1789.

"Were there any such thing as sympathy at the distance of two hundred miles, you would have been in a mightier panic than I was; for, on Saturday se'nnight, going to open the glass case in the Tribune, my foot caught in the carpet, and I fell with my whole weight (*si* weight *y a*) against the corner of the marble altar on my side, and bruised the muscles so badly, that for two days I could not move without screaming. I am convinced I should have broken a rib, but that I fell on the cavity whence two of my ribs were removed that are gone to Yorkshire. I am much better both of my bruise and of my lameness, and shall be ready to dance at my own wedding when my wives return. And now to answer your letter.

"If you grow tired of the 'Arabian Nights,' you have no more taste than Bishop Atterbury, who huffed Pope for sending him them (or the 'Persian Tales'), and fancied he liked Virgil better, who had no more imagination than Dr. Akenside. Read 'Sinbad the Sailor's Voyages,' and you will be sick of Æneas's. What woful invention were the nasty poultry that spoiled his dinner, and ships on fire turned into Nereids! A barn metamorphosed into a cascade in a pantomime is full as sublime an effort of genius. I do not know whether the 'Arabian Nights' are of Oriental origin or not: I should think not, because I never saw any other Oriental composition that was not bombast without genius, and figurative without nature; like an Indian screen, where you see little men on the foreground, and larger men hunting tigers above in the air, which they take for perspective. I do not think the Sultaness's narratives very natural or very probable, but there is a wildness in them that captivates. However, if you could wade through two octavos* of Dame Piozzi's *though*'s and *so*'s and *I trow*'s, and cannot listen to seven volumes of Scheherezade's narrations, I will sue for a

---

* Her "Observations and Reflections made in the course of a Journey through France, Italy, and Germany," honoured with a couplet in the "Baviad"—
"See Thrale's grey widow with a satchel roam,
And bring in pomp laborious nothings home."

divorce *in foro Parnassi*, and Boccalini shall be my proctor. The cause will be a counterpart to the sentence of the Lacedæmonian, who was condemned for breach of the peace, by saying in three words what he might have said in two.

"So, you was not quite satisfied, though you ought to have been transported, with King's College Chapel, because it has no aisles, like every common cathedral. I suppose you would object to a bird of paradise, because it has no legs, but shoots to heaven in a trail, and does not rest on earth. Criticism and comparison spoil many tastes. You should admire all bold and unique essays that resemble nothing else; the 'Botanic Garden,' the 'Arabian Nights,' and King's Chapel are above all rules: and how preferable is what no one can imitate, to all that is imitated even from the best models! Your partiality to the pageantry of popery I do approve, and I doubt whether the world would not be a loser (in its visionary enjoyments) by the extinction of that religion, as it was by the decay of chivalry and the proscription of the heathen deities. Reason has no invention; and as plain sense will never be the legislator of human affairs, it is fortunate when taste happens to be regent."

During the absence of his young favourites, he amuses himself with visiting his neighbours, and grumbling at his "customers," as he called the strangers who came to view his villa and grounds:

"Richmond is in the first request this summer.

Mrs. Bouverie is settled there with a large court. The Sheridans are there, too, and the Bunburys. I have been once with the first; with the others I am not acquainted. I go once or twice a week to George Selwyn late in the evening, when he comes in from walking:—about as often to Mrs. Ellis here, and to Lady Cecilia Johnston at Hampton; but all together cannot contribute to an entertaining letter, and it is odd to say that, though my house is all the morning full of company, nobody lives so much alone. I have already this season had between seventy and fourscore companies to see my house; and half my time passes in writing tickets or excuses. I wish I could think as an old sexton did at King's College. One of the fellows told him he must get a great deal of money by showing it: 'Oh, no! master,' replied he; 'everybody has seen it now.' *My* companies, it seems, are more prolific, and every set begets one or two more."

About the same date, he writes to Mary and Agnes:

"Strawberry Hill, Thursday evening, Aug. 27, 1789.

"I jumped for joy; that is, my heart did, which is all the remains of me that is *in statu jumpante*, at the receipt of your letter this morning, which tells me you approve of the house at Teddington. How kind you was to answer so incontinently! I believe you borrowed the best steed from the races. I have sent to the landlord to come to me to-morrow: but I could not resist beginning my letter to-night, as I am at home alone, with a little pain in my left wrist; but the right one has no brotherly feeling for it, and would not be put off so. You ask how you have deserved such attentions? Why, by deserving them; by every kind of merit, and by that superlative one to me, your submitting to throw away so much time on a forlorn antique; you two, who, without specifying particulars, (and you must at least be conscious that you are not two frights) might expect any fortune and distinctions, and do delight all companies. On which side lies the wonder? Ask me no more such questions, or I will cram you with reasons. . . .

Friday.

"Well! I have seen him, and nobody was ever so accommodating! He is as courteous as a candidate for a county. You may stay in his house till Christmas if you please, and shall pay but twenty pounds; and if more furniture is wanting, it shall be supplied."

" Don't bring me a pair of scissors from Sheffield. I am determined nothing shall cut our loves, though I should live out the rest of Methusalem's term, as you kindly wish, and as I can believe, though you are my wives; for I am persuaded my Agnes wishes so too.— Don't you?"

The French Revolution was now in full progress: the Bastile had been stormed and demolished; anarchy reigned in Paris; châteaux in the provinces were being plundered and burnt by the peasants; refugees, in terrified crowds, were pouring over to England. Some of the exiles presently found their way into Walpole's neighbourhood. "Madame de Boufflers," he tells Lady Ossory, "and the Comtesse Emilie, her daughter-in-law, I hear, are come to London; and Woronzow, the Russian Minister, who has a house at Richmond, is to lend it to her for the winter, as her fortune has received some considerable blow in the present commotions." Besides these foreigners, other important personages had come or were coming into the district. The Duke of Clarence had a house in the middle of Richmond "with nothing but a green short apron to the river, a situation only fit for an old gentlewoman who has put out her knee-pans and loves cards. The Prince of Wales has taken a somewhat better place at Roehampton, and enters upon it at Christmas." "My Straw-Berries," he adds, "are not yet returned, but I expect them next week, and have found a house for them at Teddington very near me." A little later, he writes, "My neighbour, the Duke of Clarence, is so popular, that if Richmond were a borough, and he had not attained his title, but still retained his idea of standing candidate, he would certainly be elected there. He pays his bills regularly himself, locks up his doors at night, that his servants may not stay out late, and never drinks but a few glasses of wine. Though the value of crowns is mightily fallen of late at market, it looks as if his Royal Highness thought they were still worth waiting for; nay, it is said that he tells his brothers that he shall be king before either—that is fair at least."*

In July, 1790, Walpole is alarmed by the intelligence that the Berrys have arranged to make a long visit to Italy. He writes to Miss Berry, then at the sea with her sister:

"I feel all the kindness of your determination of coming to Twickenham in August, and shall certainly say no more against it, though I am certain that I shall count every day that passes; and when *they are passed*, they will leave a melancholy impression on Strawberry, that I had rather have affixed to London. The two last summers were infinitely the pleasantest I ever passed here, for I never before had an agreeable neighbourhood. Still I loved the place, and had no comparisons to draw. Now, the neighbourhood will remain, and will appear ten times worse; with the aggravation of remembering *two months* that may have some transient roses, but, I am sure, lasting thorns. You tell me I do not write with my usual spirits: at least I will suppress, as much as I can, the want of them, though I am a bad dissembler."

The months pass, and we have the following farewell letter:

---

* One half the prediction was fulfilled, since the Duke of Clarence outlived the Duke of York, and came to the throne in 1830, on the death of his eldest brother, at this time, 1789, the Prince of Wales.

"Sunday, Oct. 10, 1790. The day of your departure.

"Is it possible to write to my beloved friends, and refrain from speaking of my grief for losing you; though it is but the continuation of what I have felt ever since I was stunned by your intention of going abroad this autumn? Still I will not tire you with it often. In happy days I smiled, and called you my dear wives: now I can only think on you as darling children of whom I am bereaved! As such I have loved and do love you; and, charming as you both are, I have had no occasion to remind myself that I am past seventy-three. Your hearts, your understandings, your virtues, and the cruel injustice of your fate,[*] have interested me in everything that concerns you; and so far from having occasion to blush for any unbecoming weakness, I am proud of my affection for you, and very proud of your condescending to pass so many hours with a very old man, when everybody admires you, and the most insensible allow that your good sense and information (I speak of both) have formed you to converse with the most intelligent of our sex as well as your own; and neither can tax you with airs of pretension or affectation. Your simplicity and natural ease set off all your other merits—all these

---

[*] This alludes to Miss Berry's father having been disinherited by an uncle, to whom he was heir-at-law, and a large property left to his younger brother.—MARY BERRY.

graces are lost to me, alas! when I have no time to lose.

"Sensible as I am to my loss, it will occupy but part of my thoughts, till I know you safely landed, and arrived safely at Turin. Not till you are there, and I learn so, will my anxiety subside and settle into steady, selfish sorrow. I looked at every weathercock as I came along the road to-day, and was happy to see everyone point north-east. May they do so to-morrow!

"I found here the frame for Wolsey,* and to-morrow morning Kirgate† will place him in it; and then I shall begin pulling the little parlour to pieces, that it may be hung anew to receive him. I have also obeyed Miss Agnes, though with regret; for, on trying it, I found her Arcadia would fit the place of the picture she condemned, which shall therefore be hung in its room; though the latter should give way to nothing else, nor shall be laid aside, but shall hang where I shall see it almost as often. I long to hear that its dear paintress is well; I thought her not at all so last night. You will tell me the truth, though she in her own case, and in that alone, allows herself mental reservation.

"Forgive me for writing nothing to-night but about you two and myself. Of what can I have thought else? I have not spoken to a single person but my own

---

* A drawing by Miss Agnes Berry.
† His secretary.

servants since we parted last night. I found a message here from Miss Howe* to invite me for this evening. Do you think I have not preferred staying at home to write to you, as this must go to London to-morrow morning by the coach to be ready for Tuesday's post? My future letters shall talk of other things, whenever I know anything worth repeating; or perhaps any trifle, for I am determined to forbid myself lamentations that would weary you; and the frequency of my letters will prove there is no forgetfulness. If I live to see you again, you will then judge whether I am changed; but a friendship so rational and so pure as mine is, and so equal for both, is not likely to have any of the fickleness of youth, when it has none of its other ingredients. It was a sweet consolation to the short time that I may have left, to fall into such a society; no wonder then that I am unhappy at that consolation being abridged. I pique myself on no philosophy, but what a long use and knowledge of the world had given me—the philosophy of indifference to most persons and events. I do pique myself on not being ridiculous at this very late period of my life; but when there is not a grain of passion in my affection for you two, and when you both have the good sense not to be displeased at my telling you so, (though I hope you would have despised me for the contrary,) I am not ashamed to say that your loss is heavy to me; and that I am only reconciled to it by hoping that a winter in Italy, and the journeys and sea

---

* An unmarried sister of the first Earl Howe, who then lived at Richmond.

air, will be very beneficial to two constitutions so delicate as yours. Adieu! my dearest friends. It would be tautology to subscribe a name to a letter, every line of which would suit no other man in the world but the writer."

CHAPTER X.

Walpole's love of English Scenery.—Richmond Hill.—Burke on the French Revolution.—The Berrys at Florence.—Death of George Selwyn.—London Solitude.—Repairs at Cliveden.—Burke and Fox.—The Countess of Albany.—Journal of a Day.—Mrs. Hobart's Party.—Ancient Trade with India.—Lady Hamilton.—A Boat Race.—Return of the Berrys.—Horace succeeds to the Peerage.—Epitaphium Vivi Auctoris.—His Wives.—Mary Berry.—Closing Years.—Love of Moving Objects.—Visit from Queen Charlotte.—Death of Conway.—Final Illness of Horace.—His Last Letter.

It cannot, we fear, be said with truth that Walpole had much eye for the greater beauties of nature. When he recalls the travels of his youth, it is on the Gallery at Florence and the Fair of Reggio that his memory dwells, rather than on his ride to the Grande Chartreuse or his visit to Naples. But of the modest charms of English scenery he had a real and thorough enjoyment. The enthusiasm expressed in his Essay on "Modern Gardening" has a more genuine ring about it than is often found in his writings. In reading it, one does not doubt that his praises of "the rich blue prospects of Kent, the Thames-watered views in Berkshire, and the magnificent scale of nature in Yorkshire," were something more than compliments to friends who happened to have seats in those districts.

Yet there was one spot which he admired more than even these captivating scenes. At the bottom of his heart, he was persuaded that no stream in the world could compare with his own reaches of the Thames, nor any mountain or hill with Richmond Hill. And what he believed in his heart, he was not always slow to proclaim with mouth and pen. Thus in describing the effects of a tempest, he writes: " The greatest ruin is at my nephew Dysart's at Ham, where five-and-thirty of the old elms are blown down. I think it is no loss, as I hope now one shall see the river from the house. He never would cut a twig to see the most beautiful scene upon earth." Again, after visiting Oatlands, then recently purchased by the Duke of York, Horace says: "I am returned to my own Thames with delight, and envy none of the princes of the earth." He sneers bitterly at Mr. Gilpin, who " despised the richness, verdure, amenity of Richmond Hill, when he had seen rocks and lakes in the north; for size and distance of place add wonderfully to loveliness." And when he is trying to coax his Straw-Berries home from Florence, he tells them there is not an acre on the banks of the Thames that should vail the bonnet to Boboli. With the exception of an occasional visit paid during the absence of these ladies to Conway at Henley, the six last summers and autumns of Walpole's life seem to have been spent almost uninterruptedly at Twickenham. Some little time after Mrs. Clive's death, Cliveden, or Little Strawberry Hill, was let for a short time to Sir Robert Goodere; but it seems that, before his young friends left England, Horace had determined, on their return, to give Miss Berry and her sister this house for their lives, that he might have them constantly near him. The design succeeded. Mary and Agnes became attached to the place; it continued to be their country residence for many years; and when, after surviving their aged admirer for more than half a century, they died, both unmarried, within a few months of each other, they were buried in one grave in Petersham churchyard, opposite Twickenham, "amidst scenes," as their epitaph records, "which in life they had frequented and loved."

After despatching the farewell letter given at the end of our last chapter, Walpole lingered at Strawberry Hill, consoling himself with the society of Richmond, and with Burke's "Reflections on the Revolution in France." The shock of that earthquake had already made him half a Tory, and he welcomed the great orator's declamation with delight. "His pamphlet," he tells Miss Berry, "came out this day se'nnight, and is far superior to what was expected, even by his warmest admirers. I have read it twice, and though of three hundred and fifty pages, I wish I could repeat every page by heart. It is sublime, profound, and gay. The wit and satire are equally brilliant; and the whole is wise, though in some points he goes too far; yet in general there is far less want of judgment than could be expected from *him*. If it could be translated, which, from the wit and metaphors and allusions, is almost impossible, I should think it would be a classic book in all countries, except in *present* France. To their tribunes it speak daggers; though, unlike them, it uses none. Seven thousand copies have been taken off by the booksellers already, and a new edition is preparing. I hope you will see it soon." In a subsequent letter to both his favourites, dated Strawberry Hill, Nov. 27, 1790, he says: " I am still here: the weather, though very rainy, is quite warm; and I have much more agreeable society at Richmond, with small companies and better hours, than in town, and shall have till after Christmas, unless great cold drives me thither." Two days later, having heard of the arrival of the Berrys at Florence, he writes to Agnes:

" Though I write to both at once, and reckon your letters to come equally from both, yet I delight in seeing your hand with a pen as well as with a pencil, and you express yourself as well with the one as with the other. Your part in that which I have been so happy as to receive this moment, has singularly obliged me, by your having saved me the terror of knowing you had a torrent to cross after heavy rain. No cat is so afraid of water for herself, as I am grown to be for you. That panic, which will last for many months, adds to my fervent desire of your returning early in the autumn, that you may have neither fresh water nor the ' silky ' ocean to cross in winter. Precious as our insular situation is, I am ready to wish with the Frenchman, that you could somehow or other get to it by land,—
' Oui, c'est une isle toujours, je le sçais bien ; mais, par

exemple, en allant d'alentour, n'y auroit-il pas moyen d'y arriver par terre ?' . . .

"Richmond, my metropolis, flourishes exceedingly. The Duke of Clarence arrived at his palace there last night, between eleven and twelve, as I came from Lady Douglas. His eldest brother and Mrs. Fitzherbert dine there to-day with the Duke of Queensberry, as his Grace, who called here this morning, told me, on the very spot where lived Charles the First, and where are the portraits of his principal courtiers from Cornbury. Queensberry has taken to that palace at last, and has frequently company and music there in an evening. I intend to go."

He was detained in the country longer than he had intended by an attack of gout; on his return to town he announces his recovery to Lady Ossory.

"Berkeley Square, Jan. 28, 1791.

"You and Lord Ossory have been so very good to me, Madam, that I must pay you the first tribute of my poor reviving fingers—I believe they never will be their own men again; but as they have lived so long in your Ladyship's service, they shall show their attachment to the last, like Widdrington on his stumps. I have had another and grievous memento, the death of poor Selwyn! His end was lovely, most composed and rational. From eight years old I had known him intimately without a cloud between us; few knew him so well, and consequently few knew so well the goodness of his heart and nature. But I will say no more—*Mon*

Chancelier vous dira le reste.*—No, my chancellor shall put an end to the session, only concluding, as Lord Bacon would have done for King James, with an apologue, 'His Majesty's recovery has turned the corner, and exceeding the old fable, has proved that the stomach can do better without the limbs than they could without him.'"

About the same date he describes his life in London to the Berrys:

"I wish that complaining of people for abandoning me were an infallible recipe for bringing them *back!* but I doubt it will not do in acute cases. To-day, a few hours after writing the latter part of this, appeared Mr. Batt.† He asked many pardons, and I easily forgave him; for the *mortification* was not begun. He asked much after you both. I had a crowd of visits besides; but they all come past two o'clock, and sweep one another away before any can take root. My evenings are solitary enough, for I ask nobody to come; nor, indeed, does anybody's evening begin till I am going to bed. I have outlived daylight as well as my contemporaries. What have I not survived? The Jesuits and the monarchy of France! and both without a struggle! Semiramis seems to intend to add Constantinople to the mass of revolutions; but is not her permanence almost as wonderful as the contrary explosions! I wish—I wish we may not be actually flippancying our-

---

* Here begins Kirgate's handwriting in the MS.

† A friend of the Berrys. He was then one of the Commissioners for Auditing the Public Accounts.

selves into an embroil with that Ursa-major of the North Pole. What a vixen little island are we, if we fight with the Aurora Borealis and Tippoo Saib at the end of Asia at the same time! You, damsels, will be like the end of the conundrum,

"'You've seen the man who saw these wondrous sights.'

"I cannot finish this with my own hand, for the gout has returned a little into my right arm and wrist, and I am not quite so well as I was yesterday; but I had said my say, and have little to add. The Duchess of Gordon, t'other night, coming out of an assembly, said to Dundas, 'Mr. Dundas, you are used to speak in public; will you call my servant?' . . . Adieu! I will begin to write again myself as soon as I can."

In the middle of March he wrote from Strawberry Hill to Miss Berry: "As I have mended considerably for the last four days, and as we have had a fortnight of soft warm weather, and a south-west wind to day, I have ventured hither for a change of air, and to give orders about some repairs at Cliveden; which, by the way, Mr. Henry Bunbury, two days ago, proposed to take off my hands for his life. I really do not think I accepted his offer." All the spring he vibrates between London and Twickenham. He writes again from the latter place to Miss Berry towards the end of April:

"To-day, when the town is staring at the sudden resignation of the Duke of Leeds,* asking the reason,

* Secretary of State for Foreign Affairs. He was succeeded in the office by Lord Grenville.

and gaping to know who will succeed him, I am come hither with an indifference that might pass for philosophy ; as the true cause is not known, which it seldom is. Don't tell Europe ; but I really am come to look at the repairs of Cliveden, and how they go on; not without an eye to the lilacs and the apple-blossoms : for even *self* can find a corner to wriggle into, though friendship may fit out the vessel. Mr. Berry may, perhaps, wish I had more political curiosity; but as I must return to town on Monday for Lord Cholmondeley's wedding, I may hear before the departure of the post, if the seals are given."

Among the letters written to Miss Berry from town during this season, one gives an account of the famous quarrel between Burke and Fox in the House of Commons:

"Mr. Fox had most imprudently thrown out a panegyric on the French Revolution. His most considerable friends were much hurt, and protested to him against such sentiments. Burke went much farther, and vowed to attack these opinions. Great pains were taken to prevent such altercation, and the Prince of Wales is said to have written a dissuasive letter to Burke; but he was immovable; and on Friday, on the Quebec Bill, he broke out, and sounded a trumpet against the plot, which he denounced as carrying on here. Prodigious clamours and interruption arose from Mr. Fox's friends ; but he, though still applauding the French, burst into tears and lamentations on the loss of Burke's friendship, and endeavoured to make atonement; but in vain, though Burke wept too. In short, it was the most affecting scene possible; and undoubtedly an *unique* one, for both the commanders were earnest and *sincere*.* Yesterday, a second act was expected; but mutual friends prevailed, that the contest should not be renewed: nay, on the same Bill, Mr. Fox made a profession of his faith, and declared he would venture his life in support of the *present* constitution by Kings, Lords, and Commons. In short, I never knew a wiser dissertation, if the newspapers deliver it justly; and I think all the writers in England cannot give more profound sense to Mr. Fox than he possesses. I know no more particulars, having seen nobody this morning yet."

Another refers to the trial of Hastings, and sundry matters of public interest:

* The following anecdote, connected with this memorable evening, is related by Mr. Curwen, at that time member for Carlisle, in his " Travels in Ireland :"—" The most powerful feelings were manifested on the adjournment of the House. While I was waiting for my carriage, Mr. Burke came to me and requested, as the night was wet, I would set him down. As soon as the carriage-door was shut, he complimented me on my being no friend to the revolutionary doctrines of the French; on which he spoke with great warmth for a few minutes, when he paused to afford me an opportunity of approving the view he had taken of those measures in the House. At the moment I could not help feeling disinclined to disguise my sentiments: Mr. Burke, catching hold of the check-string, furiously exclaimed, ' You are one of these people! set me down !' With some difficulty I restrained him;—we had then reached Charing Cross: a silence ensued, which was preserved till we reached his house in Gerard Street, when he hurried out of the carriage without speaking."

"After several weeks spent in search of precedents for trials* ceasing or not on a dissolution of Parliament, the Peers on Monday sat till three in the morning on the report; when the Chancellor and Lord Hawkesbury fought for the cessation, but were beaten by a large majority; which showed that Mr. Pitt has more weight (at present) in that House too, than—the diamonds of Bengal. Lord Hawkesbury protested. The trial recommences on Monday next, and has already cost the public fourteen thousand pounds; the accused, I suppose, much more.

"The Countess of Albany† is not only in England, in London, but at this very moment, I believe, in the palace of St. James's—not restored by as rapid a revolution as the French, but, as was observed last night at supper at Lady Mount-Edgcumbe's, by that topsy-turvy-hood that characterises the present age. Within these two months the Pope has been burnt at Paris; Madame du Barry, mistress of Louis Quinze, has dined with the Lord Mayor of London, and the Pretender's widow is presented to the Queen of Great Britain! She is to be introduced by her great-grandfather's niece, the young Countess of Aylesbury. That curiosity should bring her hither, I do not quite wonder—still less, that

---

* He means impeachments.

Louisa Maximiliana de Stolberg Gœdern, wife of the Pretender. After the death of Charles Edward in 1788, she travelled in Italy and France, and lived with her favourite, the celebrated Alfieri, to whom she is stated to have been privately married. She continued to reside at Paris, until the progress of the revolution compelled her to take refuge in England.

she abhorred her husband; but methinks it is not very well-bred to his family, nor very sensible; but a new way of *passing eldest*.*

"Thursday night.

"Well! I have had an exact account of the interview of the two Queens, from one who stood close to them. The Dowager was announced as Princess of Stolberg. She was well-dressed, and not at all embarrassed. The King talked to her a good deal; but about her passage, the sea, and general topics: the Queen in the same way, but less. Then she stood between the Dukes of Gloucester and Clarence, and had a good deal of conversation with the former; who, perhaps, may have met her in Italy. Not a word between her and the Princesses; nor did I hear of the Prince; but he was there, and probably spoke to her. The Queen looked at her earnestly. To add to the singularity of the day, it is the Queen's birth-day. Another odd accident: at the Opera at the Pantheon, Madame d'Albany was carried into the King's box, and sat there. It is not of a piece with her going to Court, that she seals with the royal arms. . . .

"Boswell has at last published his long-promised 'Life of Dr. Johnson,' in two volumes in quarto. I will give you an account of it when I have gone through it. I have already perceived, that in writing the history of Hudibras, Ralpho has not forgot himself—nor will others, I believe, forget *him!*"

The next is also to Miss Berry:

* A loo phrase.

"Berkeley Square, May 26, 1791.

"I am rich in letters from you: I received that by Lord Elgin's courier first, as you expected, and its elder the next day. You tell me mine entertain you; *tant mieux*. It is my wish, but my wonder; for I live so little in the world, that I do not know the present generation by sight: for, though I pass by them in the streets, the hats with valences, the folds above the chin of the ladies, and the dirty shirts and shaggy hair of the young men, who have levelled nobility almost as much as the mobility of France have, have confounded all individuality. Besides, if I did go to public places and assemblies, which my going to roost earlier prevents, the bats and owls do not begin to fly abroad till far in the night, when they begin to see and be seen. However, one of the empresses of fashion, the Duchess of Gordon, uses fifteen or sixteen hours of her four-and-twenty. I heard her journal of last Monday. She first went to Handel's music in the Abbey; she then clambered over the benches, and went to Hastings's trial in the Hall; after dinner, to the play; then to Lady Lucan's assembly; after that to Ranelagh, and returned to Mrs. Hobart's faro-table; gave a ball herself in the evening of that morning, into which she must have got a good way; and set out for Scotland the next day. Hercules could not have achieved a quarter of her labours in the same space of time."

Before the middle of June he is settled at Twickenham. He condoles with the Berrys:

"Strawberry Hill, June 14, 1791.

"I pity you! what a dozen or fifteen uninteresting letters are you going to receive! for here I am, unlikely to have anything to tell you worth sending. You had better come back incontinently—but pray do not prophesy any more; you have been the death of our summer, and we are in close mourning for it in coals and ashes. It froze hard last night: I went out for a moment to look at my haymakers, and was starved. The contents of an English June are, hay and ice, orange-flowers and rheumatisms! I am now cowering over the fire. Mrs. Hobart had announced a rural breakfast at Sans-Souci last Saturday; nothing being so pastoral as a fat grandmother in a row of houses on Ham Common. It rained early in the morning: she despatched post-boys, for want of Cupids and zephyrs, to stop the nymphs and shepherds who tend their flocks in Pall Mall and St. James's Street; but half of them missed the couriers and arrived. Mrs. Montagu was more splendid yesterday morning, and breakfasted seven hundred persons on opening her great room, and the room with the hangings of feathers.* The King and Queen had been with her last week. I should like to have heard the orations she had prepared on the occasion. I was neither City-mouse nor Country-mouse. I did dine at Fulham on Saturday with the Bishop of London [Porteus]. Mrs. Boscawen, Mrs.

---

* "There [at the opening of Hastings's trial] were the members of that brilliant society which quoted, criticised, and exchanged repartees, under the rich peacock-hangings of Mrs. Montagu."—*Macaulay's Essay on "Warren Hastings."*

Garrick, and Hannah More were there; and Dr. Beattie, whom I had never seen. He is quiet, simple, and cheerful, and pleased me. There ends my tale, this instant Tuesday! How shall I fill a couple of pages more by Friday morning! Oh! ye ladies on the Common, and ye uncommon ladies in London, have pity on a poor gazetteer, and supply me with eclogues or royal panegyrics! Moreover—or rather more under—I have had no letter from you these ten days, though the east wind has been as constant as Lord Derby.* I say not this in reproach, as you are so kindly punctual; but as it stints me from having a single paragraph to answer. I do not admire specific responses to every article; but they are great resources on a dearth.

"Madame de Boufflers is ill of a fever, and the Duchesse de Biron goes next week to Switzerland;—*mais qu'est que cela vous fait?*"

"June 23, 1791.

"Woe is me! I have not an atom of news to send you, but that the second edition of Mother Hubbard's Tale [Mrs. Hobart's party] was again spoiled on Saturday last by the rain; yet she had an ample assemblage of company from London and the neighbourhood. The late Queen of France, Madame du Barry, was there; and the late Queen of England, Madame d'Albany, was not. The former, they say, is as much altered as her kingdom, and does not retain a trace of her former

* To Miss Farren.

powers. I saw her on a throne in the chapel of Versailles; and though then pleasing in face and person, I thought her *un peu passée.*

"What shall I tell you more? that Lord Hawkesbury is added to the Cabinet-Council—*que vous importe?* and that Dr. Robertson has published a 'Disquisition into the Trade of the Ancients with India;' a sensible work—but that will be no news to you till you return. It was a peddling trade in those days. They now and then picked up an elephant's tooth, or a nutmeg, or one pearl, that served Venus for a pair of pendants, when Antony had toasted Cleopatra in a bumper of its fellow; which shows that a couple was imported: but, alack! the Romans were so ignorant, that waiters from the Tres Tabernæ, in St. Apollo's Street, did not carry home sacks of diamonds enough to pave the Capitol—I hate exaggerations, and therefore I do not say, to pave the Appian Way. One author, I think, does say, that the wife of Fabius Pictor, whom he sold to a Proconsul, did present Livia* with an ivory bed, inlaid with Indian gold; but, as Dr. Robertson does not mention it, to be sure he does not believe the fact well authenticated."

In one of our last extracts, Walpole refers to some of the French exiles, who were now assembled in large numbers at Richmond. Shortly afterwards came the

* This alludes to the stories told at the time of an ivory bed, inlaid with gold, having been presented to Queen Charlotte by Mrs. Hastings, the wife of the Governor-General of India.

news of the escape and recapture of the French King and Queen. Horace writes, " I have been very much with the wretched fugitives at Richmond. To them it is perfect despair; besides trembling for their friends at Paris!' Nevertheless, their distresses did not prevent them from taking part in the gaieties of Richmond :

" Berkeley Square, Tuesday, Aug. 23, 1791.

"On Saturday evening I was at the Duke of Queensberry's (at Richmond, *s'entend*) with a small company: and there were Sir William Hamilton and Mrs. Harte;* who, on the 3rd of next month, previous to their departure, is to be made Madame l'Envoyée à Naples, the Neapolitan Queen having promised to receive her in that quality. Here she cannot be presented, where only such over-virtuous wives as the Duchess of Kingston and Mrs. Hastings—who could go with a husband in each hand—are admitted. Why the Margravine of Anspach, with the same pretensions, was not, I do not understand; perhaps she did not attempt it. But I forget to retract, and make *amende honorable* to Mrs. Harte. I had only heard of her attitudes; and those, in dumb show, I have not yet seen. Oh! but she sings admirably; has a very fine, strong voice; is an excellent buffa, and an astonishing tragedian. She sung Nina in the highest perfection; and there her attitudes were a whole theatre of grace and various expressions.

* Shortly afterwards Lady Hamilton—Nelson's Lady Hamilton.

"The next evening I was again at Queensberry House, where the Comtesse Emilie de Boufflers played on her harp, and the Princesse di Castelcigala, the Neapolitan minister's wife, danced one of her country dances, with castanets, very prettily, with her husband. Madame du Barry was there too, and I had a good deal of frank conversation with her about Monsieur de Choiseul; having been at Paris at the end of his reign and at the beginning of hers, and of which I knew so much by my intimacy with the Duchesse de Choiseul.

"On Monday was the boat-race. I was in the great room at the Castle, with the Duke of Clarence, Lady Di, Lord Robert Spencer, and the House of Bouverie, to see the boats start from the bridge to Thistleworth, and back to a tent erected on Lord Dysart's meadow, just before Lady Di.'s windows; whither we went to see them arrive, and where we had breakfast. For the second heat, I sat in my coach on the bridge; and did not stay for the third. The day had been coined on purpose, with my favourite southeast wind. The scene, both up the river and down, was what only Richmond upon earth can exhibit. The crowds on those green velvet meadows and on the shores, the yachts, barges, pleasure and small boats, and the windows and gardens lined with spectators, were so delightful, that when I came home from that vivid show, I thought Strawberry looked as dull and solitary as a hermitage. At night there was a ball at the Castle, and illuminations, with the Duke's cypher, etc., in coloured lamps, as were the houses of his

Royal Highness's tradesmen. I went again in the evening to the French ladies on the Green, where there was a bonfire; but, you may believe, not to the ball."

At the end of September, Walpole writes to Hannah More:

"I thank you most cordially for your inquiry after *my* wives. I am in the utmost perplexity of mind about them; torn between hopes and fears. I believe them set out from Florence on their return since yesterday se'ennight, and consequently feel all the joy and impatience of expecting them in five or six weeks: but then, besides fears of roads, bad inns, accidents, heats and colds, and the sea to cross in November at last, all my satisfaction is dashed by the uncertainty whether they come through Germany or France. I have advised, begged, implored, that it may not be through those Iroquois, Lestryons, Anthropophagi, the Franks and then, hearing passports were abolished, and the roads more secure, I half consented, as they wished it, and the road is much shorter; and then I repented, and have contradicted myself again. And now I know not which route they will take; nor shall enjoy any comfort from the thoughts of their return, till they are returned safe.

"I am happy at and honour Miss Burney's resolution in casting away golden, or rather gilt chains: others, out of vanity, would have worn them till they had eaten into the bone. On that charming young woman's chapter* I agree with you perfectly."

Shortly after the date of the last letter, the Berrys were back in England. Their stay in Italy, which had been determined partly by motives of economy, was shortened in consequence of Walpole's eagerness for their return. In his anxiety, he entreated them to draw on his bankers in case of any financial difficulty; and in November, 1791, he had the satisfaction of installing them at Little Strawberry Hill. This was not accomplished without some vexation both to him and them. An ill-natured rumour, which found its way

---

* Miss Burney had recently resigned her situation about the Queen's person. Madame d'Arblay (Miss Burney) has entered in her Diary the following portion of a letter addressed to her by Walpole:

"As this will come to you by my servant, give me leave to add a word on your most unfounded idea that I can forget you, because it is almost impossible for me ever to meet you. Believe me, I heartily regret that privation, but would not repine, were your situation, either in point of fortune or position, equal in any degree to your merit. But were your talents given to be buried in obscurity? You have retired from the world to a closet at Court— where, indeed, you will still discover mankind, though not disclose it; for if you could penetrate its characters, in the earliest glimpse of its superficies, will it escape your piercing eye when it shrinks from your inspection, knowing that you have the mirror of truth in your pocket? I will not embarrass you by saying more, nor would have you take notice of, or reply to what I have said: judge only, that feeling hearts reflect, not forget. Wishes that are empty look like vanity; my vanity is to be thought capable of esteeming you as much as you deserve, and to be reckoned, though a very distant, a most *sincere* friend,—and give me leave to say, dear Madam, your most obedient humble servant, HOR. WALPOLE.

"Strawberry Hill, October '90."

into the newspapers, attributing the attachment shown by the Berry family for Walpole to interested motives, aroused the indignation of Miss Berry, and for the moment threatened to produce an estrangement. The cloud, however, blew over: the intimacy was resumed, and in a subsequent letter to the sisters, the old man expresses his gratitude at finding that they could bear to pass half their time with an antediluvian without discovering any ennui or disgust.

Almost immediately after he had recovered the Berrys, Walpole became Earl of Orford by the death of his nephew. He refers to this event, and his feelings respecting it, in the following letter to Lady Ossory:

"Berkeley Square, Dec. 10, 1791.

" Your Ladyship has so long accustomed me to your goodness and partiality, that I am not surprised at your being kind on an occasion that is generally productive of satisfaction. That is not quite the case with me. Years ago, a title would have given me no pleasure, and at any time the management of a landed estate, which I am too ignorant to manage, would have been a burthen. That I am now to possess, should it prove a considerable acquisition to my fortune, which I much doubt, I would not purchase at the rate of the three weeks of misery which I have suffered, and which made me very ill, though I am now quite recovered. It is a story much too full of circumstances, and too disagreeable to me to be couched in a letter; some time or other I may perhaps be at leisure and composed enough to relate in general.—At present I have been so overwhelmed with business that I am now writing these few lines as fast as I can, to save the post, as none goes to-morrow, and I should be vexed not to thank your Ladyship and Lord Ossory by the first that departs. As, however, I owe it to you and to my poor nephew, I will just say that I am perfectly content. He has given me the whole Norfolk estate, heavily charged, I believe, but that is indifferent. I had reason to think that he had disgraced, by totally omitting me—but unhappy as his intellects often were, and beset as he was by miscreants, he has restored me to my birth-right, and I shall call myself obliged to him, and be grateful to his memory, as I am to your Ladyship, and shall be, as I have so long been, your devoted servant, by whatever name I may be forced to call myself."

This letter has no signature. The writer for some time rarely used his new title when he could avoid it. Some of his letters after his succession to the peerage are signed "the late H. W.," and some, "the uncle of the late Earl of Orford." In 1792, he wrote the following " Epitaphium vivi Auctoris:"

> "An estate and an earldom at seventy-four!
> Had I sought them or wished them 'twould add one fear more,
> That of making a countess when almost fourscore.
> But Fortune, who scatters her gifts out of season,
> Though unkind to my limbs, has still left me my reason,
> And whether she lowers or lifts me I'll try,
> In the plain simple style I have lived in, to die :
> For ambition too humble, for meanness too high."

He could not escape the suspicion of having meditated the folly referred to in these lines. His much talked of devotion to his "sweet damsels" rendered this impossible. There is a tradition, handed down by the Lord Lansdowne of the last generation, that he would have gone through the ceremony of marriage with either sister, to make sure of their society, and confer rank and fortune on the family; as he had the power of charging the Orford estate with a jointure of £2,000 a year. There is just so much evidence in support of this story that he does appear to have avowed in society his readiness to do this for Mary Berry, who was clearly the object of his preference. But he does not seem to have ever made any such proposal to her, nor even to have spoken to her on the subject. In a letter to a friend written at the time, Miss Berry says: "Although I have no doubt that Lord Orford said to Lady D. every word that she repeated—for last winter, at the time the C's.* talked about the matter, he went about saying all this and more to everybody that would hear him—but I always thought it rather to frighten and punish them than seriously wishing it himself. And why should he? when, without the ridicule or the trouble of a marriage, he enjoys almost as much of my society, and every comfort from it, that he could in the nearest connexion?" Walpole was almost certainly of the same opinion as Miss Berry. He would have shrunk from the lasting stigma of a marriage, though he was content to bear passing jests which, perhaps, the attention of his young friends rendered

* The Cholmondeleys.

even agreeable. In May, 1792, he writes to Lady Ossory:

"I am indeed much obliged for the transcript of the letter on my 'Wives.' Miss Agnes has a *finesse* in her eyes and countenance that does not propose itself to you, but is very engaging on observation, and has often made herself preferred to her sister, who has the most exactly fine features, and only wants colour to make her face as perfect as her graceful person; indeed neither has good health nor the air of it. Miss Mary's eyes are grave, but she is not so herself; and, having much more application than her sister, she converses readily, and with great intelligence, on all subjects. Agnes is more reserved, but her compact sense very striking, and always to the purpose. In short, they are extraordinary beings, and I am proud of my partiality for them; and since the ridicule can only fall on me, and not on them, I care not a straw for its being said that I am in love with one of them—people shall choose which: it is as much with both as either, and I am infinitely too old to regard the *qu'en dit on*."

Nothing could be more sentimental than Walpole's language to and about these ladies, but his admiration and regard for them were rational enough. There was no dotage in the praises he lavished on their attractions and accomplishments. However much of their first social success may have been due to him, they proved able to perpetuate and extend it by their personal qualities alone, without the aid of large fortune or family connexion. And the tenor of his latest letters seems to show that this old man of the world derived benefit as well as amusement from their conversation. Their refinement and unpresuming moral worth were perhaps the highest influences to which his worn brain and heart were susceptible. One cannot help remarking that the respect with which he treats Mary Berry is a much stronger feeling than that which he displays for Hannah More. Though a good deal younger, Miss Berry had travelled more, and seen more of society, than the excellent schoolmistress from the West of England; and with this more varied experience came wider sympathies and larger toleration. Madam Hannah's fervent desires for the improvement of her friends, though always manifest, were not always accompanied by skill to make her little homilies acceptable. Her letters to Walpole betray some consciousness of a deficiency in this respect, and her embarrassment was not lost upon "the pleasant Horace," as she called her correspondent. He complained of the too great civility and cold complimentality of her style. The lady of Cowslip Green, who dedicated small poems to him, adorned her letters with literary allusions, and dropped occasional hints for his benefit, was always, in his eyes, a blue-stocking; and this the ladies of Cliveden never were. He was incessantly divided between his wish to treat the elder lady with deference, and a mischievous inclination to startle her notions of propriety. When he is tempted to transgress, he checks himself in some characteristic phrase: "I could titter *à plusieurs reprises;* but I am too old to be im-

proper, and you are too modest to be *impropered* to."
But the temptation presently returns. In short, Walpole subscribed to Miss More's charities, echoed her denunciations of the slave-trade, applauded her Cheap Repository Tracts, and was ever Saint Hannah's most sincere friend and humble servant ; but he could not help indemnifying himself now and then by a smile at her effusive piety and bustling benevolence. On the other hand, the entire and unqualified respect which Lord Orford entertained for Miss Berry's abilities and character was shown, not merely by the particular expressions of affection and esteem so profusely scattered through his letters to her, and by the whole tone of the correspondence between them, but still more decisively by the circumstance that he entrusted to her the care of preparing a posthumous edition of his works, and bequeathed to her charge all necessary papers for that purpose. This he did in fact, for though in his will he appointed her father[*] as his editor, it was well understood that that was merely a device to avoid the publication of her name, and the task was actually performed by her alone.

During the rest of Walpole's life, three-fourths of each year were spent by him in constant association with the Berrys either at Twickenham or in London. The months which they employed in visits to other friends or to watering-places, he passed for the most part at Strawberry Hill, sending forth constant letters

[*] The weak and indolent character of Mr. Berry made him always and everywhere a cipher.

to Yorkshire, Cheltenham, Broadstairs, or wherever else his wives might be staying. He laughs at his own assiduity. "I put myself in mind of a scene in one of Lord Lansdowne's plays, where two ladies being on the stage, and one going off, the other says, 'Heaven, she is gone! Well, I must go and write to her.' This was just my case yesterday." The postman at Cheltenham complained of being broken down by the continual arrival of letters from Twickenham. At other times, Walpole's pen was now comparatively idle. When in town, he beguiled the hours as best he could with the customers who still resorted to his coffee-house to discuss the news of the day. But he generally preferred his villa till quite the end of autumn. "What could I do with myself in London?" he asks Miss Berry. "All my playthings are here, and I have no playfellows left there! Reading composes little of my pastime either in town or country. A catalogue of books and prints, or a dull history of a county, amuse me sufficiently; for now I cannot open a French book, as it would keep alive ideas that I want to banish from my thoughts." At Strawberry, accordingly, he remained, trifling with his endless store of medals and engravings, and watching from his windows the traffic up and down the Thames. He has expressed his fondness for moving objects in a passage dated in December, 1793:

"I am glad Lord and Lady Warwick are pleased with their new villa [at Isleworth]: it is a great favourite with me. In my brother's time [Sir Edward

W.'s] I used to sit with delight in the bow-window in the great room, for besides the lovely scene of Richmond, with the river, park, and barges, there is an incessant ferry for foot passengers between Richmond and Isleworth, just under the Terrace; and on Sundays Lord Shrewsbury pays for all the Catholics that come to his chapel from the former to the latter, and Mrs. Keppel has counted an hundred in one day, at a penny each. I have a passion for seeing passengers, provided they do pass; and though I have the river, the road, and two foot-paths before my Blue Room at Strawberry, I used to think my own house dull whenever I came from my brother's. Such a partiality have I for moving objects, that in advertisements of country-houses I have thought it a recommendation when there was a N.B. of *three stage-coaches pass by the door every day.* On the contrary, I have an aversion to a park, and especially for a walled park, in which the capital event is the coming of the cows to water. A park-wall with ivy on it and fern near it, and a back parlour in London in summer, with a dead creeper and a couple of sooty sparrows, are my strongest ideas of melancholy solitude. *A pleasing melancholy* is a very august personage, but not at all good company."

This love of life and society clung to him till the end. Notwithstanding his crippled condition, he entertained the Duchess of York at Strawberry Hill in the autumn of 1793, and received a visit from Queen Charlotte there as late as the summer of 1795. He was probably honest in disclaiming all vanity at being the poorest Earl in England. When pressed by Lady Ossory to take his seat in the House of Peers, he replied: "I know that having determined never to take that unwelcome seat, I should only make myself ridiculous by fancying it could *signify* a straw whether I take it or not. If I have anything of character, it must dangle on my being consistent. I quitted and abjured Parliament near twenty years ago: I never repented, and I will not contradict myself now." If, however, there was any occasion on which his earldom gave him pleasure, it was undoubtedly when the Seneschal of Strawberry Castle was to do homage to Royal guests. Referring to Macaulay's taunt that Walpole had the soul of a gentleman usher, Miss Berry remarks that the critic only repeated what Lord Orford often said of himself, that from his knowledge of old ceremonials and etiquettes he was sure that in a former state of existence he must have been a gentleman usher about the time of Elizabeth. Walpole sends Conway a brief account of the Queen's visit:

"Strawberry Hill, July 2, 1795.

"As you are, or have been, in town, your daughter [Mrs. Damer] will have told you in what a bustle I am, preparing, not to visit, but to receive an invasion of royalties to-morrow; and cannot even escape them, like Admiral Cornwallis, though seeming to make a semblance; for I am to wear a sword, and have appointed two aides-de-camp, my nephews, George and

Horace Churchill. If I *fall*, as ten to one but I do, to be sure it will be a superb tumble, at the feet of a Queen and eight daughters of Kings : for, besides the six Princesses, I am to have the Duchess of York and the Princess of Orange! Woe is me, at seventy-eight, and with scarce a hand and foot to my back! Adieu!

"Yours, etc.,

"A Poor Old Remnant."

"July 7, 1795.

"I am not dead of fatigue with my Royal visitors, as I expected to be, though I was on my poor lame feet three whole hours. Your daughter, who kindly assisted me in doing the honours, will tell you the particulars, and how prosperously I succeeded. The Queen was uncommonly condescending and gracious, and deigned to drink my health when I presented her with the last glass, and to thank me for all my attentions. Indeed, my memory *de la vieille cour* was but once in default. As I had been assured that her Majesty would be attended by her Chamberlain, yet was not, I had no glove ready when I received her at the step of her coach ; yet she honoured me with her hand to lead her upstairs ; nor did I recollect my omission when I led her down again. Still, though gloveless, I did not squeeze the royal hand, as Vice-Chamberlain Smith did to Queen Mary."*

---

* Queen Mary asked some of her attendant ladies what a squeeze of the hand was supposed to intimate. They said "Love." "Then," said the Queen, "my vice-chamberlain must be violently in love with me, for he always squeezes my hand."

Conway died suddenly two days after the date of the last letter. He had received the truncheon of a Field-Marshal less than two years before. Like his old friend Horace, he attained the last distinction of his life when he was too old to enjoy it. Horace lingered on twenty months longer in constantly increasing debility. In the latter part of December, 1796, he was seen to be sinking, and his friends prevailed on him to remove from Strawberry Hill to Berkeley Square, to be nearer assistance in case of any sudden seizure. The account of his last days is thus given by Miss Berry: "When not immediately suffering from pain, his mind was tranquil and cheerful. He was still capable of being amused, and of taking some part in conversation; but during the last weeks of his life, when fever was superadded to his other ills, his mind became subject to the cruel hallucination of supposing himself neglected and abandoned by the only persons to whom his memory clung, and whom he always desired to see. In vain they recalled to his recollection how recently they had left him, and how short had been their absence; it satisfied him for the moment, but the same idea recurred as soon as he had lost sight of them. At last nature, sinking under the exhaustion of weakness, obliterated all ideas but those of mere existence, which ended without a struggle on the 2nd of March, 1797.

Horace Walpole's last letter was addressed, as was fitting, to Lady Ossory, then almost the sole survivor of his early friends:

"Jan. 15, 1797.

"My dear Madam,—

"You distress me infinitely by showing my idle notes, which I cannot conceive can amuse anybody. My old-fashioned breeding impels me every now and then to reply to the letters you honour me with writing, but in truth very unwillingly, for I seldom can have anything particular to say; I scarce go out of my own house, and then only to two or three private places, where I see nobody that really knows anything, and what I learn comes from newspapers, that collect intelligence from coffee-houses; consequently what I neither believe nor report. At home I see only a few charitable elders, except about four-score nephews and nieces of various ages, who are each brought to me about once a year, to stare at me as the Methusaleh of the family, and they can only speak of their own contemporaries, which interest me no more than if they talked of their dolls, or bats and balls. Must not the result of all this, Madam, make me a very entertaining correspondent? And can such letters be worth showing? or can I have any spirit when so old, and reduced to dictate?

"Oh! my good Madam, dispense with me from such a task, and think how it must add to it to apprehend such letters being shown. Pray send me no more such laurels, which I desire no more than their leaves when decked with a scrap of tinsel, and stuck on twelfth-cakes that lie on the shop-boards of pastrycooks at Christmas. I shall be quite content with a sprig of rosemary thrown after me, when the parson of the parish commits my dust to dust. Till then, pray, Madam, accept the resignation of your

"Ancient Servant,
"ORFORD."

Besides numerous portraits of Horace Walpole, we have two pen-and-ink sketches of him, one by Miss Hawkins, the other by Pinkerton. The lady describes* him as she knew him before 1772: "His figure was not merely tall, but more properly long and slender to excess; his complexion, and particularly his hands, of a most unhealthy paleness. His eyes were remarkably bright and penetrating, very dark and lively; his voice was not strong, but his tones were extremely pleasant. . . . I do not remember his common gait; he always entered a room in that style of affected delicacy which fashion had then made almost natural: *chapeau bas* between his hands, as if he wished to compress it, or under his arm; knees bent, and feet on tiptoe, as if afraid of a wet floor. His dress in visiting was most usually, in summer, when I most saw him, a lavender suit, the waistcoat embroidered with a little silver, or of white silk worked in the tambour; partridge silk stockings, and gold buckles; ruffles and frill, generally lace. I remember, when a child, thinking him very much under-dressed, if at any time, except in mourning, he wore hemmed cambric. In summer no powder, but his wig combed straight, and showing his

* 'Anecdotes,' etc., by Lætitia Matilda Hawkins, 1822.

very smooth, pale forehead, and queued behind; in winter, powder."

Miss Hawkins, who was recording in her old age the impressions of her girlhood, is clearly mistaken as to the height of Walpole's figure. Pinkerton paints him as he was at a later period, and adds several details of his domestic habits. We give the main part of the antiquary's description,* and generally in his own words: The person of Horace Walpole was short and slender, but compact and neatly formed. When viewed from behind, he had somewhat of a boyish appearance, owing partly to the simplicity of his dress. His laugh was forced and uncouth, and his smile not the most pleasing. His walk was enfeebled by the gout, which not only affected his feet, but attacked his hands to such a degree that his fingers were always swelled and deformed, and discharged large chalk-stones once or twice a year. When at Strawberry Hill, he generally rose about nine o'clock, and appeared in the breakfast-room, his favourite Blue Room overlooking the Thames. His approach was proclaimed, and attended, by a favourite little dog, the legacy of the Marquise du Deffand; and which ease and attention had rendered so fat that it could hardly move. The dog had a liberal share of his breakfast; and as soon as the meal was over, Walpole would mix a large basinful of bread and milk, and throw it out of the window for the squirrels, who presently came down from the high trees to enjoy their allowance. Dinner was served in the

* 'Walpoliana,' Preface.

small parlour, or large dining-room, as it happened; in winter, generally the former. His valet supported him downstairs; and he ate most moderately of chicken, pheasant, or any light food. Pastry he disliked, as difficult of digestion, though he would taste a morsel of venison pie. Never but once that he drank two glasses of white wine,* did Pinkerton see him taste any liquor, except ice-water. A pail of ice was placed under the table, in which stood a decanter of water, from which he supplied himself with his favourite beverage. If his guests liked even a moderate quantity of wine, they must have called for it during dinner, for almost instantly after he rang the bell to order coffee upstairs. Thither he would pass about five o'clock; and generally resuming his place on the sofa, would sit till two o'clock in the morning, in miscellaneous chit-chat, full of singular anecdotes, strokes of wit, and acute observations, occasionally sending for books or curiosities, or passing to the library, as any reference happened to arise in conversation. After his coffee he tasted nothing; but the snuff-box of *tabac d'étrennes*, from Fribourg's, was not forgotten, and was replenished from a canister lodged in an ancient marble urn of great thickness, which stood in the window-seat, and served to secure its moisture and rich flavour. Such was a private rainy day of Horace Walpole. The forenoon quickly passed in roaming through the numerous apartments

* As early as 1754 he wrote to Bentley: "You know I **never** drink three glasses of any wine."

of the house, in which, after twenty visits, still something new would occur ; and he was indeed constantly adding fresh acquisitions. Sometimes a walk in the grounds would intervene, on which occasions he would go out in his slippers through a thick dew ; and he never wore a hat.* He said that, on his first visit to Paris, he was ashamed of his effeminacy, when he saw every little meagre Frenchman, whom even he could have thrown down with a breath, walking without a hat, which he could not do without a certainty of that disease which the Germans say is endemical in England, and is termed by the nation *le catch-cold*. The first trial cost him a slight fever, but he got over it, and never caught cold afterwards: draughts of air, damp rooms, windows open at his back, all situations were alike to him in this respect. He would even show some little offence at any solicitude expressed by his guests on such an occasion; and would say, with a half smile of seeming crossness, " My back is the same with my face, and my neck is like my nose."

* "A hat, you know, I never wear, my breast I never button, nor wear great coats, etc."—Letter to Cole, Feb. 14, 1782.

THE END.

THE 'FANNY BURNEY' SERIES.

POPULAR EDITIONS OF THE

'EIGHTEENTH CENTURY' BIOGRAPHICAL SERIES.

Each in one volume, crown 8vo., cloth, with a Portrait, price $1.25.

---

1. FANNY BURNEY AND HER FRIENDS. Select Passages from her Diary and other Writings. Edited by L. B. SEELEY. With Portrait. New and Cheaper Edition. Crown 8vo., cloth. *(Now Ready.)*

    The *New York Times* wrote of this book on its first appearance: 'Mr. Seeley modestly calls himself the Editor of Select Passages from Fanny Burney's Diary, but he really gives, in a very direct and charming way, a biography of the demure little lady, drawing largely from the Diary, and sometimes freely from other writings.'

2. HORACE WALPOLE AND HIS WORLD. Select Passages from his Letters. Edited by L. B. SEELEY. With Portrait. New and Cheaper Edition. Crown 8vo., cloth. *(Now Ready.)*

    The *Pall Mall Gazette* wrote of this volume: 'Mr. Seeley's plan is to let Walpole tell his story as far as possible for himself. The most interesting and representative of his letters are selected, and they are linked together by biographical and explanatory passages, and the result is a very lively, fresh-coloured picture of the interests and fashions and follies of that day. Taking it altogether, we do not often meet with a more entertaining volume.'

3. LADY MARY WORTLEY MONTAGU. 1 vol.
    (Ready Autumn, 1896.)

4. SIR JOSHUA REYNOLDS.
    (Ready Autumn, 1896.)

5. MRS. THRALE, AFTERWARDS MRS. PIOZZI.
    (Ready Autumn, 1897.)

6. DEAN SWIFT: HIS LIFE, ETC.
    (Ready Autumn, 1897.)

NEW YORK: CHARLES SCRIBNER'S SONS.

In 8vo., cloth, $4.50.

MADAME

Memoirs of Henrietta, Daughter of Charles I. and Duchess of Orleans.

By JULIA CARTWRIGHT (Mrs. H. Ady), Author of 'Sacharissa.'

With Two Portraits on Copper. Demy 8vo.

₊ *This Volume contains Ninety Unpublished Letters of Charles II.*

SACHARISSA

Some Account of Dorothy Sidney, Countess of Sunderland, her Family and Friends.

By JULIA CARTWRIGHT (Mrs. Henry Ady).

With Portrait after Vandyke. Demy 8vo., cloth, $3.75.

'A thoroughly interesting book, with selections sometimes most felicitous.'—*National Observer.*

'Mrs. Ady is much to be congratulated on this volume, in which she collects and gives to the world all that can be gathered together concerning the life and times of a most delightful and remarkable woman.'—*Saturday Review.*

'Not only is it a valuable history of the great people of the time, but it is interesting reading throughout.'—*Pall Mall Gazette.*

'In this attractive book a new light is cast on her great-hearted brother, Algernon Sidney, her famous son-in-law, Lord Halifax, and half the notables of that stormy age.'—*Leeds Mercury.*

'We have nothing but praise for the way in which Miss Cartwright has done her work.'—*Spectator.*

'Mrs. Ady has brought together an abundance of interesting details which make her volume delightful reading.'—*Glasgow Herald.*

'This is a delightful book, and the story is pleasantly and sympathetically told. We are grateful to Miss Cartwright for thus preserving to us, in these pages, the memory of one who so fitly deserves our remembrance and our gratitude.'—*Guardian.*

NEW YORK: CHARLES SCRIBNER'S SONS.

The Eighteenth Century Biographical Series.

SIR JOSHUA REYNOLDS. By CLAUDE PHILLIPS. With Portraits on Copper. Cloth, $2.50.

'A whole library has been written about Sir Joshua, but this is the best digest of the subject we know.'—*Athenæum.*

DEAN SWIFT: HIS LIFE AND WRITINGS. By GERALD MORIARTY, Balliol College, Oxford. With Nine Portraits. Crown 8vo., $2.50.

'Mr. Moriarty is to be heartily congratulated upon having produced an extremely sound and satisfactory little book.'—*National Observer.*

HORACE WALPOLE AND HIS WORLD. Select Passages from his Letters. With Eight Copper Plates, after Sir JOSHUA REYNOLDS and THOMAS LAWRENCE. Crown 8vo., cloth, $2.50.

'A compact representative selection, with just enough connecting text to make it read consecutively, with a pleasantly-written introduction.'—*Athenæum.*

FANNY BURNEY AND HER FRIENDS. Select Passages from Her Diary. Edited by L. B. SEELEY, M.A., late Fellow of Trinity College, Cambridge. With Nine Portraits on Copper, after REYNOLDS, GAINSBOROUGH, COPLEY, and WEST. Cloth, $2.50.

'The charm of the volume is heightened by nine illustrations of some of the masterpieces of English art, and it would not be possible to find a more captivating present for anyone beginning to appreciate the characters of the last century.'—*Academy.*
'A really valuable book.'—*World.*

MRS. THRALE, AFTERWARDS MRS. PIOZZI. By L. B. SEELEY, M.A., late Fellow of Trinity College, Cambridge. With Nine Portraits on Copper, after HOGARTH, REYNOLDS, ZOFFANY, and others. Cloth, $2.50.

'Mr. Seeley had excellent material to write upon, and he has turned it to the best advantage.'—*Pall Mall Gazette.*
'This sketch is better worth having than the autobiography, for it is infinitely the more complete and satisfying.'—*Globe.*

LADY MARY WORTLEY MONTAGU. By ARTHUR R. ROPES, M.A., sometime Fellow of King's College, Cambridge. With Nine Portraits, after Sir GODFREY KNELLER, etc. Crown 8vo., $2.50.

'Embellished as it is with a number of excellent plates, we cannot imagine a more welcome or delightful present.'—*National Observer.*

NEW YORK:
CHARLES SCRIBNER'S SONS, 153-157, FIFTH AVENUE.

PRESS NOTICES.

DEAN SWIFT.

'It is a singularly bright and readable account of Swift and his works. Those who know their Swift will enjoy the book as offering a pleasant reminder of many good things; while those to whom Swift is little more than a great name will be able to gather, with little or no exertion, a very vivid picture of the man and his life. ... Very readable, too, is the chapter on "Swift in the Great World." Mr. Moriarty has there strung together, chiefly from Swift's journals and letters, a number of most entertaining examples of Swift's tyrannical behaviour in society.'—*Spectator.*

'Mr. Moriarty is to be heartily congratulated upon having produced an extremely sound and satisfactory little book. He states his facts with candour and accuracy, choosing rather that his readers should draw their own inferences than be fatigued by his; but he is no wobbler, and where a bold touch is required, his hand is decided and firm. ... The reproductions of portraits (in particular those of Stella and Vanessa) are a highly interesting and attractive feature in a highly interesting and attractive book.'—*National Observer.*

SIR JOSHUA REYNOLDS.

'The book is extremely well done, and it fulfils excellently its appointed task of standing between the literary essay and the extremely bulky and voluminous memoir.'—*Academy.*

'It is well written and beautifully illustrated with reproductions of the master's work. The author has drawn his biography from numerous sources, and pursued Sir Joshua industriously through many and varied volumes, in which characteristic glimpses of him appear.'—*Black and White.*

MRS. THRALE.

... 'Before the appearance of the present volume there was no regular biography of the lady whose name is often associated with some of her most famous contemporaries. Mr. Seeley has performed his task with skill and excellent judgment. Though he writes in evident sympathy with his subject, he is rigidly impartial.'—*Athenæum.*

'Mr. Seeley had excellent material to work upon, and he has turned it to the best advantage. The volume, which will be a fit companion to the editor's "Fanny Burney," contains some excellent illustrations.'—*Pall Mall Gazette.*

www.ingramcontent.com/pod-product-compliance
Lightning Source LLC
Chambersburg PA
CBHW022109230426
43672CB00008B/1323